Blacklisted

English editions of other books by Paul Lendvai:

Eagles and Cobwebs: Nationalism and Communism in the Balkans
Anti-Semitism in Eastern Europe
The Bureaucracy of Truth
Hungary: The Art of Survival

BLACKLISTED

A Journalist's Life in Central Europe

Paul Lendvai

I.B.Tauris *Publishers*
LONDON • NEW YORK

Published in 1998 by I.B.Tauris & Co Ltd
Victoria House, Bloomsbury Square, London WC1B 4DZ
175 Fifth Avenue, New York NY 10010

In the United States and Canada distributed by St. Martin's Press
175 Fifth Avenue, New York NY 10010

ISBN 1 86064 268 3

A full CIP record for this book is available from the British Library
A full CIP record for this book is available from the Library of Congress

Library of Congress catalog card: available

Typeset in Sabon by Dexter Haven, London
Printed and bound in Great Britain by WBC Ltd, Bridgend

Dedicated to the memory of

CARL LUTZ

GIORGIO PERLASCA

NUNCIO ANGELO ROTTA

RAOUL WALLENBERG

who in Budapest in the winter of
1944/45 risked their lives in order
to help the persecuted.

CONTENTS

PREFACE

This book is a deeply personal account of a witness to the startling developments in Central and Eastern Europe which in one form or another have shaped our time. The corner of the earth in which I was born and have spent all my life has, in the twentieth century been a cockpit for struggle, conflict and cultural ferment. In this region we have, over an eighty-year period, seen terrible wars, massive destruction, unfathomable genocide, strident nationalism, ethnic hatred, anti-semitism in both its virulent and more subtle forms, massive migration and population explosions, as well as some of the most astonishing and enduring expressions of civilisation, creativity and intellectual achievement. It is a region with a complex, chilling and sometimes even inspiring history.

I have in this memoir attempted to provide an account of a life which in its own way was caught up in and buffeted by the turbulent history of twentieth-century Europe. I have tried, as best I could, candidly to portray my own participation in some of the follies which affected our times, first as an ardent young leftist, then as an ambitious communist activist and journalist.

Born and brought up in Hungary, my early life as a child and young man was shaped by the killers and victims, traitors and heroes who occupied Hungary's dramatic history between 1944 and 1956. After my flight to Vienna, where I have worked as a foreign correspondent (with 22 years on the *Financial Times*) and as a political writer and television producer of historical documentaries, I had plenty of time to reflect on the sinister forces which have shaped the twentieth-century history for Central and Eastern Europe. The demons of nationalism and ethnic hatred have presented themselves in this region in many different guises – fascism, Nazism, communism and post-communism ferment. Each of these I have been able to observe at one time or another in my life. Each of these periods and movements has played on the intricate weft of ethnicities, religions, sects, languages and cultures which make up Central Europe to advance the prevailing political fashions of the time. This depressing reality seems to continue well into the third millennium.

In these memoirs I have been able to use hundreds of pages from files compiled on me by the secret police networks of Hungary, Czechoslovakia and the German Democratic Republic, all of whom were interested in my work as a journalist and observer of the political scene in the communist bloc. Reports on me were fed to the KGB, which functioned as a clearing house and central exchange for information gathered on their key targets. It is an interesting reflection on the changes which have taken place in the former Warsaw Pact countries that many of the persons and structures from those dark days are still very much in place whether in Budapest or in Moscow.

As a Hungarian-born Austrian author with Jewish parents and an English wife, now living in Vienna but travelling and lecturing frequently around the world, I have been blessed with a distrust of excessive partisanship for any nation or cause. I am, of course, grateful to the people of Austria who took me – along with over 600,000 other refugees since 1945 – into their world and gave me the opportunity to develop a new life. But this has not prevented me from looking critically at Austrian leaders, which I hope my chapters on Bruno Kreisky and Kurt Waldheim make clear.

My intention with this book has been to make a modest contribution to the study of contemporary history in Europe before, during and after the Cold War. If I have done this in a manner which holds the attention, however briefly, of a curious reader I will consider the effort to have been worthwhile.

I would like to record my gratitude to the Bank of Austria for their generous assistance in funding the translation costs of this book from German to English. I am also grateful for the help extended by the Austrian Cultural Institutes in London and New York.

Paul Lendvai, Vienna, March 1998

PROLOGUE
In the cell – facing the camera

I wanted to go back into the prison, but they wouldn't let me in. It did not matter that I had been waiting for that moment for days, even weeks. The producer of the TV documentary in which I was to appear as a witness to contemporary history, having received clearance for her project, was convinced that she would have no trouble shooting her film in Budapest's notorious detention centre on Fo Street. But for some reason or other, things did not work out as planned. At the rear entrance on Gyorskocsi Street, where for so many years thousands of people disappeared into this infamous police prison, we were brusquely turned away.

Twice I tried in my best Hungarian to explain our undertaking to the sceptical plain-clothes security man. Neither he nor his superiors knew anything about it. After one final phone call, he advised us to pursue the matter of this alleged filming permit with the police authorities on the other bank of the Danube, in Pest. The door leading into the prison was firmly shut in our faces. Almost enviously our little group watched the automatic gate opening and closing as cars drove in and out. To pass the time, our cameraman kept on shooting the front of the building, the plaque commemorating Imre Nagy, the Premier during the 1956 Revolution, and his comrades, executed in June 1958 following a secret trial in this very building.

As a last resort our producer decided to phone her official contact, but unfortunately she had forgotten both his name and position. After rummaging through her papers she finally found his telephone number and we clung to the hope that this mysterious person could actually be found. She came back in high spirits: Mr S. – head of the military prosecutor's office, the top official with the rank of colonel – was waiting for us in the reception room of the imposing building. He apologised for the administrative muddle, engaged us in polite conversation, and in our presence phoned the commandant of the section of the prison we wanted to visit. Within minutes we were on our way to the interrogation centre.

To a bystander, an ordinary visitor, the building looked like any other prison. For me, however, this return was unique, unforgettable. My heart began to pound. I could hardly keep up with the young captain who was escorting us. We arrived at the hallway where some 40-odd years ago we were escorted from our cells for questioning. Day and night the opening and shutting of cell doors could be heard, the murmuring of the guards, the whispered passwords they exchanged to avoid a chance meeting of the prisoners in the corridor. Our escort, who was joined by some curious colleagues, now unlocked an unoccupied cell. Above the massive iron door I saw a light bulb encased by wire. In those days it was never turned off. On the opposite wall there was a ventilation shaft. The dominant feature, then as now, was the peephole, which the guard would open and close every half hour or so. Now the door stayed open.

The cameraman and sound technician set up the lights and asked me to sit down on one of the wooden bunks. In the dark, tiny room I spoke briefly about my experiences 'back then', about the overcrowded cells which during the time I spent on Fo Street were hermetically sealed off from the outside. We had no contact with our families or with other prisoners. We had no books, no cigarettes, no information. Nor did we receive permission to take walks or write letters. Particularly after Stalin's death – that period of 'highest alert' – everything was in high gear. Cells meant for two would sometimes house five.

The cameraman went on making shots of the sombre background, 'just in case'. Then the producer asked me to stand outside, in front of the cell, and repeat what I had said inside. The team would use the better of the two versions. The cell may have been too dark she said, visibly pleased with our excursion.

I, on the other hand, was agitated and confused, and as our little contingent walked toward the exit accompanied by the friendly captain, my thoughts kept on returning to that memorable winter and spring of 1952/53 which I had spent under the watchful eye of the secret police, in the very same prison in which some eight years earlier the Gestapo had conducted its brutal interrogations of resistance fighters, anti-Nazis and Jews. To this day, this huge building housing military courts, state prosecutors, secret police and their prisons fills me with foreboding. Fo Street is a place that will never lose its horror for me.

Who would have thought that I would ever again set foot in those eerie corridors, let alone this very cell, that I would one day appear as a 'contemporary witness' to this bizarre world of bygone police terror?

True, during the Kadar regime and after the fall of Communism, on the way to my hotel from the Hungarian foreign ministry on the banks of the Danube, I would occasionally drive by that imposing building. Because of heavy traffic, and perhaps also out of a subconscious timidity, I would never stop. All I would do was cast a furtive glance at a building that had played such a crucial role in my life. It took the idea and push of a determined, energetic documentary filmmaker to bring me back to this place and the most secret recesses of this depressing building.

If only Gyuri, Colonel F., a man with whom I had spent the worst months here, could see me now. He used to be the only one who was brought here not in one of those broken-down Soviet vehicles but in an elegant gray Humber; something of which he was inordinately proud.

And what would Pista S. have thought? Pista, to the annoyance of his fellow prisoners, would recite the poems of József Attila over and over again until even I knew them by heart.

How amused the engineer Joska F. would have been. Shortly after Stalin's death he had jokingly remarked that 'nevertheless' he hadn't lost any sleep. To his utter astonishment he wound up in our cell ten hours later. And what about young Feri? He was a conscript and requested my father as his defence lawyer. Through this stroke of luck, my father found out at last where his son, who had disappeared without a trace, was being detained.

The people I had encountered on my way from the 'elitist' sixth floor to the communal cell and finally the Kistarcsa internment camp and not the guards escorting us, should have been here with me now in this cell, in the hallway, or in the building itself. All my fellow inmates were witnesses. They all should have been here to sign each page of this account, as was the case after every interrogation.

I was neither beaten nor tortured, nor engaged in philosophical discussions about party loyalty similar to Koestler's 'Darkness at Noon'. I must have been one of the youngest political prisoners. How, even in those 'dark days', did a twenty-three-year-old journalist who had just completed his military service get caught up in the ever-faster rotating machinery of purges in late Stalin era? And what were my feelings during those days and nights?

The other prisoners were periodically taken away for interrogation. Only I was spared. Had they forgotten me? Or was the whole thing one horrendous mistake for which they would eventually apologise? During the first few weeks I was still in rather good spirits. If in the morning the key in the cell door turned and the guard handed me a tin cup of what passed for coffee and a thin slice of bread I thought they were about to send for me and it would all turn out to be a bad dream. As a matter of fact I dreamt that a special issue of the party paper, *Szabad Nep*, had appeared with proof of my innocence. I even managed to convince my initially sceptical cell mates that the authorities had obviously made a mistake, that today – or at the latest tomorrow – would be my last day here. A couple of them even asked me to memorize the name and address of their families and get word to them as soon as I got out.

But as time went on, my confidence became increasingly shaky. Did they want to bury me alive here? Was a close friend involved in some crime against the party, or had they perhaps been recruited without my knowledge?

While the camera, spotlight, cables and all the other paraphernalia were being loaded into the van outside, unforgettable pictures of my arrest flashed before me. I saw myself during that first night lying on the wooden plank, pressed against my cell mates, my hands resting on the thin blanket, and with open eyes staring at the wire-enclosed light-bulb.

They had come for me on a cold, damp evening in January 1953 at about 7pm. Because we were suffering from a cold my wife and I were in bed when the door-bell rang. My elderly mother-in-law opened the door to five secret policemen with search warrants in hand. It was bitterly cold; the heating wasn't working. We had been drinking rum, which in Hungary was considered the ideal medicine against 'flu. That is probably why I saw what was taking place in our small apartment – my eight-year-old stepdaughter continued to sleep peacefully – as though through a fog. I dressed quickly. In conformity with what they called 'socialist legality', the policemen had summoned a neighbor and the janitor as witnesses. I greeted these two terrified people, and then two men grabbed hold of me and led me away.

It's only a stone's throw from Kigyo Street in Budapest's inner city to the interrogation centre on Fo Street. Fifteen minutes later I had already become a number with no name, without shoelaces or belt, expelled from society, buried alive, forgotten by the outside world. For the secret police, the AVH (formerly AVO), I was a closed file.

Three of the men from the arresting party meanwhile continued to turn the apartment upside-down. With unshakable poise my wife watched as they rummaged through closets and leafed through every book on our shelves. Despite my wife's objections they took with them numerous books, including some on loan from the parliament's library, and also all written material, family photographs, even the autographs and pictures of foreign and Hungarian movie stars. The apartment had belonged to the ex-husband of a famous musical-comedy star, Hanna Honthy, and the uninvited guests found and took with them a metal box with money (around 10,000 forints), a silver cigarette case and a gold watch-chain, items that had been stored in our apartment without my knowledge. In addition they also removed some pornographic classics, like the Hungarian translation of the memoirs of Josefine Mutzenbacher, 'a Viennese prostitute', allegedly the work of Felix Salten, the author of *Bambi*. One of the secret policemen was fascinated by Mutzenbacher's reminiscences and left the more arduous task of searching to his colleagues. After more than five hours looking for subversive materials they left, and the two witnesses were sent home; one of the policemen stayed for yet another hour to guard my wife, or rather to keep her from phoning.

Another smaller group of secret policemen had meanwhile gone to my parents' house. When they pushed their way into the living room my mother, who had never recovered from the nervous breakdown she had suffered during the fascist Arrow Cross terror regime in the winter of 1944-45, collapsed on the couch. Neither she nor, fortunately, the policemen knew that a carton under that sofa held far more 'subversive' material. While still living with my parents I had stashed away things like old issues of *Time* and *Newsweek* and some books that might now be considered subversive, stuff for which I just had no room. My parents knew nothing about any of this, but were so frightened that they decided to get rid of anything compromising and possibly treasonous that very night. My father, a highly decorated World War I officer, even started to destroy maps of the Austro-Hungarian empire and documents dating back to the years he spent as a prisoner-of-war in Siberia. But where to dispose of it all? They cut up the maps, thinking they would flush them down the lavatory; however, they had not taken into account the quality of the paper of those old documents. It became clogged in no time. Only the next day were they able to get it going with the help of a reliable neighbour and burn those dangerous papers in two ovens.

By that time my wife had managed to let my parents know about my puzzling arrest. My father, even though he was a lawyer still licensed to represent defendants before the military court, could not find out anything about my situation, let alone what I was charged with. I had disappeared in the heart of Budapest as though swallowed up.

To relate all this in the ten or 12 minutes foreseen for my interview in the documentary would have been impossible. In the meantime we were already in the midst of arranging next day's schedule, a trip to Kistarcsa, the internment camp on the outskirts of Budapest, and were discussing the most favorable locations for filming reminiscences of the 1956 Revolution.

Yet during my conversations with my colleagues I saw my life unrolling before me. Again and again I kept on asking myself why I, so young, and under normal circumstances 'free of any guilt', had to go through prison, internment camp, and three years of enforced unemployment, a total of almost four years of fear, degradation, and 'non-existence?' Why?

I

The Heights
and Depths
of Youth

1

Farewell to the 'Golden Era'

It was a glorious Sunday, that 19 March 1944. My soccer team, Ferencvaros, in the traditional green-and-white kit, was at home and played very well to beat the visiting team, Ujpest, 4-1. As always after a game at the Ferencvaros Stadium, the trolley line that stopped in front of our apartment, at the intersection of Liliom Street and Ulloi Street, was packed. Jammed together but in high spirits we rode home. Like my friends, I was elated by the brilliant strategy of the famous Sarosi brothers.

When I opened the door to our apartment my father, his face ashen, was shouting, 'Where've you been so long?' I could not understand why he was so worked up. He knew that after a victory by the home team it wasn't so easy to get out of the stadium. But I soon learnt the reason for his agitation. The German army was invading Hungary. Since four o'clock tanks, troop carriers and motorcycles had been moving toward Budapest. Early that morning paratroopers had occupied the airport, bridges and other strategic points.

Even though I was only fourteen I knew immediately that this day, 19 March, spelt danger. It was in fact a turning point in the history of Hungarian Jewry and, as it turned out, the death sentence for well over half a million people. All of us had waited for the invasion of France by the Allies, but what we got instead was Hitler's army. Was Hungary no longer a faithful ally of the Third Reich?

Today we know almost everything about the events preceding this occupation: about Hitler's ultimatum to Admiral Horthy, the aged regent who was bamboozled in the talks held at Klessheim Castle, about Hitler's order to march into Hungary and the scenario devised in Berlin; the long-planned dismissal by force of Prime Minister Kállay. As a result, right-wing extremist politicians allied for better or worse with Hitler's Germany came to power. About 3000 'anti-Nazis', patriotic and pro-Western politicians and officials, aristocrats and intellectuals, were arrested by the Gestapo within days of the occupation and taken to German concentration camps. But for one group of the population the invasion and, above all, the simultaneous arrival of Eichmann's special commandos, meant more than mere arrest; in the long run it spelled certain death for Jews, or Christians who according to the racial laws were considered Jews.

To this day historians disagree about the unique tragedy of Hungarian Jewry. Would it have been possible to ward off the German invasion through a more restrained foreign policy or a more determined resistance, and thus save the lives of hundreds of thousands?

Outside Hungary hardly anyone knows the history of the apparently successful symbiosis of the small Hungarian nation and the Jews of the former Hapsburg multinational empire who became patriotic Hungarians, and the abrupt, puzzling turn to political anti-semitism and ultimately to the Hungarian dimension of the 'final solution'. All this was also to be found in the microcosm of our own widely-dispersed family. We had at varying times seen the pendulum swing between assimilation and exclusion, between the national decline of Hungary and the fate of Hungarian Jewry. Now that fate seemed sealed.

The reverberations of the shock of the precipitous events after that drastic day in March 1944, can be understood only against the historical background. Ever since the settlement in the Carpathian Basin in around 896 the Magyars are among the great losers of European history. With the possible exception of the Albanians, they are the loneliest nation of Europe. The original home of the Hungarians lies west of the Urals, and their closest surviving linguistic relatives are the 30,000 or so Ostiaks and Vogules of the Finno-Ugrian family of nations. Despite their membership of the so-called Ugrian group, Hungarians and Finns cannot cummunicate with each other.

The political unity and territorial integrity of Hungary were destroyed by the Ottoman victory in the fateful battle of Mohacs in 1526: The country was divided into three parts. The heartland, the Great Hungarian Plain, became part of the Ottoman Empire. In the long run, the most crucial effect of the devastation and depopulation of vast territories during Ottoman rule was the slow but unstoppable transformation of the lands under St Stephen's crown into a multi-national state in which the Magyars at the end of the eighteenth century (even without Croatia-Slavonia) constituted only about 40-45 percent of the population. A planned settlement policy brought more and more Serbs and Germans, Slovaks and Croatians into the territory. Separately from the pendulum swings between the failed battle of independence against the Hapsburg monarchy of 1848-49 and the successful Austro-Hungarian Agreement that in 1867 turned the Austrian Empire into the dual monarchy, the mood of the dominant Magyars vacillated between their mission as founders of a great St Stephen's Crown empire in the Carpathian Basin and the profound fear of dying out, the slow death of an isolated nation without relatives between hostile Rumanians, Slavs and Germans.

The Hungarian concept of statehood as well as the suppression of the national minorities were not racist but cultural. All who affirmed their Hungarian identity enjoyed equal opportunities. Instead of working towards consensus among the nationalities, the Hungarian government championed the policy of Magyarisation in all areas. Only Croatia-Slavonia succeeded in winning a special place as a country under St Stephen's crown with administrative, judicial and educational autonomy, and with appropriate representation at the centre.

But at the turn of the century, and above all as a result of the in-toxicating national euphoria sparked off by the celebration of the millennium of the settlement, the Magyarisation measures became government policy without regard for nationalities, and thus the basis of a completely unrealistic vision of the future role of St Stephen's realm in Central and Eastern Europe.

That almost all Hungarian parties and politicians underestimated the dynamics of the nationalism of the non-Hungarian population groups for so long was linked to the impressive, almost sensational, increase in the Magyar-speaking population. It was not merely a matter of linguistic and political assimilation, but also of the widespread effects of economic growth, urbanisation and social mobility. Between 1787 and 1910, that is to say in less than 125 years, the Hungarian population increased by 210 percent, while the non-Magyar peoples grew by only 71 percent. According to the statistical estimates cited by the Hungarian historian Péter Hanák, the number of Germans choosing to be Hungarians exceeded one million, whereas the assimilated Slovaks numbered somewhat more than half a million, and Jews opting for

Magyarhood amounted to approximately 700,000. It is estimated that even prior to World War I the proportion of assimilated Germans, Slavs and Jews reached more than 25 percent of the statistically counted Magyars, or to put it differently the share of the Hungarian-speaking population rose from 46.6 percent in 1880 to 51.4 percent in 1900, and to 54.5 percent by 1910.

When I went to school our textbooks and history teachers swept under the carpet not only the role of Turkic peoples like the Petschenegs and Kumans in Hungarian history, but also the part played by Serbs and Croats, Greeks and Germans, Slovaks and Jews. The fact that János Hunyadi, possibly the greatest military hero of the Turkish wars, the celebrated saviour of the West, whose son, King Mátyás I, became the most outstanding ruler in Hungary's history, was a descendant of Rumanian immigrants from Walachia; that the great writer and general Count Nikolaus (Miklós) Zrinyi alternately called himself a Hungarian and a Croat; that his brother Peter claimed allegiance to the Croatians; that the great national poet and revolutionary Sándor Petöfi was of Slovak-Serbian descent; that of the 13 Honved generals executed on 6 October for plotting revolution and Hungarian liberation, only five were 'pure' Hungarians, and that of these not all of them spoke or understood Hungarian. These and many similar facts show the absurdity of excessive Hungarian national assertiveness, particularly on this 'permament battleground'.

It was a German writer, Horst Krueger, who, as one of the few outside observers, wrote a sensitive essay in which he compared the Hungarians with the Jews: 'Actually, the Hungarians like the Jews are a dispersed people, a people that has repeatedly been subjugated and disenfranchised but who, like the Jews, never gave up... They practiced the art of survival.'

Even though these words were written in connection with the 1956 Revolution crushed by Soviet tanks they nonetheless hold a deeper meaning for the 'golden era' between the Austro-Hungarian Agreement and the collapse of the dual monarchy (1867 to 1918). Even though in its last session of the Assembly in late July 1849, preceding the capitulation before the Austro-Russian armies, Lajos Kossuth's revolutionary government had ordered the emancipation of the then more than 300,000 Jews, it was not until the emancipation edict of 1867 that Magyars of the Jewish faith were granted full civil and legal rights. This was not because of a charitable attitude on the part of the nobility nor because of a Jewish conspiracy to take over economic and financial power, as future anti-semitic ideologues were to claim. The unique relationship between Hungarians and Jews came into being because on the one hand the Jews almost without exception identified with the Hungarian national movement, the Hungarian language, and Hungarian culture during the 1848 revolution, and on the other hand, because Hungary needed people who were loyal and statistically expanded the Hungarian share within the limits of St Stephen's realm and at the same time were prepared (together with Greek and German groups) to fill the jobs disdained by Hungary's middle and lower nobility in the economic and financial sectors and the free professions.

Although it is documented that Jews had lived in the Carpathian Basin for more than a 1,000 years, they did not settle *en masse* until the eighteenth and nineteenth centuries. In 1787 the area held 83,000 Jews; by 1805 that number had risen to 126,620; in 1857 to 413,000, and by 1910 to 911,000. That meant that about five percent of the population of Greater Hungary (excluding Croatia-Slavonia), belonged to the Jewish community. Yet even these figures do not really reflect the role of Hungarian Jewry as pioneers and carriers of the economic and cultural revolution. They formed the middle layers between the landed aristocracy, the impoverished nobility – every tenth Hungarian was a member of the nobility, referred to as 'gentry' since 1870 – as well as the bureaucracy dominated by these groups on the one hand and the millions of agricultural workers and small landowners on the other. The assimilated Jews were both the backbone of capitalism and the conveyors of liberal and socialist ideas. Even though Theodor Herzl, the founder of modern Zionism, was born in Hungary, neither then nor later was Zionist influence a factor in Hungary. The historian John Lukacs has rightly concluded that the exceptional symbiotic relationship between Hungarian Jews and non-Jewish Hungarians in Budapest around the turn of the century was unique. The free development of the cultural and scientific, financial and professional influence of the Jews made Budapest the biggest financial and media centre of Europe east of Vienna. In 1906, 39 daily papers were published in Hungary's capital, including one German-language paper, compared with 24 in Vienna, 25 in London and 36 in Berlin.

The aged Count Gyula (Julius) Andrássy, the first prime minister after the Austro-Hungarian Agreement, had said he would like to see more Jews in Hungary, not fewer. According to Lukacs, Budapest was a reflection of this inseparable and seemingly permanent link. At the turn of the century Jews constituted 16.5 percent of all industrial workers, 54 percent of merchants, 49 percent of physicians, 45 percent of lawyers, one-third of journalists and 25 percent of artists and writers. In Budapest more than 20 percent of the population and as many as 40 percent of voters (given their higher level of education and civic involvement they were committed voters) were Jews, which led the anti-semitic mayor of Vienna, Karl Lueger, to dub Vienna's sister city 'Judapest'.

Despite the predominance of the gentry in the administrative bureaucracy, the judiciary, the political administration, diplomacy and the army, by the turn of the century the parliament had 16 Jewish members and the university two dozen Jewish tenured professors. And Jews who converted soon began to advance in the government. Thus in 1910 Baron Samu Hazai became minister of defence and another convert, Janos Teleszky, finance minister; in 1913 Herzl's nephew, Ferenc Heltai, was elected Mayor of Budapest. But the truly symbolic breakthrough came in 1917 with the appointment of Vilmos Vazsonyi, a practicing Jew, as minister of justice.

Parallel to developments in Austria, Germany and France, anti-semitic tendencies naturally also occurred in Hungary, but not, as is often claimed, against the 160,000 largely Orthodox Yiddish-speaking 'Eastern Jews' in the Carpthian Ukraine and the northern border regions of Transylvania; the primary targets were the assimilated successful Jews of Hungary, above all the Jewish bourgeoisie of Budapest, not only the thousand or so top industrialists and bankers. Despite the resentment of the Christian middle-class against successful Jewish competitors and their conspicuous consumption, the pact between Hungary's nobility and its political elite on the one hand, and the assimilating, loyal Hungarian Jews on the other survived.

The Hungarian Jews proved their loyalty in the First World War as soldiers in the Imperial Army. About 10,000 died in battle, tens of thousands were wounded and decorated for bravery in action. In addition to Colonel General Baron Hazai there were 24 other Jewish generals; General Márton Zöld was one of the most highly decorated officers in the army.

My father, a lawyer, and my uncle, a physician, were among the 25,000 officers of Jewish descent. Both were wounded and decorated for bravery. As soon as the war broke out my father joined the Sixth Infantry Regiment, and on 1 January 1916, was commissioned as a reserve lieutenant. In July 1917 he was taken prisoner by the Russians and did not return home for three years from the prison camp in Vladivostok. On the occasion of his thirtieth birthday he wrote a sad though not desperate letter to his younger sister, saying that he had lost six years of his life in war and as a prisoner in Siberia.

When I began to delve into my ancestry in connection with this book and wanted to know where they came from, who they were, and what they had experienced, I found that most documents were lost and almost all the relatives who were the guardians of the family history were dead. But even the little I found or heard has allowed me to trace the story of my paternal family as members of the Hungarian-speaking bourgeoisie in commerce and industry, and the second and third generation's professional careers.

What has been established is that all of them came from the Bohemian-Moravian provinces or small towns of present-day Slovakia, some on the border of the Carpathians, and that they had been a part of Hungarian culture even prior to the emancipation laws. Yet according to the census of 1910, half of the Jews who claimed allegiance to Hungary also spoke German. Of course at the time this was not extraordinary, since some five million people, about a quarter of the population of Greater Hungary, spoke two or more languages.

Many of the time-worn family documents, above all employment records and school reports, were written in two languages. Baron Edmund von Beust thus certified in August 1869 in Hungarian and German that my great-grandfather, Ignac Loffler, after having worked 'for the past twelve years with great success' was to be named manager of his mill with full power of attorney.

His daughter Ilona, my grandmother, attended the Ursuline Catholic Teachers' Training Academy in the city of Kassa (Kosice) and received her certificate in 1881. At that time this could not have been the usual educational route followed by a girl of the Jewish faith. Looking through her school papers I was startled to see that at the age of thirteen she was licensed to teach in primary schools. She must have been a near-genius. Only later did I discover that, for whatever reason, she had 'corrected' her year of birth from 1863 to 1868. This yen for artificial rejuvenation was passed on to her oldest daughter, Aunt Olly, who managed to reduce her documented age by ten years, and that under communist rule to boot.

Mixed marriages were not a rarity in my grandmother's family: the numerous offspring of her two sisters were spread throughout the world, from Hungary to Great Britain and Canada. Lawyers and pilots, engineers and administrators, as well as an expressionist painter and a theatre director were part of the so-called 'Loffler line'. The most brilliant figure was the husband of my grandmother's youngest sister, Tivadar Farkas, whom the family initially admired from afar and later on ridiculed. He had become wealthy in a rather mysterious fashion, spent a great deal of time on the Riviera, and sent his two sons to Swiss boarding schools. And then came the crash. 'The baron', as the family dubbed him, suddenly had nothing but debts. The older of his two sons went to England, and the younger one, Imre, became the proverbial black sheep. The tabloids featured stories about this 'linguistically gifted telephonist' of Budapest able to chat with the guests of the Japan Coffee House in five or six languages. But his character was so flawed and in some respects possibly damaged that he ended up doing menial work to support his wife and children. At any rate, whenever Imre showed up at our house silent alarms went off. Make sure, the internal message warned, that he does not leave with more than he came with.

Grandfather Leimdorfer, a native of Hlinik, formerly in Hungary and now in Slovakia, after attending commercial schools in Budapest and Vienna worked as a bookkeeper, cashier and secretary, and ultimately became the administrative head of sawmills and steelmills throughout the country. The plants in question were in what today is Slovakia and Transylvania, and for more than three years he worked in Zagreb, the capital of Croatia. His employers lauded him for his efficiency, industriousness and reliability. His children, two sons and two daughters, grew up in the cities and towns of the dual monarchy, and all of them pursued professional careers. Their lives and hopes, their very names, reflected the complete assimilation of Hungary's bourgeoisie. The Leimdorfers, like so many upwardly-mobile people of German and Slovak descent, Magyarised their names to Lendvai. One of the four children, Father's youngest sister, went one step further. Prior to her marriage she converted to Catholicism and became a devout member of her church.

It is safe to assume that her uncle, Grandfather's brother, knew nothing of her break with Judaism. David Leimdorfer, also a native of Hlinik, was then the highly respected Chief Rabbi of the Jewish community of Hamburg. Not in his wildest dreams would he have imagined that a niece of his would one day become the mother of a Cistercian priest.

Unlike this intellectual and internationalist paternal family, my mother's was probably in part the product of a later Eastern immigration, although my great-grandmother is said also to have had Spanish forebears. At any rate, this family group lived in the centre of the Hungarian settlement region of Transylvania. Most of them, like my grandfather Armin Polacsek, were in commerce and, unlike the Lendvais, were very devout. The relatives I met during my school holidays in Transylvania or during their visits to Budapest spoke flawless Hungarian and considered themselves Hungarians.

The break-up of the Austro-Hungarian monarchy was a victory for modern nationalism, and simultaneously the tragic defeat for the idea of a multicultural society and the multinational state built on political equality and minority rights. Whatever the reasons for the collapse of the empire, it was symbolic that the group that had profited from this unique structure, the Jews, became, alongside Austria and Hungary, the biggest losers of World War I.

For Hungarians, a single word, Trianon, came to symbolise the greatest tragedy of its modern history. In the Trianon at Versailles the thousand-year-old history of St Stephen's realm came to an end. Not only did Hungary lose two-thirds of its territory and three-fifths of its population, but more than three million Hungarians were destined to live under foreign rule, even though half of them had their own compact settlements on the periphery of the successor states (Czechoslovakia, Rumania and Yugoslavia). The Hungarian nation had been dismembered. On the day the Versailles Treaty was signed church bells tolled throughout the country, all traffic came to a halt, and in the churches symbolic funeral services were conducted. Almost every Hungarian family was directly affected by the tragedy of Trianon, including our uncles, aunts, and cousins living in towns like Pressburg (known to Hungarians as Pozsony and to Slovaks as Bratislava), Klausenburg (Kolozsvar to Hungarians, Cluj to Rumanians), Kaschau (Kassa, or Kosice), or in villages like my grandparents', Parajd (Praid). Overnight they had all been turned into 'foreigners'. This shock reverberated throughout all of former Hungary, and to this day Hungarians, regardless of political affiliation, have not recovered from it. In kindergartens and schools, at divine service in churches, and in the press, the idea of the return of territories lost to despised neighbours was kept alive.

The incessantly proclaimed slogan 'No, no, never' of course did not come to terms with the question of whether the revision of the hated Trianon treaty was to be won by peaceful means or by force. After Trianon, and in the context of the encirclement of the rump state by the Little Entente (the alliance of Czechoslovakia, Rumania and Yugoslavia championed by France), the Budapest-born writer Arthur Koestler said: 'Perhaps this unique solitude accounts for the strange intensity of its existence; to be a Hungarian is a collective neurosis'.

At any rate, Trianon proved to be a 'fatal obstacle to democratisation' (Thomas von Bogyay). Even twenty years later the politics of revisionism continued to colour daily life in our schools. Our generation was raised in the spirit of 'No, no, never' and 'Rump Hungary is not a state, Greater Hungary is the kingdom of Heaven'. In the illiberal, authoritarian, unrestrained nationalistic climate of the Horthy era, the myth of an out-of-control revisionist campaign formed the basis of that fatal course which ultimately led Hungary, as the satellite of Hitler's Germany, into yet another catastrophe.

However, it would be wrong to believe that the nationalist course was unpopular with or rejected by the cultural elite. On the contrary, the belief that the Versailles Treaty was an unconscionable injustice was the overwhelming sentiment in rump Hungary and also of us in the high school. Hungary's government and political parties sought to win over the British newspaper magnate Lord Rothermere, Mussolini, and later also Hitler, to their cause – at least to the return of the territories in the border regions settled largely by Hungarians.

When the Axis powers returned some border regions of dismembered Czechoslovakia and Rumania to Hungary, I, then an eleven-year-old, and my fellow-pupils were jubilant. With tears in our eyes we sang our national anthem. All our relatives, from Bratislava to Parajd, were just as elated. An uncle, Dr Oszkar Lendvai, who was living in the Slovakian capital, was as great a Hungarian patriot as the relatives in Transylvania who repeatedly risked their fortune, professions and even their freedom in their identification with Hungary's cause. At any rate, within 30 months the then governnment was able to expand Hungary's territory by 85 percent and the population by 58 percent, to almost 15 million. The fact that even though 2 million Hungarians had been reincorporated, 3 million non-Magyars (Rumanians, Slovaks, Serbs, etc) now were subject to Hungarian rule did not disturb the enthusiastic population nor the virulently nationalistic officers and bureaucrats put in charge of the administration of the acquired territories.

Trianon did not merely spell the end of the dream of Hungarian hegemony in the Pannonian Basin. The collapse of Austro-Hungary followed by the 133 days of the Communist republic enthusiastically welcomed by Lenin – on 21 March 1919, it replaced the democratic government that had been peacefully established – also destroyed the historic pact between the ruling political class and Hungarian Jewry.

Many leaders of the Communist regime under Béla Kún were of Jewish descent. This gave rise to the glib equating of Jews and

Communism and the 'Red terror' of the short-lived dictatorship, even though the overwhelming majority of Jews never sided with Bolshevism. When Admiral Miklós Horthy rode into Budapest in November 1919 at the head of the 'White' national army on a white horse, he called Budapest that 'sinful city', thereby setting off vehement anti-semitic outbursts. The pent-up dissatisfaction of the impoverished middle class and the vast number of refugees from the territories of the successor states had finally found an outlet. The 'Red terror' of the Soviet dictatorship was soon replaced by a far more relentless 'White terror' of the officer commandos and paramilitary organisations. According to the German historian Jorg K. Hoensch, the vengeance campaign carried on until the early summer of 1920 victimised real and alleged Communists and innumerable Jews, as well as workers and peasants who had played a role in the implementation of social programmes.

The horrors that were perpetrated after 19 March 1944 (and in part earlier as well) obscured the roots from which they had sprung. That is why one must not forget the chaotic origin of a 25-year-old era that is identified with Miklós Horthy, the regent elected on 1 March 1920.

Randolph Braham, the historian of the Hungarian Holocaust, rightly pointed to this unique paradox: 'The Hungarian Jewish community, which after its emancipation in 1867 experienced an unparalleled rise, was the first to be subjected to anti-Jewish legislation in Europe after World War I'. What he had in mind is the law on the admission of Jewish students to the universities passed by Parliament on 22 September 1920. It was only a trial run and its implementation was attenuated during the ten-year reign of István Count Bethlen, unquestionably the most able and relatively moderate politician of the interwar years. Nonetheless, this 'numerus clausus' regulation marked the overt start of the official anti-semitism of the Christian-nationalist, right-conservative counterrevolution.

Even though the number of Jews in post-Versailles Hungary amounted to a mere 400,000, 4.3 percent of the population, their leading role in high finance, commerce, and industry remained unchanged up to the late 1930s. However, due to the economic crisis, the numerous unemployed academics, together with the inflated officers' corps and bureaucracy, became the props and followers of right-radical ideologies and movements. Intellectuals of Jewish descent were consequently hit especially hard because they either were not admitted to the universities or excluded from government service and university faculties. Moreover, after Hitler's rise to power the various governments took a rightward turn, and the growing influence exerted by the extreme Right, and of National Socialist groups, proved alarmingly successful in the elections of May 1939, in which they won almost a million votes in working-class districts.

Even though only 40 percent of the population had the right to vote, the early successes of the politics of revisionism and the economic upturn resulting from the armaments industry and their exports, above all to the Third Reich, as well as the diplomatic victories of the Axis powers, changed the domestic political situation to the detriment of the liberal and leftist groups. Public opinion overwhelmingly believed that Germany would win a war.

Amidst this atmosphere, Parliament passed the first 'anti-Jewish law' in May 1938, and the second the following April. The classification 'Jew' initially was a religious category and served as the basis for the economic quotas in the professions and admission to institutions of higher learning. The ruin of livelihoods was sealed by the third 'Jewish law' and completed after Hungary's entry into the war on the side of Hitler Germany against the Soviet Union in August 1941. Not only did quota regulations become more stringent, but – and this was a major defeat of the Christian churches – National Socialist race ideology became the basis for discrimination and persecution.

As Raoul Hilberg, the historian of the Holocaust, has pointed out in his chapter on Hungary, Hungarian legislation was harsher than the Nuremberg laws. People with two or more Jewish grandparents were considered Jews, whereas in Germany a half-Jew who did not practice the Jewish religion and was married to a quarter-Jew was not classified as Jewish. In Hungary a half-Jew in a similar situation was regarded as a Jew according to the 1941 law. In addition, Hungary also barred intermarriage, and extramarital intercourse between Jews and non-Jews was classified as 'race defilement'.

István Bibó, the great thinker, in his essay 'On the Jewish Question' puts his finger on the wound that so many 'populist' writers and right-wing historians have ignored, namely that the anti-Jewish laws marked the 'moral decay of Hungarian society'.

These laws gave broad segments of the middle-class and lower middle-class the possibility, to get ahead easily, without personal effort, thanks to the state and at the expense of other livelihoods. Broad segments of Hungarian society welcomed the idea that they could advance not just through work and enterprise but also by homing in on someone else's business, denouncing its owner, checking out his ancestry, provoking his dismissal, and laying claim to his enterprise, and thus in fact completely taking over such a livelihood.

Bibó concluded that all this 'showed an alarming picture of greed, unrestrained dishonesty, and at best the calculated ambition of a substantial portion of that society. This constituted an unforgettable upheaval not only for the victimised Jews but for all decent Hungarians'.

In our day-to-day life our family at first did not feel the effects of the Jewish laws. Paradoxically, in the beginning we even profited from the gradual exclusion of Jews from economic life because my father, being a lawyer, got clients, the victims of aryanisation who had been forced to hand over their property to non-Jews or who needed legal assistance in clarifying their status as citizens. After the many years of relative poverty when my mother's dowry, her valuable rugs and silverware, had to be pawned in times when she sometimes could not even afford a tram-fare, this modest upswing was like a gift from heaven. As concrete evidence that our situation had improved I was given my first bicycle. Yet despite my youth I sensed that this financial upturn of ours was deceptive.

I knew that my admission to Vörösmarty Gymnasium – quotas were in force – was made possible because a relative of my 'Aryan' uncle who was then a high-school teacher in Zalaegerszeg in western Hungary pulled some strings. Nevertheless from 1939 to 1944 I did not suffer any overt discrimination, let alone was subjected to open anti-semitism by pupils or teachers. I was even able to deliver my first lecture at our voluntary self-education group on the role of Jewish writers in Hungarian literature as exemplified by József Kiss and his periodical *The Week*. The Hungarian name of this intellectual self-education group was Onkepzokor, an institution that played an important part at Hungarian high schools under the aegis of teachers.

But then came the first blow. In 1941, my father, who only a little while before had had his picture taken in full dress uniform and all his decorations from World War I, was, like all Jewish reserve officers, stripped of his rank. If memory serves me right he had to report for labour service in Jaszbereny in the summer of 1941 or 1942. His revised identity papers said nothing about his rank, medals and war injuries. The Jews wearing yellow armbands, and the converts wearing white ones, had to perform the most menial tasks. Since he was more than fifty years of age my father came back after a few weeks. For a reserve officer who took pride in his medals, and who had given six years of his life to his country, this was an unbelievable degradation.

Meanwhile the return of the territories ceded at Versailles, welcomed by the vast majority of Hungarians regardless of faith, turned into a dual tragedy for the Jews in those areas. They, who had remained proud Hungarians whether in Greater Rumania or Yugoslavia – many refused to speak the language of those countries – had hoped for a return to the 'good old days'. Instead, they were suddenly confronted with the full harshness of the anti-Jewish laws. The men, in rags and undernourished, were sent out as labour servicemen to the Eastern front. In January 1943, in the course of the Soviet counteroffensive at Voronezh on the Don, the hurriedly-assembled, poorly-equipped Second Hungarian Army was almost completely wiped out. More than 40,000 soldiers were killed and 70,000 taken prisoners. My mother's oldest brother, my uncle Arthur, was probably among those killed, and so we devoted special care to his two children, eight-year-old Hugo and five-year-old Livia.

Alarming news also came in the spring of 1941 from Yugoslavia, reduced to rubble by Hitler, Mussolini and their Hungarian and Bulgarian vassals. Despite the impassioned appeals of Prime Minister Count Pál Teleki, the Horthy regime took part in the aggression, and in the wake of the German army reincoporated parts of Voivodina into Hungary. Scarcely four months after the signing of the agreement, Hungary stabbed its 'friend' Yugoslavia in the back, an act that so dismayed Teleki that he committed suicide on the eve of the attack. Neither his dramatic gesture nor the warnings of the opposition and the handful of far-sighted government officials against total dependence on Hitler's Germany could deter the pro-German general staff and officer corps or the politicians and bureaucrats dazzled by Germany's *blitzkrieg* strategy.

The Hungarian army staged a blood-bath in Ujvidek (Novi Sad) and Szabadka (Subotica) and surrounding areas against unarmed Serbian and Jewish civilians. The toll was 4,000 casualties, of which 1,250 were Jews. Even the Hungarian government of the day could not readily tolerate this shameful deed. The responsible generals and officers were court-martialed, but most of them managed to flee to Germany.

The massacre of Ujvidek, of which Danilo Kiš gave a shattering account in his trilogy, was an unmistakable warning sign for Hungary's Jews and those in the reclaimed Hungarian territories. Moreover, rumours about the deportation of Jews began to seep out from Slovakia and the occupied territories east and south.

A grand-daughter of the late Chief Rabbi Leimdorfer escaped to Budapest from Zagreb, the capital of the fascist Ustasha state. Since her husband was able to furnish documentary proof of his Hungarian citizenship she was permitted to stay in Budapest. Other members of his family managed to survive underground in Zagreb or linked up with the Tito partisans. But a number of them were killed.

Meanwhile we had also begun to hear of the cruel treatment of Hungarian labour servicemen with the yellow armband. Imre, my mother's younger brother, was fortunate: he was able to stay in the region of the Carpathians and survived. Many other Jews from Transylvania, about 10,000, perished in Russia. Some – among them Attila Petschauer, a Hungarian Olympic gold medalist in fencing – were literally tortured to death by the pitiless, brutal officers and NCOs.

We in Budapest felt encouraged when Horthy appointed the moderate, pro-Western Miklos Kállay as head of government. In the political discourse of the time his balancing act between the threatening Third Reich and the sceptical Allies was called the 'Kállay double-play'. That the democratic parties and the Jews, despite discrimination, were still relatively protected was to Kállay's credit. Measures instituted by his stalward defence minister, Vilmos Nagy de Nagybaconi, who was outraged by the abuse of Jewish and politically suspect labour servicemen, succeeded in saving thousands of lives.

During the first years of the extermination of Jews in the German-occupied territories of Europe, the Jews of Hungary enjoyed a degree of freedom unheard-of in the other countries under the sway of the swastika. Still we lived in fear of what the next day would bring – afraid of the future, afraid of the extremists in the government, afraid of the Arrow Cross, and above all afraid of the Germans. We all felt instinctively that our survival was a race against time.

Our imagination would not let us conjure up the unimaginable. What had happened in other parts of occupied Europe simply could not happen here. This, consciously or subconsciously, was the belief of those Hungarian democrats, Jews and non-Jews alike, who expected the speedy collapse of the Hitler regime, given the rapid advance of the Red Army and the expected invasion of the Western allies.

2

The Road to Purgatory

We Hungarian Jews, believers or non-believers, converts or those who learned only that they were of Jewish descent after 1941 when documents were sifted as required by the Nuremberg laws, all lived as though on an island until the spring of 1944. 'But an island not encircled by water,' in Hilberg's apt description of the situation. 'It was a land island set in and protected by a political boundary. The survival of the Jews depended on this boundary; and the Germans had to tear this last barrier down. In March,1944, the Hungarian border fell. The Germans overran the country and the Jews suffered a catastrophe.'

A few days after the German invasion the bad news began to pour in. Hungary's aged regent believed that the retrospective legalisation of the occupation could avert the worst. In fact, however, the country was governed by the German Minister, Hitler's Plenipotentiary, the honorary SS-General Dr Edmund Veesenmayer, with the help of a puppet regime. The extermination of the Jews was taken over by a special commando of between 150 and 200 expert deportation officials under Adolf Eichmann. They organised a Jewish Council to disseminate instructions and to reassure the Jews about their safety. The council puppets in the hands of the Germans called on the Jewish population to maintain discipline and obey orders. Only after the war did we learn that the Jewish leaders in Hungary knew what fate awaited the

Jews, that they knew precisely what had happened in the East to the Jews deported to Auschwitz and other extermination camps.

In that spring of 1944 hardly a day passed without tribulation, fear and a sense of foreboding. By the end of March the Sztójay government ordered the registration and closing of all accounts and assets, the confiscation of typewriters, radios, cameras, bicycles, cars etc, the discharge of all non-Jews working in Jewish households. Jewish lawyers, journalists, actors, and notaries were barred from employment in the public sector; doctors, however, were excepted, for one in three doctors was Jewish and there was concern that the entire hospital and health service system might otherwise collapse. New regulations were issued daily. We were barred from restaurants and cafés, theatres and cinemas; businesses and offices were closed; travel by railway required official permission. We were issued special food ration cards with smaller rations and were allowed to leave our homes for no more than two or three hours.

In the appendix of his standard work on the destruction of Hungarian Jewry, Randolph Braham cites 107 regulations that were issued after the German invasion. Veesenmayer, Hitler's envoy, enthusiastically notified Berlin that the anti-Jewish legal code was drawn up 'with unparalleled rapidity'. For me, then barely fifteen years of age, the regulation of 5 April 1944, requiring all Jews over the age of six to wear a 3.8-inch-square canary yellow Jewish star was not only demeaning – that was true of all of us – but simply incomprehensible. At the last moment, in response to the repeated intervention of Cardinal Primate Justinian Serédi, members of the clergy, highly decorated war veterans, disabled veterans and converted widows of Christians were exempted from this regulation.

Still another regulation hit home even more forcefully. On 5 May Jewish students were prohibited from wearing their school uniform. That meant that I was expelled from my class, so to say from my own society. Now I no longer belonged. Since it was only six weeks before the end of the term my best friend, not Jewish, brought the final report to my house. To this day I can still see how he stood before me, saying good-bye to me, his eyes filled with sadness. From that spring on I was no longer a true Hungarian because I was a Jew, despite my Hungarian mother tongue, despite the fact that I was the top in the class in Hungarian history and literature, despite the fact that I was a passionate fan of the Ferencvaros football team.

What did being a Jew mean for me personally? A statement by the German poet Hilde Domin echoes my feelings: 'For me being a Jew does not mean being part of a religious community or national community or a matter of race. It is a community of destiny. I was pushed into it, without being consulted, as into life itself.'

Under 'normal' conditions, this community of destiny barely manifested itself in my everyday life. The basis of my friendships, of my relationship with women, my two marriages, have never had anything to do with my Jewishness. My mother did take me as a small child to the synagogue on the High Holy days, where I was terribly bored, but she did not force me to observe Jewish traditional practices. Even with my father Jewishness was not a matter of belief, but the memory of his parents and respect for the religiosity of my mother. He did not attend religious services. In our family, Sunday was the day of rest; we celebrated Christmas and Easter, and we, that is to say my father and I, did not fast on the Day of Atonement. My knowledge of Hebrew – even at school – was hardly worth mentioning, and my knowledge of Jewish religious laws was sparse.

What therefore does being a Jew mean to me, who has always considered himself primarily a citizen of the world or a European with Hungarian-Austrian roots and only secondarily as a Jew? Perhaps the meaning lies in what Hans Jonas, the great German-Jewish philosopher, calls the collective memory of suffering. In our contemplation of the year 1944 in Hungary, Jonas's words seem highly pertinent:

> The Jews were not chosen for extermination because of their religion, so that subsequently another creed could emerge victorious, but solely because of their race. Converted Jews, even the nun Edith Stein, were exterminated the same way because of their Jewish blood or Jewish race.

Jonas concludes that Jewishness is 'an alliance of destiny, a belonging' which 'cannot be arbitrarily dissolved'. Almost all international personages in this book *Jewish Portraits*, particularly the Austrians, Germans and Hungarians, spoke of a bond forged by destiny.

What I and my generation learned was that in a single day everything can collapse, a recognition that has coloured my entire life. Even though more than 50 years have passed since that day, subconsciously I can never feel completely secure. If one recalls that we, the survivors, escaped the most cruel, concentrated, most accelerated extermination campaign of the war, probably of modern history, it will not be hard to agree with the historian Hans Kohn, that history is 'an open process in which the unexpected can occur at any time'.

The hounding of Jews – this unprecedented and unexpected phenomenom – hit us with a vengeance in the chaotic spring and summer of 1944 after years of relative calm. Yet what does 'us' mean in this context? Hungary's territory after the return of the many lost regions after April 1941 already included more than half of the pre-Versailles area; the number of Jews thus increased from 401,000 to 725,000, or to 4.9 % of the total population of Greater Hungary. This number, however, was limited to persons of the Jewish faith. If one takes into account those considered Jews under the Nuremberg laws it is estimated that the above figure was 60,000 to 100,000 larger, which would mean that between 800,000 and 825,000 human beings were poised on the brink between life and death.

The German and Hungarian killers worked at top speed to wipe out all these lives: old and young, men and women, children and infants. And for Hungary the thesis also applied that the crimes of the perpetrators were not limited to Jews as the sole victims. From the beginning of the German occupation to the bitter end in the spring of 1945 tens of thousands died, soldiers and resistance fighters and deserters, Catholic anti-Nazis and Social Democrats, members of the nobility and Communists. Yet one indisputable fact remains, as the Nobel medalist Elie Wiesel put it so succinctly: 'Not all victims were Jews – but all Jews were victims'.

Like everywhere else, the first measure taken in Hungary was to restrict freedom of movement. The country was divided into six zones, including Budapest. The concentration, ghettoisation in selected apartments, districts and cities were the logical first steps to deportation. In June the regulations were implemented for Budapest. About 190,000 people in 36,000 houses had to vacate their apartments within five days and move into 2,681 buildings marked with yellow stars. Somewhat later the number of houses bearing the star was reduced to 1,981, and the residents were given a mere eight days to vacate their quarters. To visualise this one must try to picture the population of a medium-sized city all moving out *en masse*. To make matters worse it kept on raining. The moving companies and operators of horse carts were kept busy. About 19,000 apartments had to be vacated and made available to others. Our family also had to get out of our apartments, where already my grandparents had lived and in which my father had his law office; we had to move in with an uncle of my mother.

The hour of the profiteers of aryanisation had struck. Those with connections acquired 'Jewish furniture' at bargain rates or without paying anything at all. It was a terrible shock, an unprecedented upheaval. We were thrown out of our home; my father was without a profession and without income, and we had to share a small apartment with people we hardly knew. However, that was but a prelude to what still lay ahead.

We young people adjusted relatively quickly to our new surroundings and formed new friendships. We were allowed to leave our house for no more than two hours a day. My father filed innumerable requests with various government offices for inclusion in the lists of the so-called 'privileged', based on his war-time decorations and record as a prisoner of war in Russia.

Meanwhile the 'Final Solution' was going full steam ahead although we were unaware of it. The German-Hungarian scenario was the same throughout the country, from the Carpathian Ukraine to Transylvania and the Hungarian Plain. At first the people were herded together in improvised ghettos in brick yards and subjected to brutal searches and torture. Special policemen and detectives were brought in from other parts of the country to interrogate the Jews about valuables they might have hidden or given to Christian friends for safekeeping. After being interrogated and often beaten up they were marched off to the railway stations where cattle cars were waiting. The police ordered them into the wagons, 70 persons in each freight car equipped with a full bucket of water and an empty one for excrement. In the burning heat of summer the police crammed the hapless victims into the railway carriages, sealed them and chalked the number of persons in each compartment on the outside. Each transport consisted of 45-wagon trains, which meant that the average transport held about 3,150 Jews. The Hungarians in charge proudly reported to their German masters that between 15 May and 7 July, 147 trains holding 437,402 Jews had been sent off to Auschwitz.

My grandparents from Parajd in Transylvania wrote to us in Budapest as late as 26 April. They were very worried and not well, yet they still managed to send us a little package. On 1 May my mother mailed them a card of thanks, but it was returned to us with the notation 'moved'. According to Braham's book the transport of Jews from the small towns of the Szekler region to the Marosvasarhely ghetto in fact began on 3 May. My grandparents, little Livia and my cousin Hugo, together with 29 other relatives in neighbouring villages, disappeared without a trace.

Thirty-two years later when I stood in Auschwitz in front of a pile of shoes and eyeglass frames, artificial limbs, empty suitcases and tons of hair I thought that this braid might have been little Livia's or that pair of children's shoes my cousin Hugo's – I had promised to send him the school uniform of a Budapest high school. On that summer day in Auschwitz I, a survivor who had not been in Auschwitz, felt deeply ashamed. Together with a small group of Austrian journalists I looked at the prison compound, the yard, the wall where prisoners were shot, the gas chamber and the crematorium. Standing in front of that mountain of hair and remembering Livia I broke down in tears. Our group left the camp and took the bus back to Cracow, but Auschwitz never left me. Over and over again I read Paul Celan's 'Death Fugue': 'Keep playing the violins darkly then you rise up as smoke in the air, then you have a grave in the clouds where you do not lie close'. For us in Budapest, too, a grave in the air had long been prepared.

The destruction of the Jewish community of Budapest was to be the crowning glory of the exemplary work of Veesenmayer, Eichmann and their Hungarian henchmen. The evacuation of the 200,000 Jews of Budapest was to be completed by the end of July. The chief of the Jewish affairs section of the German Foreign Office, Eberhard von Thadden, had spoken of the plan as early as May. On a specified day the Jews were to be brought to an island in the Danube outside Budapest. All bus and tram traffic was to be halted on that day. Eichmann's special commando, Hungarian police and gendarmerie forces from the provinces, together with the mailmen and chimney sweepers from Budapest, were to participate in this 'monster action'.

After the failure of that plan Veesenmayer and Eichmann tried to persuade Horthy to open three huge mass camps in Budapest and to begin with the deportations on 27 August. Six trains were to transport 20,000 people to the extermination camps, followed by three trains a day carrying 9,900 people.

I don't remember exactly whether we left that house of our relatives with the yellow star mid-July or in August and secretly returned to our old, still-unoccupied apartment. It was a daring move. We decided to spend the night in my father's office. My parents were very excited and kept on whispering throughout the night, but I fell asleep in a comfortable easy chair even though I knew that we were in extreme danger. After all, the deportations from the countryside were taking place openly before the eyes of the world. And rumours abounded. Our night-time, dangerous excursion to our old apartment in the face of curfews and prohibitions of free movement was basically one last desperate gesture of revolt.

Suddenly, however, there came a let-up, even though only temporarily. The deportations were halted because of world-wide protests. The aged nominal head of state, Miklós Horthy, convened some loyal units in the capital and yielded to the protests of President Roosevelt, the Swedish King, the highly active Papál Nuncio, Angelo Rotta, and to a note of the neutral states. He put a stop to the deportations and ordered the withdrawal of the police forces secretly ordered to Budapest from the countryside.

Nonetheless, Eichmann and his SS troops managed at the last moment to arrange for the deportation of 4,000 Jews from the suburbs of Budapest, including Kispest, to Auschwitz, and of some thousands of internees from the Kistarcsa camp. This raised the number of deportees to 444,152.

These cold statistics included people we loved, close friends and relatives of my mother, the Rozsa family form the Kispest suburb, who ended up in Auschwitz. Only the then thirteen-year-old daughter Kato survived, because she looked older, was strong, and was put to work. Her mother died shortly after being liberated following a death-march to another concentration camp. She was 38, the same age as my mother at the time. Kato's future husband was sent to work in the Serbian copper mines of Bor. At the request of Hitler's Minister, Albert Speer, the Hungarian authorities had to send almost 10,000 Jews to Bor in 1943, since almost all Serbian Jews had been killed the year before and new slave labourers were urgently needed. In September 1944 the Germans and Hungarians had to vacate this territory. During the retreat the Hungarian accomplices of the Waffen SS executed about 2,000 unarmed, starved slave labourers. Kato's husband for some reason or other missed the first transport and had to join the second one. This group was luckier. Tito partisans attacked the escort troops and at the last moment prevented the liquidation of the prisoners. The fate of this one Budapest family is a telling example of the chain of accidental breaks, of persecution and flight, of massacres and miracles of survival throughout Jewish history.

Aside from these hapless victims of the special commandos in the suburbs, the Jews of Budapest escaped certain death only because the news of the landing of the Allies in France, the rapid advance of the Soviet forces and, above all, the defection of Rumania on 23 August 1944 radically changed the situation and substantially strengthened the resistance of the moderate circles around the aged Horthy. With the appointment of his loyal aide General Géza Lakatos as Prime Minister on August 29, Horthy signaled his wish for a *volte-face*, for switching sides.

Meanwhile the world learned of the fate of Hungarian Jews who had been hurriedly deported, two-thirds of whom had been sent to the gas chambers or murdered in the camps. In July Churchill wrote to his

Foreign Secretary, Antony Eden: 'There is no doubt that this is probably the greatest and most horrible crime ever committed in the whole history of the world'.

Numerous books and articles have been written about the 'conspiracy of silence' surrounding Auschwitz, particularly about the tragedy of Hungary's Jewry. In my opinion one of the most candid testimonies is that of the then head of the Department of Emigration of the Swiss Legation, Consul Carl Lutz:

> When I saw that many persons were in mortal danger I knew that I had to act. My conscience compelled me to do something for the hundreds of thousands of defenseless people and consequently I acted even though I did not have my government's permission. In 1944 I witnessed the bloodthirsty fury of the Nazis and their Hungarian vassals in Budapest. I was ashamed of the British, the Americans, and also of my own country. I was ashamed above all because all stood by and watched the deportation of almost half a million people, among them the sick and the old, in the spring of 1944, and by their inaction assisted in the deed. The majority of the persecutors were members of the corrupt Hungarian middle class. These people had been inculcated with hatred of Jews since the end of the First World War. For 25 years incitement against Jews had been stirred up, but all of us share in the guilt. All the diplomats of the democratic countries. All of us knew everything – and kept silent. In truth I was active only in the very last part of the tragedy, in 1944. My conscience bothers me because for more than two years, while in Budapest, I kept silent about the atrocities even though I knew.

As we shall see, Carl Lutz did everything he could on behalf of the victims, and he should be the last person to blame himself. The responsibility for inaction lies with the political leaders of the West and the Red Cross as well as Pope Pius XII and the Vatican – and the officials of the various Jewish organisations in the West and in Palestine as well as Hungary. But in the final analysis, it was the Germans and their Hungarian henchmen who were responsible for a systematic extermination which even within the framework of the 'Final Solution' shows some unique features.

Horthy, contrary to the evidence, claims in his memoirs not to have been informed about the deportations between May and July 1944. Despite his awareness of the deportations and his attempts to deny his responsibility, for which he stands condemned, it must be acknowledged that during that summer of 1944 he did prevent the deportation of Budapest's Jews to Auschwitz. This intervention is one of the few bright spots in an otherwise bleak balance sheet.

While the Lakatos government was conducting secret truce negotiations with the Soviets a number of measures somewhat easing the restrictions on Budapest's Jews were issued. On 15 October 1944, Horthy, after months of irresolution and hesitation, broadcast an appeal to the nation. The news about his order to cease military action against the Red Army and his change of allegiance spread like wildfire.

For the first time in six months we went for a walk without wearing the hated yellow star. 'Come with me,' my father said to me in an almost festive manner, and in a firm voice added, 'See, my supreme commander doesn't desert us'. I still remember how free and happy the two of us felt. But our elation was short-lived. Within a couple of hours everything collapsed.

Horthy's preparations to proclaim an armistice and to effect a disengagement were amateurish, naive and had the ingredients of a tragicomedy. The German occupation troops and their Hungarian henchmen, the Arrow Cross gangs, had long known of the plan, and they promptly struck back. Now, as in March, the old regent had to yield, revoke his proclamation and even legitimise the appointment of Ferenc Szálasi, the head of Arrow Cross, as Prime Minister. Had he refused, the Germans would have murdered his younger son whom a special SS unit had kidnapped. Taken into German 'protective custody,' the broken head of state left the country, never to return. Five days later we were already in mortal danger.

On 20 October 1944, early in the morning, a number of uniformed Arrow Cross men and policemen with swastika arm bands entered in 'our' yellow-star house. They picked up all able-bodied men between the ages of 16 and 48. Later the age limit was raised to 60. I had just turned 15. According to that regulation they were not supposed to take me along, but that kind of legalism did not bother these men in uniform.

My mother was full of bitter recriminations, accusing my father of being impotent and confused. He hadn't done a thing, she said, to save me from the reach of the Arrow Cross. A few days later my fifty-four-year-old father was also taken away. Because of the deteriorating military situation they couldn't ship us to the extermination camps in the East. Consequently 50,000 'loaned Jews' were sent to German arms factories. Later Eichmann and Veesenmayer wanted another transfer of 50,000 Budapest Jews sent to Germany. But when the Red Army on December 8 closed in on the capital these plans proved too ambitious.

The small group from our building together with men from other houses was taken to the Budapest race track where thousands of others were already waiting. Over and over again I tried to convince the policemen that I should be sent home because of my age. 'Shut up; once you're wherever you'll be sent your case will be straightened out'.

We were shifted from place to place. In the outskirts of Budapest we had to dig ditches to prepare for the defence of the city. In November, in wind and rain and hail, we dragged ourselves in the direction of Austria. We were supposed to be the vanguard of the infamous death-march, that ultimate satanic action of the SS. It was bitter cold and we slept in close embrace either in the concrete hangars of the Ferihegy airport, out in the open or in ditches.

When I try to conjure up what I remember most from those days after being abducted and the beginning of the death-march I always see the same image: the murder of an older journalist with whom I had talked the evening before about his profession, the war and many more things. Hopeful that he would survive, he whispered to me that he had hidden bank-notes in his shoe; only hours later he was executed in full daylight somewhere in the outskirts of Budapest by a Danubian Swabian speaking perfect Hungarian wearing either a Waffen SS or Arrow Cross uniform. My friend the journalist was shot because he was suffering from diarrhea and was not able to climb out of the ditch quickly enough and join our contingent. I heard the shot quite close by. The lifeless body of this friendly man who seemed to me, a teenager, old but who probably was not yet fifty, symbolises death for me.

We had to keep on marching. The guards prodded me to hurry up. From time to time I would hear a shot. In the ditches exhausted men and women were lying around.

While my father and I were taken away separately, my desperate mother was left alone in the apartment in the house with the yellow star. She already knew that her parents had been murdered, that her older brother had been missing in the East for almost two years, and that her younger brother was in a labour camp somewhere in Transylvania. And now her husband and only child had been taken away. These shocks and tragedies left her with an irreversible facial paralysis, a serious depressive neurosis, and a hearing defect. She never recovered from these blows.

After a week my father managed to escape from an improvised camp in a school in Budapest. And I owe my survival at least in part to my friendship with Dönci, the son of the building's wealthy owner. He had built a hiding-place behing a wall in the caretaker's apartment, but the Arrow Cross had caught Dönci. The caretaker's wife, not herself Jewish, had witnessed the arrest.

To this day I still don't know how this very resolute and reliable woman found where Dönci had been taken. At any rate one day she appeared in Pecel, near Budapest, and engaged our two middle-aged, approachable guards in a lively conversation. Soon after that she signaled us to make ourselves scarce. Had we been older we would probably have been more wary. But Dönci and I did not hesitate for a moment. Without exchanging a single word we dissappeared in the bushes. After removing our yellow arm bands and a long walk we reached the end stop of the Budapest comuter train and took the next back to the capital. We were particularly proud of taking this dangerous trip without paying.

I have forgotten, or perhaps I never knew, how much our caretaker paid the guards. In any event it was a sort of exchange. My mother had hardly any money left, but the well-to-do owner of the apartment building knew that I even though two years younger than Dönci, was more determined and quick-witted than his somewhat spoiled son. Whatever the circumstances it was not until much later I realised that this intervention had saved me from the fatal trek to the Austro-Hungarian border. On this death-march the SS guards and the fanatical adherents of the Szálasi regime and their like-minded Austrian comrades murdered about 40,000 people.

Appalled, the Red Cross representative Born reported on this as follows:

> The agreement between Germany and Hungary to send 50,000 Hungarian Jews to Germany for forced labour in the joint war effort must be one of the most shameful pacts ever. In columns of thousands these inconsolably unhappy people, bone-tired and starved, dragged themselves westward. Old people, men and women. Young boys and girls, but also children, driven by the perverted Arrow Cross troopers, staggered slowly on the edge of the road toward the setting sun. The lightest bags proved too heavy after a couple of miles and were simply left on the road. Cowering on the edge of the road, without blankets, without food, desperate and uncertain where their journey would end, these unfortunate people spent the cold autumn nights, only to be driven on the next morning. Often shots were fired when those too tired couldn't go on. The road to Vienna became a road of horror and will live on in memory as the road of hatred. Forty columns of thousands of people had to start out on their death-march to Germany.

Among the victims was one of the great modern poets of Europe, the 35-year-old Miklós Radnóti, who wrote his most beautiful poems on this death-march. He carried his last manuscript, a little black notebook, in his pocket when, half-starved and unable to keep on going, he was liquidated by a shot in the neck, on the outskirts of the west Hungarian city of Gyor. In five languages he 'politely requested' the finder to send the notebook which 'contains poems' to the address noted therein. After almost two years his body and those of 20 other victims who, like Radnóti, had been driven westward from the copper mine near Bor south of Belgrade clear across Hungary were found – together with the miraculously preserved notebook. It contains his last magnificent poem, written on 31 October 1944, a few days before his murder: Radnóti considered himself a Catholic since his youth. Abbot Sándor Sik, himself a poet, had baptised him. Sik, also of Jewish descent, had been hidden by the fellow-members of his order and thus had been saved. Other prominent writers and critics who were murdered also regarded themselves as devout Christians.

The escape from the death-march by no means guaranteed safety, only a breathing space. No sooner did we think that we were relatively safe in the house with the yellow star when the unpredictable Szálasi regime hit out again. It had decided to establish a ghetto. With that all Jews were subjected to the dual terror of the Germans and the Arrow Cross. About half of the Jews of Budapest survived largely because the Red Army captured the partially destroyed city, but were it not for the unparalleled humanitarian actions by a handful of courageous diplomats few would have been saved. The world knows the story of the legendary Raoul Wallenberg, who rescued countless people and disappeared without trace after the arrival of the Russians. But practically nothing is known of the heroism of two other men, Carl Lutz, the Swiss Consul, whom I mentioned earlier, and Giorgio Perlasca, an Italian businessman who passed himself off as a Spanish diplomat.

Switzerland was able to play a key role when the Swiss Embassy, particularly Consul Lutz as chief of its foreign affairs section, was allowed to issue immigration certificates to Palestine (then a British mandate) for 788 families as well as a maximum of 7,800 protective passes. With Lutz's approval 30,000 such protective certificates were issued. Young Zionist groups working in the embassy's building took over the potentially highly dangerous task of issuing genuine or forged documents to the persecuted persons living in the houses with the yellow star. These documents also gained exemption from labour service. To mislead the Arrow Cross every protective pass was numbered, but the number sequence varied so that not a single one showed a number above 7,800 (the maximum allowed by the government).

While I was still in the forced labour unit my father got us a Swiss protective passport. I still don't know whether it was genuine or phoney. Since after 15 November all Jews or Christians who, according to the racial laws, were considered Jews were to be herded together in an 'international ghetto' of protected buildings controlled by neutral states, that document establishing a claim to apartments was of vital importance. This quarter in the centre of town comprised 125 buildings. Most of the people, about 17,000, lived in the so-called Swiss buildings, followed by the Swedish houses with 4,500 inmates; then came Spain, the Vatican and Portugal.

In the middle of November we, with only a handful of belongings, together with other holders of protective passes, were sent to a nearby house, 47 Hollan Street. A protective house turned out to be better than the large ghetto, which was sealed off on 10 December. Between 65,000 and 70,000 people were concentrated there. In the ghetto as well as in the protective houses anywhere from 30 to 50 people were crammed into two- and three-room apartments, the difference being that it was easier for non-Jewish friends to get food and medications to the people in the protective houses than to the ghetto, which was more strictly controlled.

Even more important was the matter of safety. True, the Arrow Cross gangs and their bureaucratic henchmen were active everywhere. They looted, robbed, murdered; they did not even stop at hospitals and children's homes. Jews everywhere were in constant danger, but the diplomats and their Hungarian aides were able to protect the people in these specially marked houses with more success if word came to them in time, often passed along by neighbours.

For a teenager like me the terror reign of the Szálasi bandits, group living, spending time with emotionally fragile people and the mass feeding was easier than for older people. We half-children-half-adults occasionally even became frivolous. One day my father sent me to a client to pick something up. Since I had plenty of time I removed my star and went to a movie and then took a trolley-bus back home. When I saw that a checkpoint had been set up at the next intersection I got off and walked back to our house. Back home I told of my heroic deed and instead of praise I got slapped – a rare case of physical punishment. Under these special conditions my father's reaction was probably pedagogically correct; but very soon these sorts of excursion became impossible.

Our guardian angels Wallenberg and Lutz as well as the Papal Nuncio Angelo Rotta and the Red Cross representative Friedrich Born saved the lives of tens of thousands, Jews and Christians alike, but the bravest of them all was undoubtedly Giorgio Perlasca. This Italian businessman and ex-Fascist had met the future Spanish Ambassador to Budapest during the Spanish Civil War. Perlasca spent the last war years in Hungary, and even obtained a Spanish passport. When the Soviet troops surrounded Budapest the Spanish ambassador, like most other diplomats, left the capital. Perlasca, instead of seeing to his personal safety, claimed to be an official representative of Spain. Soon stories about a Spanish diplomat by name of Jorge Perlasca who ran the risk of taking endangered Jews into a building enjoying Spanish diplomatic immunity, of saving others after negotiations with and threats to the Germans and Hungarian Nazis began to circulate. According to official reports about 3,000 (some estimates put the number at no fewer than 5,200) Jewish men, women and children owe their lives to this strange man. At the end of the war Perlasca returned to Italy to lead a completely ordinary life until many years later Hungarian Jews who owed him their life found him by pure accident. This fantastic story about the 'banality of good' was subsequently made into an Italian television film, and a book about him was published. In 1990 Perlasca was honoured by Hungary, Israel and Italy.

In his old age Perlasca recalled the brutalities, particularly the mass shootings, on the banks of the Danube:

> Hundreds, even thousands, were driven to the bank of the river. Some tried to get to the near-by international protective houses. All were shot. When they were driven down to the quay where the shootings were taking place they tearfully pleaded for help. They had to take off their shoes and then were handcuffed to one another in twos and threes, but only one was shot, and he'd pull the others with him into the icy water.

That's exactly what happened. And occasionally uniformed Arrow Cross guards would grab Jews or other suspects on the street and throw them into the freezing Danube from a bridge. We on our street also feared for our lives when, living as we did only a few hundred metres from the river, heard the thundering marching columns of the Hungarian Nazis. Once a diplomat from a neutral country together with a Hungarian interpreter appeared literally at the last moment as a protective house was being broken into. We never found out whether it was Wallenberg, Lutz or Perlasca, but whoever it was managed to save the people living under Swiss and Swedish protection.

All chronicles of this gruesome winter as well as Perlasca's memoirs noted that while thousands of people were being murdered and the thunder of canons could be heard in the eastern suburbs, cinemas and theatres continued to operate, and coffee houses and restaurants were open. During the Christmas season the bookstores advertised their new books. The nightclubs and café terraces were crowded, Perlasca says, even though executions were taking place up to the very end. 'I saw,' he writes, 'how the victims (a few hundred) were forced to march in twos with handcuffs, bare feet, and no clothes for two kilo-metres. Then they were made to kneel down on the river bank in front of the Hungaria and Negresco coffee houses and shot in the neck.'

In the big ghetto in the seventh district Wallenberg, Perlasca and Lutz saw hundreds of frozen bodies in the garden of the main syna-gogue, in shops and the offices of the Jewish community. When the Red Army liberated the ghetto on January 18 more than 3,000 bodies were lying in the streets, according to official reports. During raids and lootings, massacres and shootings, neither the police nor the Hungarian army stood up to the murderous Arrow Cross. But the more intelligent perpetrators already knew as they were committing their crimes that the war was lost, and some of them tried in the final days to make contact with Jewish activists and the few resistance groups to prevent a general massacre, possibly in the ghetto.

Budapest paid a high price for Hitler's order to defend 'fortress Budapest from house to house'. The Pest side was largely liberated on 17-18 January, we on Hollan Street as early as the thirteenth. The night of 18 January the Germans blew up all the Danube bridges. For us and many on the Pest shore, the war nonetheless continued because we were being fired on from the hills and the Buda Castle on the other side of the Danube. Not until 13 February did the futile battles in the castle area cease.

'In Budapest Vienna was being defended,' so said the National Socialist weekly *Das Reich*. The scorched earth policy cost 20,000 civilian lives and tens of thousands of Hungarian, German, and Soviet soldiers. Entire city blocks, more than 30,000 buildings, were destroyed.

Despite the weakness of the Hungarian resistance it is nonetheless true that about 25,000 people, in part with forged papers, in part hid-den by friends and non-Jewish relatives, survived in Budapest. Thus I learned after the war that the principal of my high school, Dr József Hittrich, had hidden dozens, at times as many as 50 Jews, deserters and resistance fighters in the air-raid shelter and other areas of the school.

Looking the other way and plugging their ears, and not the active participation in the extermination process, was probably the position of the overwhelming majority of those Hungarians who neither stood up to the German occupation and the Arrow Cross terror nor took part in the 'aryanization' and the subsequent overt robberies. At the same time the deportation of 440,000 people and the later death-march did not elicit any noticeable protests.

The fate of one of my aunts, Izabella Rajna (nee Lendvai), who lived in the provincial city of Zalaegerszeg in western Hungary, bears out the fact that the regional administrations controlled by the extreme Right and Arrow Cross continued on their frenzied course even after the capture of Budapest. I recently received documentary evidence that my aunt, a Roman Catholic married to an 'Aryan' high school teacher, a resident of the town for two decades, had been put under police surveillance in October 1944, after the Arrow Cross took power. Even though she was married to a first lieutenant on active service, she had to report to the police every Monday, Wednesday and Saturday, was allowed to leave her apartment only for an hour between 11am and noon, was not allowed to receive visitors nor make phone calls nor send telegrams, and her mail was censored by the police. The reason: 'The free movement of the above-named individual of the Jewish race is not desirable and therefore must be subjected to intensive observation'. Between October 1944 and 8 January 1945, my aunt reported to the police 31 times. Then she and other partners of mixed marriages who according to the racial laws were considered Jewish were arrested and jailed. Since my officer uncle, a '100%, Aryan', feared the worst, he asked to be demobilised to be around to assist his wife. With the help of doctors he knew my uncle at last managed to have my aunt certified as ill and have her transferred to the gynecological clinic of a hospital outside the town. Thus she survived to be reunited with her son, who was later ordained a priest; he had survived the war in a Cistercian seminary under the aegis of a friendly abbot. Had it not been for the energetic efforts of her husband and the help of friends she might well have died in a death-march to Austria or in a German concentration camp. And who knows how many similar cases ended less happily?

During the final months and weeks of the terror regime of the Arrow Cross the non-Communist political and military leaders of the underground in Sopronkohida on the Hungarian-Austrian border were executed and countless intellectuals and members of the clergy, including József Mindszenty, the Bishop of Veszprem and future Cardinal Primate, were arrested.

World War II claimed many victims in Hungary. Between 400,000 and 500,000 lost their lives, including 297,000 Jews in Hungary proper. In the territories reincorporated during the war and then lost again in 1944-45 267,000 Jews died. For the survivors, including my family, 18 January in Pest and 4 April in the rest of Hungary meant liberation. Soon thereafter we reclaimed our old apartment. The bar owner from across the street who had made himself at home there moved out relatively quickly. The old neighbours were still there and pretended to be glad to see us back. One of them had seen us there on that critical night in July, but despite the orders of the then government had 'kept her mouth shut,' as she told us.

What the writer Jean Améry said in his excellent essay ('Beyond Guilt and Forgiveness') holds true for Hungary as well, although the circumstances were different: 'Nobody can say how many saw the crimes, approved of them, committed them or, in their impotent aversion, allowed them to be committed in their name'. The Hungarian historian László Varga drew what I think is the right conclusion: 'The fate of the Hungarian Jews, the extermination of the overwhelming majority of them, weighs down German and Hungarian history in equal measure'.

It would be a dangerous oversimplifcaton to claim that the defeat of Hitler's Germany and the entry of the Red Army was seen as liberation only by the Jews or those of Jewish descent. Numerous non-Jewish citizens, Catholics, Protestants, and agnostics – democrats, Socialists, landholders, liberals – welcomed the collapse not only of the Arrow Cross regime of terror but of 'historic Hungary'.

The conduct of the 'liberators' was – as in all Soviet-occupied territories – not exactly designed to create feelings of friendship for the Soviet Union. Rape, looting and brutal intervention in internal politics managed to add to the naked hatred that many already nursed. With the passage of time the uncertain fate of prisoners of war, the abduction of tens of thousands of civilians to forced labour camps and the Soviet support of the Communist offensive persuaded an overwhelming majority of Hungarians to see the new era under the Red Star as the beginning of yet another bondage.

But in Year Zero, in the spring of 1945, everything was still undecided, including our fate. No sooner were we liberated and able to rejoice over the newly-won life when the sudden disappearance of my father threw us into despair. What had happened? At a Soviet checkpoint he showed them, either out of exuberance or more probably ignorance, a Russian document, a sort of identity card. What he had not taken into account was that this paper dating back to 1918 or 1919 had been signed by a White officer, the commander of a prison camp in Siberia, obviously a 'counter-revolutionary' for the Soviets. Consequently my father was accused of counter-revolutionary activity.

After a numer of interrogations he was brought to Retsag, a special section of military intelligence (incidentally where Cardinal Mindszenty was interned for a time). In what was probably the best plea of his career my father finally managed to convince the suspicious officers that he was a minor, politically utterly harmless, Budapest lawyer, that he had never had anything to do with the 'Whites' or 'Reds' in the Russian civil war, let alone now, after the so-longed-for liberation. After a few days he returned home, but the incident stayed with us a long time.

After this experience, my father had all three of us enrolled in the Hungarian Social Democratic Party so that we could obtain clear, unambiguous documents in Hungarian and Cyrillic. This move as well as my passionate interest in Stefan Zweig and his work soon brought me into the exciting and increasingly dangerous world of Hungarian politics.

3

From Stefan Zweig to Lenin

Everything began with Stefan Zweig. Sad to say I no longer know which of his books was the first to capture my imagination. Could it have been *The Royal Game*? I had been a member of my school's chess team and was passionately involved with the game, buying chess books. Or was it perhaps his three novella volume *Conflict* or one of his biographies? Or *Brazil, Land of the Future*? Many years later when I found myself in Rio de Janeiro I fulfilled one of my fondest dreams by driving to the small town Petropolis. There stood the house in which this profoundly pessimistic homesick writer committed suicide in 1942 with his second wife. But I was bitterly disappointed to find that the house itself did not have a memorial plaque. The only commemoration note is the German and Hebrew inscription on the gravestone of the two Zweigs.

His last book, which I read during the war in Budapest, *The World of Yesterday*, probably made the strongest impression on me. In this strangely magical work, written so far from his homeland, Zweig presents a captivating picture of the never-to-return world of the 'great peace'.

The young people of today cannot possibly imagine how extremely popular Stefan Zweig was both in Europe and the former Soviet Union. Even in the hermetically sealed Albania of Enver Hoxha I found books by Zweig in a shop in Tirana in the eighties. Fifty years after his suicide critics tend to discuss the weakness of his *oeuvre*, and the biographies and publishers of his voluminous correspondence give us a far more differentiated picture of his personality. But for us his work was a sort of revelation. And as for me, the gentle pacifism, the deeply-rooted internationalism and psychological insight of this cosmopolitan Austrian still moves me deeply. Having taken two of the most important steps of my life under Zweig's influence – first my involvement with the socialist youth movement in Hungary and ten years later my move to Austria – I was and still am so strongly affected by his life and work that I probably will never be able to take a more dispassionate view of him.

I was introduced to the Hungarian translations of Zweig's work at a tiny lending library across the street from where we lived. For a minimal fee my mother and I were able to borrow books there. We were probably its best customers. The well-read owner, Florika, and her friend Karcsi, an antiquarian, became my intellectual guides. My father was almost forty years old when I was born. We did not have many conversations with each other, particularly during the war years, and even afterward I treated him with a sort of shy respect. And so the shop with its piles of books became my second home. Karcsi encouraged me to finish a long-planned essay on Stefan Zweig, giving me advice about the style and structure of my planned piece. But the dream of seeing my essay in print was never realised. However, by sheer accident this unpublished Zweig essay had far-reaching political consequences. In view of the tough competition between the political parties and their youth organisations the local socialist youth group – SZIM, an acronym of the Hungarian words for socialist youth group – decided to activate the so-called 'file bodies', enrolled members who did not have any active contact with the Social Democratic Party. I was one such case.

In any event, in the spring of 1946 or perhaps somewhat earlier, two youths appeared in the hallway facing the room in which I usually did my homework or read and asked me to become an active participant in the district organisation. With a detached air of superiority I told them that I was busy working on an 'extremely important' essay on Stefan Zweig and was not interested in political activity. 'That's no problem,' one of them said. 'Come and talk to us about Stefan Zweig, and then you can read us your essay.'

That was a surprising and very clever move of these two young activists. As so often in my life, my pride in the written or spoken word proved to be an irresistible incentive. A few days later I went to the headquarters of the young socialists to introduce myself. In either March or April 1946 I delivered the first public address of my life, a talk about Stefan Zweig and his work, to about 30 SZIM members. My mother and my intellectual guides, Florika and Karcsi, sat in the last row. My father did not attend. I had begun to get more and more involved in politics and with that growing involvement the tensions between my father and myself also grew.

I liked the SZIM activists from the very first. They were open, involved, tireless, and their heart was with the Left. Not yet 17 years old, I was one of the youngest. The organisation in my district had between 100 and 150 active members. I was invited to seminars, talks and other such activities. I learned and read about the history, ideas and activities of the Social Democrats, the oldest political party in the new, democratic Hungary. Under the influence of the best public speakers and teachers of the party it was only logical for me to become a Marxist but, from the Marxist perspective, for all the wrong reasons. What drove me was what Marxists would call 'bourgeois alienation' and 'humanist-ethical motives' not any indignation over exploitative capitalism.

The story I have to tell about the SZIM and its role as accomplice in the murder of Social Democracy is like that which Hegel said was inscribed on the empty pages of the great book of memory. In retrospect the domestic policy of the time resembled a collective plot: 'Let us keep reality a secret'. In a country in which unspeakable crimes had been committed with the tacit acquiescence of the majority of the people, self-deception had become commonplace. How could the Social Democrats proclaim slogans like 'Today for democracy – tomorrow for socialism?' How could it be assumed that in a city which between October 1944 and February 1945 had been the scene of death and disaster the same people who for 25 years had been living under a miasma of nationalism, revisionism and anti-semitism would overnight turn into democrats, let alone socialists?

Yet that is the vision the self-satisfied membership statistics of the governing coalition parties tried to present. That summer the Social Democrats claimed a membership of half a million. The Communists, who during the war had shrunk from 1,000 activists to about 80 (according to the János Kádár), proudly claimed 150,000 members, and by early 1946 more than 600,000. It was an open secret that a party headed largely by Jewish 'Muscovites' built its base, above all in the early days, on 'little Arrow Crossists', marginal groups – unskilled workers and petty bourgeois and bureaucrats – who felt threatened by the change in government and in part by the unexpected return of Jewish owners of 'aryanised' businesses, plants, and apartments.

However, by far the largest political entity, the Smallholder Party, was seen as the upholder of the bourgeois-democratic form of government, private property and national values; as early as summer 1945 it could lay claim to more than 900,000 members. The democratic trustworthiness of their leading representatives was beyond doubt, and after their overwhelming victory in the first free elections in Hungarian history, the head of state, the Prime Minister and the president of the parliament were all of that party. With 57 percent of the votes and 245 representatives out of 409, the electorate showed its preference for a liberal-democratic order. The Social Democrats got 17.41 percent, the Communists a little less than 17, and the left-wing populist National Peasant Party almost seven percent of the votes.

In the first phase the Socialists behaved in a far more radical fashion and were further to the left than the widely-feared Communist Party (CP), which enjoyed the support of the Soviet occupation power. The Communist leader, Mátyás Rákosi, who in 1940, after 15 years' imprisonment, had been exchanged for Hungarian flags captured by the Russians in 1849, did not return from Moscow to Budapest until February 1945. In his opinion and that of his closest advisers, stamping out the deep-seated mistrust of the Communists was the highest priority. To do so they had to don an antifascist-democratic, coalition-building disguise, to discard socialist slogans, and in contrast to the outspoken socialists avoid the very word socialism. We now know from numerous sources that this 'soft line', which stretched from East Berlin to Budapest and Prague, was based on directives issued by Stalin personally. In Hungary, too, the leaders of the CP had counted on a long transitional period before the economy could be collectivised and total political power achieved.

However that did not prevent the predominantly Jewish leadership of the CP from cynically and unscrupulously exploiting anti-Jewish resentments. Thus the very first issue of the Communist paper *Szabad Nep* carried a page-long article by the left-wing populist writer József Darvas with the highly suggestive title 'A Frank Word about the Jewish Question'. This crypto-Communist who was later appointed Minister of Education alluded to the fact that 'the Jews were capitalising on their suffering as though they were the only ones who had suffered'. Rákosi was the only Number One leader of Jewish descent in the Eastern bloc. Throughout his career, this extremely distasteful 'court Jew' serving the anti-semite Stalin in his quest for power proved more eager than any of the other party heads of the satellite states to tolerate anti-semitic tendencies or, if necessary, even stir them up. Thus in the spring of 1945, his demagogic speeches set off demonstrations against black marketeers which, as was to be expected, turned into anti-semitic excesses: 'In a democracy there is room for spontaneous mass actions and it is only right and proper that the people take justice into their own hands'.

In a depressed economic situation it is not too difficult to stir up a people suffering from runaway inflation. When in May and July 1946 pogroms broke out in Kunmadaras and Miskolc, one of Hungary's bigger cities, the Communist leadership retreated into embarrassed silence, not least because, as has since been admitted, the local Communist Party organisations initially played a role in the 'spontaneous' riots.

'Those who didn't experience it can't really imagine it, and those who experienced it can't forget it.' These words of Arnulf Baring, the German political writer, in a different context about the new beginning, about the feeling of being newborn, in Berlin in May 1945, also apply to the immediate post-war period and the politicised youth of Budapest.

It would be a mistake to describe the atmosphere at that time and the political battles from today's vantage point. Many of us in the Socialist Youth and most likely our contemporaries in the Communist movement, in the Peasant Party and the Smallholders Party were attracted to those who were against oppression, discrimination and injustice and who wanted equal justice for all.

Moreover there is no denying that the economic and social structure of Horthy's Hungary was more in line with the nineteenth century than with ours. For example, half of all arable land belonged to about 10,000 families, and the thousand wealthiest owned a quarter of all arable land. Land reform – pushed through by the Communists and the National Peasant Party for obvious reasons, but ultimately also supported by the other coalition partners – was enacted as early as the spring of 1945, 650,000 agricultural workers and small landowners receiving 1.9 million hectares of farm land.

Another welcome change was the proclamation of the republic by the new National Assembly on 1 February 1946.

The punishment of the ultra rightist pillars of the Horthy regime and the top functionaries during the Arrow Cross reign of terror was agreed to by all democratic parties. However, the disputed creation of special tribunals to try war criminals and later also 'enemies of the people', on which political party and trade union delegates sat in as observers, opened the door to the later arbitrary actions of the Communists. Between the end of the war and March 1948 the People's Courts sentenced 16,273 people, though half of them to less than a year; of the 322 death sentences, 146 were carried out. Among those executed were major war criminals like Ferenc Szálasi, the 'leader of the nation', who incidentally was of partly Armenian descent, and the former prime ministers László Bárdossy, Béla Imrédy, and Döme Sztójay, as well as those members of the police and the Ministry of the Interior directly responsible for the deportation of Jews.

All Hungarian parties protested the efforts of the Czechoslovak government, paralleling the expulsion of the Sudeten Germans, to cause the 600,000-strong Hungarian minority in Slovakia to disappear through persecution, enforced population exchange and expulsion. But it must be admitted that all parties approved the unconscionable, wholesale, frequently inhuman resettlement of a quarter of a million Hungarian Germans.

The democratic new beginning did not last long. The differences over the control of the police, the judiciary and the defence forces, but also over the course and tempo of economic policy and the introduction of socialism, against the background of the interventions of the Soviet occupiers, continued to undermine the cohesion of the government and the heterogeneous leading party, the Smallholders. Rákosi, in a famous speech, coined the term 'salami tactics' to describe the gradual wearing down and smashing of political rivals.

The main attack naturally was directed against the Smallholders, which in the course of less than a year lost its parliamentary majority through engineered splits and after the arrest of its general secretary, Béla Kovács, on the charge of spying levelled by the Soviet occupation forces. The Communists also continued to keep a watchful eye on other left-wing parties allied with them. Like the Soviet-occupied zone of Germany, Hungary also heeded the advice of Walter Ulbricht, the architect of the future German Democratic Republic, who at the very first meeting of his adherents in Berlin on 2 May 1945, advised that 'It must seem democratic, but we must keep control of everything'. That was by no means achieved exclusively through police power or overt Soviet interference.

An important role was played by crypto-Communists recruited to infiltrate the other parties. They carried two party membership cards, a 'nominal' one in their own group and a 'real' one in the CP. Some did not even have a membership card yet but were still regarded as highly reliable by the Communist leadership. Between 1945 and 1948, and also prior to and after the October Revolution of 1956, these people leading a double life were vital factors in the crushing of all opposition and the cementing of the dictatorship. Two heads of state and two prime ministers as well as three secretaries general and a number of well-known ministers who were representatives of non-Communist parties were in fact either dyed-in-the-wool Communists or men forced to give allegiance to the Party. The mask worn by some of these famous public personages may indeed have been more genuine than the reality it hid. Yet the left-wing Social Democrats in particular nursed the illusion that a 'genuine change' in the Hungarian Communists and in the role of the Soviet Union was possible. I recently had the opportunity to see the mimeographed original documents which were distributed to the Party speakers by the central office for their weekly meetings. I was flabbergasted by the mixture of self-overestimation and almost absurd misjudgment of domestic and international relations between July 1945 and March 1948.

Such illusions about the strength of the Socialists and their desire for unity under the sign of the ritually proclaimed 'unity of action' probably also coloured the speeches I delivered as early as November 1946 before various local Social Democratic membership meetings in factories in the 9th district. We young people showed initiative and enthusiasm for the 'movement'. Overbearing, self-confident yet at the same time idealistiic, not motivated by personal gain, we pledged ourselves to free discussion and to what we believed to be democratic socialism.

In stark contrast to the personality cult of Stalin or Rákosi, the relationship between the leadership of the Social Democrats and their young supporters was relaxed, non-bureaucratic and in no way hierarchical, particularly as regards the left-wingers who in many respects, including age, were closer to us than the elders of the movement.

In this connection I had an unforgettable experience. The then mayor of Vienna and later head of state, Theodor Körner, came to Budapest on 9 February 1947, at the invitation of Mayor József Kovago (Smallholders Party). In addition to attending the various official receptions, Mayor Körner also visited our Social Democratic organisation. Why he chose our district I no longer know, nor the reason why I, a member of the district leadership of the youth organisation, was chosen to greet the Austrian dignitary in the name of the Social

Democratic youth. With the help of my Aunt Olly, in charge of the German language correspondence of a firm, we drafted a friendly welcoming speech which I spent days memorizing and delivered without too many mistakes – carrying a bouquet of red carnations in my right hand and, for reassurance, the crumpled text of my speech in my sweaty left. Whether the tall, elderly man said anything to me beyond a friendly handshake I do not remember, but the fact of this personal encounter has remained with me.

An important subjective proof of our independence as a socialist force was the fact that the party's leadership not only turned down repeated Communist feelers in favour of a united youth organisation, under the slogan of 'unity of the working class', but even underscored its position by setting up its own organisation of high school students in the late autumn of 1946. Thus we – a group of reliable young socialists – formed a student organisation, the Ady Student Circle, on the orders of the party. Beginning in December 1946 we held a weekly forum in the basement of a coffee house. With that we were continuing an honourable tradition: coffee houses had long been the meeting place of writers, journalists and, in times of crisis, of revolutionary intellectuals. The great national revolution against Hapsburg rule was launched on 15 March 1848 at the centrally located Café Pilvax which still exists. According to a three-volume history of Budapest's cafés, coffee drinking in Hungary predates Vienna and Paris by 100 years. In 1900 Budapest already had about 600 coffee houses. Our choice of a centrally located café as our meeting place thus made sense.

I was elected educational secretary of the Ady Circle, yet I no longer remember whose idea it was to name our group after the poet Endre Ady. Our president was the recently returned émigré György Faludy, the author of a controversial Villon translation. It is entirely possible that our name, Ady, was his idea or that of our champion in the party executive, Pál Justus. At any rate the name Ady was symbolic: Ady (1877-1919) was not only a great poet but also a 'historic, political, and literary phenomenon' (according to John Lukacs). His poetry was a breakthrough into modernity and he became the spiritual pioneer of the bourgeois-republican revolution of October 1918.

Thus by choosing Endre Ady's name we presented ourselves as a progressive, open, Western-oriented student group rather than a Social Democratic one. Everyone knew that the members of the executive board were Social Democrats, but we carried on primarily as a literary-cultural organisation. The Communists also formed a student group under the name Petöfi Circle, and I think the other parties set up similar clubs. My duties included organising the weekly programmes together with Faludy and other executive board members, to get the speakers, and from time to time chair the weekly meetings.

We succeeded in making the Ady Circle known throughout the high schools, and we soon had between 220 and 250 enrolled members, who often brought friends to the meetings. In August 1947, differences between the official leadership and the young leftists broke out, but by then I was already involved in the university student movement.

4

Left-wing Socialist Illusions

At a lecture series for young socialist activists at the former Palace Hotel, the headquarters of the Social Democratic Party, in the summer of 1946 or possibly somewhat later, I met the man who quite literally changed my life. The young woman sitting next to me whispered to me that the man speaking was Pál Justus, the chief ideologue of the Party, or more accurately its left wing. This slender, good-looking, bespectacled 40-year-old man charmed not only women, regardless of age. 'Pali', as we all called him, became the idol of the young socialist Left. I do not remember what Justus said at this first encounter, but all of us were captivated by his persuasiveness and candour. He had set out on a search for a third road to Socialism, which many at the time, and later many more, called 'naive': a road between the petrified, intellectually unappealing, uninspired reformism of the prewar party and the rigid, unyielding claim to ultimate truth of the Communist Party.

Justus, who had been active in the Social Democratic movement since his twenties, had studied in Bologna and Paris. When he lost his job after a failed strike of bank employees the young intellectual spent a year in Vienna and another three years in Paris before returning to

Budapest before the outbreak of the war. Even back then, Justus was already an intellectual catalyst. He dominated debates about political, economic and cultural problems. His major work, *The Road to Socialism*, completed in 1942, could not be published until after the war. The book was one of the earliest socialist theoretical works to treat the phenomenon of fascism as a mass movement. In a postscript he admitted that he also underestimated the impact of fascism on the working class. Having been fortunate enough to survive the grueling years in the infamous copper mine at Bor in Serbia and the death-march of the starving conscripts to Hungary, Justus in 1945 quickly rose in the Social Democratic Party hierarchy to the 21-member executive committee. He became a parliamentary deputy, editor-in-chief of *Szocializmus*, the theoretical Party monthly, and the ideologue who authored and co-edited most of the party's weekly guidelines for its speakers and propagandists.

Few knew that this outstanding speaker and tireless teacher of the young generation was primarily a poet. In his early youth he had contributed poems to Lajos Kassák's *Munka* (*Labour*), the avant-garde periodical published by the leftist pioneering editor who had been harassed by all regimes. Justus's first volume of poetry, *Under Dark Peaks*, had been published in 1925, when he was twenty years of age. Five years later a second volume, *The Song of the Road*, appeared. I came across this slim volume published by an obscure publisher or perhaps by himself in a second-hand bookstore, and at our next meeting I asked Justus to inscribe it: 'Seventeen years later...' To my shame I must confess that in 1949 I shredded the little volume with the highly personal inscription after the Rajk trial, or rather after Justus's life sentence. To this day I feel ashamed of this cowardly act, yet it is possible that it saved me from a worse fate after I myself was arrested.

My participation in the so-called Justus Seminar was a clear sign that I too now belonged to the small circle of disciples of this brilliant loner. Up to 30 young socialists were personally invited by Justus to the biweekly Saturday afternoon seminar at the Palace Hotel, a group of close friends interested in socialist theory and talented young people who had come to his attention in the party school of higher education.

The discussions in the Justus Seminar were memorable because there even the youngest participants were accepted and respected as equal intellectual partners. As a rule Justus gave us books on the topics under discussion. Since he himself knew English, French, German and Italian, he took it for granted that we could also read the works of Karl Korsch, Karl Mannheim, Ferdinand Fried, Fritz Sternberg, Rosa

Luxemburg, and Georg Lukács on theoretical Marxism in the original language in the two weeks between sessions and be able to discuss them intelligently.

In the course of my political activities as a functionary of the socialist high school students and later as the Party's political secretary at the law school, as well as a student in the evening courses of the first Diplomatic Academy, I was shocked when Communist participants responded to my support of Justus with ironic smiles. Only much later did I begin to understand what lay hidden behind their behaviour.

As secretary of one of the strongest district organisations of the Social Democratic Party in the late thirties Justus repeatedly spoke out against the Moscow show trials and even organised a small protest meeting with a dozen other left-wing socialists in front of the Soviet Embassy in Budapest. He also spoke out strongly against the Stalin-Hitler Pact of 1939. Moreover, many Communists at the time took cover in the Social Democratic Party, as for example did the future head of the Communist Party, János Kádár, as well as Julia Rajk (nee Foldi), the wife of László Rajk, the later Communist Minister of the Interior. For decades the Social Democrats had been called social fascists by the Communists. And those who criticised the Communist world movement from a left-wing socialist and Marxist perspective were labeled Trotskyites. Since Justus, despite his declared intention to enter into close political co-operation with the CP both before and after 1945, rejected such concepts as Marxism-Leninism or People's Democracy, he was considered a Trotskyite traitor by the Hungarian Communist faithful. In truth he never, neither at the socialist party school nor in the Saturday seminars, appeared to be a Trotskyite sympathiser, let alone attempt to turn us into Trotskyites.

But during the great purges truth fell by the wayside. Our group included young women and men who listened to Justus on Saturday and who on Monday or even earlier gave their controllers written or oral reports about our discussions, above all about Justus's views. Some of these Party informers, whether card-carrying Communists or not, later became executive editors, vice ministers and top functionaries of the newly created, politically cleansed youth organisations. Others, soon after the 'year of the turning point' (the term coined by the Communist leader Mátyás Rákosi), ended up in prison or internment camp. And for still others, like myself, their fate was to be sealed later. The fact remains that left-wing socialists then and later were a thorn in the flesh of the supporters of the 'real existing socialism'. The democratic Left, or rather the intellectuals who were part of it, were in the interwar years and after World War II so indoctrinated or manipulated that even in the periods of the all-out battles against 'tank Communism' (after 1956, 1968 or 1981) under no circumstances wanted to appear 'anti-Communists'. At the same time, the left-wing critics of Stalinism were reviled as 'ultraleft opportunists', or as either 'left' or 'right' revisionists, as needed, and as a prelude to the later trials as Trotskyite, Titoist or Zionist traitors or agents of American imperialism.

Originally the leadership of the CP foresaw a long transitional period to its political takeover. In its inner circle, top leaders even spoke of a ten-to-twenty-year period before the complete collectivisation of the economy. Toward the end of 1945 and early 1947, to the utter surprise of many, the opening shot was fired in the total war to seize total power. The Communist leadership had most likely recognised that political spring cleaning by democratic means was not possible. In the final analysis it does not matter whether the decision was reached in Budapest or Moscow. What counted was the now unmistakable determination of the CP to use the Military Intelligence, the army's secret service (Kat-Pol), as well as the state security service (AVH), to destroy the Smallholders Party which commanded a comfortable absolute majority.

There followed selective arrests and torture. Meetings of rightist opposition deputies and their friends were projected as a powerful antigovernment conspiracy. In seven trials a total of 260 persons were sentenced. The crucial move, which simultaneously sounded the death knell for the nascent democracy, came in February 1947 with the arrest of the General Secretary of the Smallholders Party, the deputy Béla Kovács, by the Soviet security forces. The second man in the strongest coalition party whose immunity had been guaranteed by the parliamentary majority was arrested under the pretence of 'having organised armed terrorist groups and engaged in active espionage on behalf of a Western secret service against the Soviet Union'. He was shipped to the Soviet Union and not released until 1956.

It was probably the most serious mistake of the Social Democratic leadership to brusquely reject the feelers of the two non-socialist parties. The weak, indecisive Secretary General, Árpád Szakasits, eagerly declared 'We are not a party of the centre'. While crypto-Communists in the SDP and the National Peasant Party began to take over vital positions of power within their parties, the Communist drum-beat against the strong Smallholders Party continued unabated. The passivity of the Western powers in the Allied Control Commission and the impotence of the parliament and the President made clear that the die had been cast.

After a new split in the strongest party, Prime Minister Ferenc Nagy, who was in Switzerland taking a cure, was forced to resign after rumours were circulated about a pending investigation – he was accused of a 'conspiracy against the state' – and about the fate of his young son who had stayed behind in Budapest.

A collection of secret documents, exchanged at the highest levels between Moscow and Budapest from 1944 to 1948 and acquired from Soviet Party archives by Hungarian historians in the era of Perestroika and published in 1994, reveal the grandly conceived subversion of the democratic parties by the Communist controlled secret police. As early as April 1947 the head of the political police, Gábor Péter, proudly informed the Soviet official in charge of Hungary:

> About 80 percent of our personnel are Communists; the representatives of the other parties are preoccupied with secondary matters, and we are doing everything to prevent them from finding out what they are not supposed to know... Our basic task is to find out everything in advance and to inform our leadership. That is the reason we have installed a widespread network of informers. We have our people in every political party. We managed to win over functionaries of other parties... We have people in every ministry, even in the Church. The information we have thus gained is pretty thorough.

And then the candid Peter goes even further in his eagerness to impress the Soviet comrade, or rather his superior in Moscow:

> The political police is of great help to the Party. Generally we are able to find out the political intentions of our adversaries before interparty negotiations, and thus we are able to keep the CP leadership informed in time. We have organised the tapping of phones. Now we can listen in on every important telephone conversation of the Prime Minister and Party leaders, and we report the most important matters to Comrade Rákosi.

Nobody in the socialist youth movement at the time thought that the elections scheduled for 31 August 1947 at the urging of the Communists could damage the Hungarian Social Democrats, a party founded in December 1890 and so rich in tradition. The possibility of fatal consequences never entered our minds. But these were the elections that became known as the 'scandalous elections with blue ballots'. The real scandal was the manipulation organised by the Communists: estimates put the number of blue ballots used by

Communist activists at between 100,000 to 300,000. The future Prime Minister András Hegedüs tells in his frank memoirs how he himself, as a Party functionary riding around either in a car or on a bicycle, voted at least twenty times for the CP with a single blue registration card in various polling places. Thus the CP officially received 1,113,000 votes, 300,000 more than in 1945. Nonetheless most Party historians point out that the election fraud, which incidentally has never been officially admitted by the Communists, did not play a decisive role. Even though the CP officially thus became the strongest party, still the result was a bitter disappointment for the Rákosi clique: with 22.3 percent of the votes the CP won only 100 of the 411 seats.

The ominous 'blue cards' and the election result came as a great shock, particularly to the Social Democrats, one from which they never recovered. Members and particularly activists regarded the fact that their party polled 80,000 fewer votes than in the first postwar elections in 1945 as a catastrophic result.

In the meantime the political climate continued to worsen. After the decision of the countries in the Soviet sphere of influence to refuse to participate in the Marshall Plan conference in Paris, and the founding of the Communist Information Bureau, the Cold War began to rage. With confidential internal references to a possible third world war, Stalin pushed through the 'monolithic unity of the Socialist camp'. Domestically, the head of the CP, Rákosi, Minister of the Interior Rajk, and the heads of the military and political secret services, General György Pálffy and General Gábor Péter, moved decisively against the demoralised, Communist-infiltrated bourgeois camp. Bowing to the threat of legal action, the leaders of the groupings that had split off from the Smallholders, and who even in the manipulated elections still received 30 percent of the votes and held 109 seats, were forced to flee; their parties were subsequently banned and their deputies lost their seats.

Not surprisingly, the Communists in their internal propaganda briefings bragged about 'a huge victory for democracy'. After the 'smashing of the fifth column of American imperialism' and the nationalisation of the banks it was of major importance that in the Smallholders Party and Social Democratic Party 'the Left should take over the leadership', and after that the development of Hungary's democracy could be accelerated in an unprecedented fashion, according to a CP brochure for internal consumption.

After the electoral defeat, Social Democracy became the chosen target of Communist subversive tactics. And regrettably the Socialist

Youth organisation was the most easily manipulated ally in the splitting and destruction of the SP. Many of us young left-wing socialists who took to the streets to demonstrate against the leadership of their organisation and that of their elders were naive and basically revolutionary idealists.

After I graduated from high school with honours, despite my political activities and other diversions, and won first prize in a national history contest, I devoted all my energies to the SZIM. I delivered countless speeches in enterprises and institutions in my district, and later at seminars and student discussion groups.

After enrolling in law school, to the dismay of my father, I devoted far more time to political fights than to the study of Roman law. As the political secretary of the Social Democratic student organisation, I was so successful in my political-ideological 'battle' against the right-wing students that in February 1948 – the high point of my brief and as it turned out portentous political career – I became a member of the executive committee of the Social Democratic Student Group, and its educational secretary. All this was, of course, only of theoretical importance, particularly since only weeks later the amalgamation of the Social Democratic and Communist youth organisations was decided upon.

On 18 October 1947 the first issue of our own biweekly, *The Young Socialist*, appeared. It was supposed to be the counterpart to *The Youth*, the organisation's official paper controlled by the right-wing leadership.

Friends of mine played a crucial role in the founding of the paper as well as in the sectarian battles. I also took part in a mass demonstration of left-wing Socialist Youth activists and was indignant when the party leaders in attendance – men like Minister Bán and the Hungarian Ambassador to Sweden, Vilmos Böhm, a veteran of the 1919 Soviet Republic – made fun of our resolution and called us naive (or, in the words of Bán, paid) instruments of Communist provocation.

I was soon asked to become the foreign-policy commentator of the leftist paper. We published the resolutions of the groups and party organizations controlled by the Left. We were backed by the members of the so-called 'Group of Eight' in the party leadership whose members included Justus, Ferenc Révész, Imre Vajda. They were consistently on the Left, and some of them, perhaps even the majority, were in close contact with Communist headquarters.

The second youth congress, called for November, was broken up by the leftist groups; chaos erupted. On the sixth floor of the Palace

Hotel the elected heads of the organisation were in one room; the left-wing rebels were next door on the same floor.

When decades later a former youth group functionary showed me a collection of old issues of this peculiar left-wing student paper, I had to admit that we – and that also holds true of the adults – were at best 'useful idiots' or conscious pawns of the Communists. This first encounter with a paper whose financing at the time I never paid any attention to was an eye-opening experience. I had long been attracted to journalism. Regardless of our political differences some of us 'Justus disciples' even regularly went to the editorial offices of the highly-respected Socialist daily *Nepszava* (*People's Voice*) to get first-hand insight into this prized vocation.

Apart from occasional commentaries for the left-wing youth paper of the – so it appeared to me at the time – unstoppable left-wing and 'progresive' forces, I was particularly proud of my first essay in a 'real' paper, *Kortars* (*Contemporary*), a biweekly Social Democratic cultural journal founded by Kassák and now overseen by Justus. My article, however, was merely a precis of an English book about Soviet poetry.

Meanwhile my district organisation nominated me for a position in the Party's educational department. Supported by Justus and Révész I was hired in February 1948 as a full-time employee (for the very modest monthly salary of 700 forint). Up to then – apart from getting reimbursed for street-car fares, I had never been paid for my work in the movement.

My career as Party employee lasted only briefly. By early April I went to work as a volunteer for the Social Democratic evening paper *Kossuth Nepe*, the first step in my cherished dream of becoming a journalist. It was very pleasant work, particularly since the paper went to press before 2pm and we spent the time waiting for the first copies playing ping-pong in the editorial offices. Never again have I found such an exotic clutch of journalists. The editor-in-chief, Ferenc Felkai, was a renowned dramatist whose only interest was the theatre. His second-in-command, László Hars, was the successful author of children's books. The foreign affairs editor, Endre Gaspar, a superb translator of French, German and English literature, was himself a talented poet. His youthful assistant later became a renowned translator of French poetry. The head of the business section was a seasoned sports journalist who knew far more about what was happening on the soccer front than about the consequences of the nationalisation of the Hungarian banking system. I was to earn my spurs as a reporter under his aegis.

While I and my friends enthusiastically and devotedly worked for the victory of the left wing in the youth movement and the party, preparations for the long-planned and methodically prepared organised destruction of Social Democracy by the Communists were proceeding at full steam. This clever manoeuvre was of course helped by the almost laughable naivete of the Socialist Left.

In fact the dams against Communist subversion had long been breached: every day tens of thousands of members of plants, offices, and local organizations applied for membership in the victorious CP. In these difficult months, almost coincidental with the well-publicised Communist coup in Prague, the Hungarian Communist leadership demanded a purge of the Social Democrat right wing and the Party headquarters as the price for the fusion of the two parties.

The death knell for Social Democracy sounded as early as 18 February 1948. At a mass meeting of Social Democratic activists in the sports arena, under the centralised control of the acting crypto-Communist General Secretary Marosán, the announcement of the expulsion from the party of the most respected old leaders like Kéthly, Bán and Szelig was greeted with jubilation. We have since learned from the memoirs of Szakasits's daughter that the nominal head of the party had been outmanoeuvred by an invitation to Moscow and only after his return was informed of the purge of the party leadership. Other documents and declarations of Communist witnesses to these events show that the meeting was in fact organised by the Communists, and that the decision about the merger had not been approved by any elected body. In the face of trials against various Social Democrats already under way – Gyula Kelemen, the Social Democratic State Secretary of the Ministry of Industry was, despite the protests of his Social Democratic minister, sentenced to life in prison on a flimsy pretext – Szakasits and all the other surprised functionaries had to accede.

The thirty-sixth, and as it turned out last, congress of the Social Democrats was a mere formality. The fusion of the two parties was approved on 12 June by the thirty-seventh Congress, and on 13 and 14 July 1948 formalised at a joint party conference. The left-wing gravediggers accepted seemingly leading, but in fact powerless, roles in the new 'Party of the Hungarian Workers' (MDP) while Bán, Szelig and a few other endangered leaders of the old guard were able to leave the country in time and form a party in exile. The fusion ended a war of extermination against Social Democracy which reduced it to meaninglessness. The CP now claimed that its membership had risen to 887,000 while the Social Democrats could claim only 240,000.

The victorious Communists, all of whom, even those who were subsequently imprisoned or disillusioned looked at us, the former left-wing Social Democrats, with deep suspicion, often malignant resentment. In part this had to do with the tradition of world Communism. The Social Democrats, denigrated as either social fascists or revisionists, had always been seen as the chief enemy.

Many documents that have come to light show how suicidal the wishful dreams, illusions, and delusions of the left-wing Social Democrats were, how late we became aware of the iron will of the Communists to destroy all others. But in those days all we saw was a worldwide battle between capitalism and socialism.

In his memoirs Denis Healey, the British Defence Secretary and Chancellor of the Exchequer, and in the forties the chief of the international department of the Labour Party, discusses the decline of Eastern European Social Democracy. At the Labour Party conference in 1945 Foreign Secretary Ernest Bevin said with reference to the Soviet Union that the 'Left can talk with the left'. But Healey, as International Secretary, and soon Bevin as well, realised that in the eyes of Stalin, Attlee's Socialist Britain was the main obstacle to Soviet control of Western Europe.

While in Eastern Europe the Communists were gradually swallowing up all elements of the left, in Western Europe the internal factionalism among the various socialist and social-democratic-oriented groupings was quite pronounced. And always the principal issue was the Left's attitude towards the Soviet Union. For example in Britain under its Labour Government the Left was divided between the likes of Richard Crossman, Michael Foot, Ian Mikardo and Woodrow Wyatt who attacked Foreign Secretary Ernest Bevin for being too anti-Soviet and pro-American, while others like Healey, who was better informed about bitter power struggles in Eastern Europe and who had himself been a Communist Party member, argued for more scepticism about Soviet and Communist intentions.

Meanwhile in Hungary Rákosi proclaimed that most Social Democrats had been 'police agents or British spies' before the war. That of course was nonsense. But it is true that after the Labour victory in 1945, Great Britain was a model for the Social Democrats of Central and Eastern Europe fighting for survival. There was a general feeling that despite the oppressive Soviet hegemony, international Social Democracy would survive being undermined by the Communists and that its historic tasks had by no means yet been fulfilled.

In life coincidence often plays a crucial role in the shaping of events, even if this is not clear at the time. Today with the best will in the world I can no longer remember how I fared in the essay contest sponsored by the British Council. But whatever the outcome, in the summer or early autumn of 1947 I was told that I had been awarded a scholarship at Ruskin College, Oxford. However, nothing came of it. Anna Kéthly, the President of Parliament and member of the Social Democratic executive, wanted to send another young man in my place. Even though Kéthly was on good personal terms with Healey and Secretary General Morgan Philips in London, there was only one place for Hungary. And thus it was Kéthly's candidate who went to England. I was told that my turn would come the following year. But given the rapid degeneration of relations with the West, it was no longer possible to re-establish contacts with the British Embassy. (But I did finally get a glimpse of Ruskin College for the first time in the early eighties when I delivered an address at All Souls College.)

In that spring – 1948 – of precipitous political developments, the Social Democratic left and a small portion of the centre were absorbed into the Communist Party. More precisely, the sad remnants of Social Democracy throughout Eastern Europe were swallowed up by the Communists at will. Apart from the so-called 'secret members' of the CP most of the Social Democrats in the new MDP, the united party, were somehow looked upon as 'handicapped', as retarded and as untrustworthy.

The distribution of jobs and the staffing of the Government and Party apparatus, of the nationalised plants, of the local administration as well as the important sectors of cultural, scientific and media policy were arranged by supposedly joint comittees, but with a clear nume-ri-cal superiority of Communists. The final decision was thus always made by the Communist members.

Looked at from today's perspective, and in part also on the basis of facts that have since come to light, one might get the impression that in the year of the turning point or soon thereafter, many Hungarians were either very cynical or unsuspecting. As far as I am concerned I certainly did not belong to those who in any way were forced to go along, let alone considered themselves political victims. On the contrary, we thought we had found – and were even proud to have done so – the road from Marxism to Leninism after much hesi-tation and many wrong turns. Some time in early 1948 we, together with two political friends in the Social Democratic student movement, decided to form a 'revolutionary nucleus' in the Justus seminar – and should our teacher, Justus himself, fail to lend his unambiguous support to the unification of the two working-class parties, we would break with him. The two friends, F.T. and Sz. T. (the former became a professor of economics, the latter head of a chemical institute in the Academy of Sciences) came to my apartment. After hours of discussion in my father's office we formulated our 'ideological indictment' of Justus's hesitant, irresolute line. Again and again he had given a hint of a preference for an independent left-wing Social Democracy even when most of the left-wing young socialists were already passionate supporters of the counter-offensive so cleverly set up by the crypto-Communist leaders. Sz. T. took along the draft, ostensibly to have a girlfriend make clean copies. In fact, however, he sent our personal letter intended for Justus to the leader of the Communist youth organisation and others for their approval and revision. In his eagerness Sz. T., as he later admitted in his testimony against me, even sent a copy to Zoltán Biro, Rákosi's brother and the head of the political education department of the CP.

This letter of resignation was to take on fateful significance in the lives of all of us, but particularly mine. When 47 years later I found the four handwritten pages full of platitudinous Marxist-Leninist phraseology about the role of the party, the agrarian question, the class struggle, etc, in my personnel file in the Hungarian Ministry of the Interior, I had to think of what Arthur Koestler, the Hungarian-born literary indicter of Soviet Communism once labeled 'controlled schizophrenia', a thought process which, even though intrinsically logical, even astute, has lost all relationship to reality.

The letter was signed by us, the three 'rebels'. On a flimsy pretext the other two left to me the embarrassing task of handing Justus the letter. Dated 19 March 1948, the letter was an impudent challenge by three cheeky conceited youths, yet a 'rebellion' without risk. Even though I was not privy to the background intrigues I did know the direction things were taking, namely that within a short time or at the latest by the end of the year our party would disappear from the political stage as an independent force. At any rate I followed orders and, obviously embarrassed, handed Justus the letter in his office at the Palace Hotel.

While we, the Party's grave-diggers in the youth movement, were busy, the true puppet-masters behind the scenes were making decisions about our future assignments. Our paper, *Kossuth Nepe*, like most of the old Social Democratic publications was discontinued. For the first time in my life I was given formal written notice. But there was no cause for alarm. Even though, or perhaps because, I was not yet 19, the personnel department of the united MDP – it was located in the old Communist Party headquarters – informed me that it had been decided to transfer me, the 'talented young budding journalist', to the editorial offices of *Szabad Nep* (*The Free People*), the official paper of the former CP, now of the MDP. I became the youngest editorial employee of the most important paper in Hungary.

Today it is difficult to explain the role the mouthpiece of the evolving one-party dictatorship played in the daily life of the people. Even though it seems to me that my tenure at the paper was a long one, in fact it lasted barely nine months. Recalling those days I think of the leftist futurologist's Robert Jungk's warning in his memoirs about the revisions people tend to make in their reminiscenses of the past; not that they lie consciously but that they understandably seek to bring the illogical, contradictory, and murky aspects of their lives into clear or objectively incorrect relationships.

That naturally holds true, perhaps most of all for those who in their commentaries and reportages, but also in their novels and poetry, provided the window-dressing for a regime which, misusing the emancipatory ideals of the working-class movement, was in the service of a Party dictatorship which resorted to terrorist methods of oppression. Some of my colleagues of that period were later in the frontline of those who between 1953 and 1956 sought to reform socialism and fight for the independence of the gagged country. Some, like chief commentator Géza Losonczy and the editorialist Miklós Gimes, were even to give their lives. Others, the domestic affairs editor Miklós Vásárhelyi, the agricultural expert Pál Löcsei, or the former partisan György Fazekas, received long prison sentences after the defeat of the 1956 Revolution.

However, in 1948-49, these future victims were still pillars of the system of injustice and in a sense instruments of repression. The Communist official paper, in which we were all now enthusiastic fighters in the class struggle, was after all the locomotive of the virulent campaign against the middle-of-the-road politicians, the so-called right-wing Social Democrats, the Catholic Church in general, and Cardinal Mindszenty in particular. When later, beginning in the summer of 1949, some of our own comrades were arrested and labelled 'Titoists', 'Trotskyites', and 'agents of imperialism' we were content to continue our work with undimmed enthusiasm.

An interview that the journalist Hans Habe conducted with the painter Oskar Kokoschka in 1965 in Geneva contains an astute characterisation of the atmosphere of informing:

> Human beings have all the ugly traits of animals, but they have one that makes them still uglier than animals. Animals fight one another, even songbirds fight over the tiny space in a cage; they are avid and miserly, but there is one thing they do not do: they do not denounce. Denunciation sets human beings apart from animals. From the Inquisition to world wars, from National Socialism to Comunism – denunciations head the list.

The beginning of this era of denunciation and omnipresent vigilance coincided with the beginning of my employment at the Party paper *Szabad Nep*. No sooner had I begun work there when the last whiff of tolerance evaporated. Like a bolt of lighting we were hit by the ceremonial excommunication of the Yugoslav Communists from the Cominform, the international Communist information agency founded in 1947. The 'unmasking' of the defecting Titoists, the only movement that had come to power without outside help and would not allow itself to become a mere recipient of orders from the Kremlin, was a shock not only for all who had looked on Tito's Yugoslavia as a pioneer. It was also the prelude to a new series of bloody purges. The hunt for enemies of the party, foreign agents and anti-Soviet elements became a central element in politics.

The loyalty of the Communists was to the Soviet Union, not their own country. In addition Hungary was burdened by reparation payments of $200 million to the Soviet Union ($70 million went to Yugoslavia and $30 million to Czechoslovakia). The confiscation of former German assets, the dismantling of entire industrial enterprises, and finally the creation of the notorious mixed enterprises for air and Danube transportation, for oil exploration and development, for mining and bauxite and aluminum production created even greater resentments. Up to 1954 the Soviets could syphon off more than a billion dollars in 'profits' from Hungary.

All it needed was an expression of 'suspect' ideas on the part of an employee or manager with regard to this unequal relationship, a mere rumour about anti-Soviet or 'nationalistic' resentments, an anonymous denunciation about the mood of a functionary who was suspicious of all critical thinking or independent acts, for someone to become the subject of official attention. And once that person became part of a secret police file it was almost impossible for him to go unpunished for long. More and more telephones were tapped, more and more bugs were installed in apartments and offices. Letters were opened, houses searched and neighbours questioned. And the targets of these activities often did not even know that they were being watched.

Meanwhile the extensive watching of the members of the new united party began in earnest. The former Social Democrats, or those bourgeois elements under suspicion because of their parentage or past activities, were of course the prime targets. The supposedly proletarian or working-class 'minor Arrow Crossists' were not as endangered. The commissions consisted of three to five 'reliable' comrades. At the central Party paper an old Communist and Muscovite headed the control commission. As the youngest member of the editorial staff, I had no problem.

More than 300,000 members were expelled or reduced to candidate rank, although the MDP still had a membership of 820,000. If the future purges, new admissions, the collapse in 1956, and the reconstitution of a new party under János Kádár are taken into account, the estimate of the historian Miklós Molnár in Geneva (the former cultural affairs editor of *Szabad Nep*), that between 1945 and 1985 two million Hungarians must at one time or another have been Party members seems reasonable. Or to put it differently: one of three adults at one time or another must have belonged to the Communist Party under its various names. Today this fact is largely forgotten in Hungary or, more accurately, repressed. Without the knowledge of these simple facts many of the – for outsiders so baffling – contacts and breaks in the mendacious post-Communist transition period would hardly be comprehensible.

In *The God that Failed*, in which well-known ex-Communists from Koestler to Stephen Spender talk about their break with the Party, Ignazio Silone, the Italian writer, states: 'The ex-Communists constitute a category apart, like ex-priests and ex-regular officers. The number of ex-Communists is legion today.' 'The final struggle,' I said jokingly to Togliatti [Palmiro Togliatti, the head of the Italian CP] recently, 'will be between the Communists and the ex-"Communists".' Since the revolution of 1989, however, the power struggle in the political arena in the former Soviet bloc is being carried out primarily among ex-Communists who are wearing a variety of different masks.

During my time at the Party paper, we lived in a world of delusions, in a dialectically obscured reality. The dynamics of the witch-hunt set in motion by the Tito-Stalin conflict increasingly replaced reason with fear, as the Hungarian intellectual István Bibó put it in a different context.

After the victory over the 'class enemy' – private industry, even small business and the crafts had already been nationalised or destroyed – the peasants came next. There was no longer talk of Marxism or Marxist thinkers but only about the teachings of Lenin and, above all, of those of the greatest genius of all, Joseph Vissarionovich Stalin. Marxism-Leninism, that bizarre political church, promised salvation, though not for individuals but rather for society as a whole. All one had to do was commit the sacred texts to memory to arrive at an unshakable, complete belief. Stalinism offered more than merely a programme. It laid claim to developing the type of a 'new man' out of the closed system of a philosophic-economic belief structure.

After the year of the turning point, and for decades to come, there was the belief both in the West and the East that the Soviet system, Communism – or as Ernest Gellner put it, the world religion and state ideology of Marxism – was the alternative to liberalism. As far as Marxism as 'secular religion' (Gellner) is concerned it ought perhaps be pointed out that at the high point of the Stalin era – and probably afterwards – nowhere else was Marx read as little as in the countries of the Eastern bloc. The ideological daily ration consisted of ready-made, and also simplified, Stalin and Lenin primers. Georg Lukács, the great Hungarian Marxist philosoper, once remarked in a private conversation that ideology was the connecting text between the quotations. The real bestseller was the notorious *Short Course* of the CPSU, the glorification of Stalin written under his personal supervision. This crude concoction was printed in an edition of 560,000 in Hungary. The title pages of the papers and magazines in those years featured accounts and pictures of peasant women in national dress at Party congresses or other events clutching books of Lenin and Stalin.

Stalin's teachings about the intensification of the class struggle constituted the ideological foundation of the vigilance campaigns and the political terror. As was to be expected, the editorial office of the official paper of the ruling party was a particularly fruitful hunting ground for the guardians of the discipline and morale of Party members. The ardour in matters of vigilance had comic and frequently also tragic results.

Those who committed errors in their editorial assignments were naturally punished. I no longer remember whether my inauspicious departure from the paper was due to a minor infraction or whether my lapse was simply the last straw. My case was connected with the person of Sir Stafford Cripps, the then British Chancellor of the

Exchequer. I dictated a dispatch about British politics and then handed it in at the editorial offices. However, the article contained a grave error: Cripps was described as Foreign Minister instead of Finance Minister. The fact that the stenographer was not only a former colleague from the days of the Social Democratic paper but had become my girlfriend (and later wife), may possibly have been the reason for my or our carelessness.

The consequences were unexpected. A few days after my glaring mistake a meeting of the entire staff was called. It was held in the very room in which the results of the investigations of Party members were announced. At that time I was feeling very low about the disciplining of two former Social Democratic journalists. One had been demoted to 'candidate' because of his love of gambling, and the other was found unworthy of membership because he had married the owner of a small dress shop. The question now was what fate might await us. The first item on the agenda was personnel matters. The editor-in-chief suddenly called out my name: 'Because of serious political errors Lendvai is being transferred with immediate effect to the news agency MTI'. And in order to make clear that this was not a promotion but a punitive measure he added, 'Gone is the time when someone who is being kicked out from our paper can immediately get another high position. No, Comrades: he will not fill the first- nor the second- nor the third-ranking position but must start at the very bottom to prove that he has learned from his mistakes.'

What made the entire affair so intolerable for those concerned, that is for me and the three or four colleagues who were also being disciplined, was the stage-managing of this matter like a criminal trial. It took place in a huge hall in the presence of about 100 or 150 people.

But it was also a black day for me for another reason. Nobody had prepared me nor even hinted at the possibility of such action. This was the notorious Communist Party discipline which left no room for petty-bourgeois feelings, or concern for the psychological state of a twenty-year-old. For me a world was collapsing around me: I was being driven out of the leading paper and sentenced to professional obscurity.

That I left the building with tears in my eyes and even compiled a short list of the names of those colleagues who found a few kind words for me after my expulsion may seem ridiculous or even despicable today, almost 50 years later. At the time the terrible trial of Cardinal József Mindszennty had taken place; thousands were being arrested, charged with conspiracy, speculation and of being enemies of the people. Persons who had lost everything in the war and had built new lives for themselves were caught in the toils of the nationwide nationalisations. My father had to deal with such tragic cases daily and was himself afraid that he would not be able to continue his work as a lawyer. The steamroller of Bolshevisation rode roughshod over the country. What, compared to this, was the 'expulsion' from the self-appointed elite or the personal degradation in a public forum? Compared with the misery to which so many Hungarians were sentenced in those months, and compared with the blows of fate which hit me four years later, this was a bagatelle. But for this ambitious and idealistic twenty-year-old the world had caved in.

5

Suspicion, Fear and Show Trials

According to the Party's yardstick, my transfer to the news agency MTI might have been interpreted as a demotion. In fact, however, my new job gave me a fascinating view of the mechanics of news manipulation. At the same time it made me an early witness to the reverberations of the political earthquake which in Hungary's postwar history became known as the Rajk affair, or simply the Rajk trial, in deference to its central figure.

MTI, the central news agency, like TASS in Moscow was the key instrument in the manipulation of both internal and foreign news. It was the main channel for the transmission of information thought to be politically acceptable or sufficiently manipulated to be suitable for dissemination in the press or over the air. Its second major task, which was hardly known in the West and to which I will return later, was the preparation, compilation and distribution of so-called 'confidential' news bulletins for the privileged elite of the Party and state apparatus.

At the time, MTI and radio still formed one administrative unit. In their way almost all the leading editors were interesting figures, and they were later to play an unexpectedly important role in my life. In the early fifties, when the news agencies of the Eastern bloc still based their reports on Soviet sources, two women were in charge of internal agency policy. The editor-in-chief and later acting Director General, Julia Kenyeres, was an old Communist in the truest sense of the word. Born in 1895, she had been a Communist before the October Revolution, had spent 25 years in exile, first in the West and subsequently eight years in Moscow, and did not return to Budapest until 1947. Back in the thirties she had already worked in the international press agency of the Comintern, and in the end had even taught at the Comintern Academy in Moscow. In brief, Comrade Kenyeres was a dyed-in-the-wool professional functionary. She took no risks. She once fired an editor because he had dared to cut a couple of sentences from a humdrum TASS dispatch. If she had no Soviet source to fall back on she called up Moscow and put everything on hold until she had enough background material from her Soviet sources, even if the world press had already reported the item in question. Thus when Palmiro Togliatti, the Italian Communist leader, issued a proclamation about the 'new directions' in the worldwide Communist movement, this inflexible woman succeeded in preventing its publication in the Hungarian press for a week, when the official Party paper printed edited 'extracts' from it.

Nor was I spared experiencing the vigilance of the MTI editor-in-chief at first hand. Initially I had been assigned to the paper's economic section. One day we received a report from a Western agency about the precipitous slump in American auto production. The news did not seem to pose a problem, particularly since it seemed to confirm the relentless Communist propaganda barrage about the decline of capitalism. That afternoon I was phoned by Mrs Kenyeres: 'You have committed a serious political mistake; the report you paraphrased plays right into the hands of capitalist propaganda'. I felt as though I had been hit over the head. The offending report after all had said that the previous year two to three million fewer cars had been produced in the United States than the year before. Where had I gone wrong? 'By mentioning these absolute figures you make it possible for every reader to get an idea of how many vehicles come off the assembly line. It would have suffficed to mention only the percentage of the decline.'

The lesson was clear, and it was one that was confirmed daily by TASS and the plan reports of the fraternal countries: never cite absolute figures, only percentages. In that event nothing, absolutely nothing can go wrong. Continuity or changes in the Party line on important questions of domestic and foreign policy were determined as much by that which was suppressed as by what was published. But

Kenyeres in her vigilance went far beyond censoring news items. Her careful scrutiny of everything and her watchdog mentality were probably connected with her personal history. Only much later did I learn that her husband, a former TASS correspondent in Berlin, had been called back to Moscow and been arrested. Like so many others he had disappeared without a trace.

Her actions after the death of a colleague in my department should also be seen against her personal background. Before the Communist takeover the man in question had been head of the economics department; he spoke a number of foreign langauges and had no diffculty adjusting to the new situation. His superb translations of complex economic texts made him a mainstay in the editorial offices. When this 60-year-old colleague died unexpectedly, his family asked me to deliver the eulogy. Kenyeres agreed but insisted that I clear the draft of my address with her. She carefully read the two-page paper and deleted two sentences, or rather some 'far too friendly and appreciative words'. That, she said, was excessive. The man had been, after all, a reactionary, although admittedly he had proved useful.

The funeral left a deep impression on me, not least because of the demeaning circumstances, and I kept on dreaming about it, not right away but later, in prison. It was the first time that I been to a funeral, let alone one at which I was to deliver the eulogy. But what bothered me at the time – and probably still does – is the fact that I accepted the revisions so meekly. It did not occur to me to deliver the speech in its original form. I don't even think that I acted out of fear. No, it was simply part of the personal adjustment one made in those days.

The second woman in a supervisiory position was named Julia Poll. She was the widow of a long-dead secretary of the weak underground Communist Party of the interwar years, and so reliable that she was entrusted with taking care of the private library of the almighty Party boss, Mátyás Rákosi, after business hours. Julia Poll was now the head of the department involved in the compilation of the confidential information channelled to the Party and government nomenclature.

Receiving information was a privilege. The scope and type of information one was given depended on the rank and influence of the recipient. The 'confidential editorial office' relied on the news of the Western press agencies, on Western papers and broadcasts, in brief on sources that normally editors of the general news service were not privy to – a true privilege at a time when foreign papers were not available on the newstands and translators and journalists could be fired if they lent a friend a Western periodical or paper. Information that seemed particularly explosive, like articles about Hungary itself, were given only to members of the Politburo as special bulletins in special sealed envelopes, hand-delivered by special messengers. Receipts had to be signed, making the recipient responsible for keeping these items secret. The bulletins had to be returned to the MTI within a specified period. At the time there existed at least four versions of the special bulletins and access to that information, like all perks of the elite (cars, apartments, etc) followed strict hierarchical lines. But this structured system of access to news, a scheme followed to in all Eastern bloc countries, was in fact a gigantic farce. The 'highly confidential' information in the different 'white', 'red', or 'green' bulletins was also availabe to ordinary citizens who had the patience to listen to foreign broadcasts, even if these were usually jammed. Thus, for example, my parents, who listened to the Hungarian-language broadcasts from Munich (RFE) or London (BBC), were as well-informed as the high-ranking recipients of the special bulletins. But all that did not change the significance of this confidential section at the MTI nor the power position of the woman who headed it.

I have now arrived at a somewhat sensitive chapter of my life, though as it turned out one that was to have highly important political and personal consequences for me. The feared Comrade Poll at the time was exactly 20 years my senior, and not exactly a beauty. At an office outing – in fact we were 'volunteering' to help in the construction of a housing project in the new Stalin City – the two of us had a friendly chat. Soon after that excursion my girlfriend and I had a falling out, and while this was happening Mrs Poll came down with the 'flu. Out of compassion and quite innocently I visited her at her house. Without going into details let us say that I was probably not the first and certainly not the last young editor she seduced, not by force but very authoritatively; rape would not be the right word in the case of a twenty-year-old. When I made up with my girlfriend a couple of weeks later I broke off my relationship with the far older Comrade Poll. Christmas 1949, on the occasion of Stalin's seventieth birthday, she had given me a small white Stalin bust, but not even that could change my determination to put an end to the affair.

Since the two of us continued to work in the same institution for almost two more years, both of us in executive positions, she was able to wreak terrible vengeance on me. She had even warned me before I broke up with her that she could do me great harm if... The scorned woman attacked me wherever she could, especially behind my back.

Whether she also pulled strings later when I was arrested I do not know. But as a witness she did everything possible to blacken my reputation. In jail I was shown her signed testimony according to which at the MTI I had already engaged in 'hostile activities' and 'between the lines' had inserted 'imperialist ideas' into my articles.

Before this episode which was to have dire consequences, dramatic events took place; at first these affected me only indirectly, though more directly later. When I was 'punitively' transferred to the MTI my immediate boss as head of the economic desk was György Adam, an economist and journalist who had returned from Latin America after the war and whose Communist ties went back to the illegal days of the Party. We had no close personal contacts. I had been at the MTI for only a short time, and initially the age difference as well as his superior position probably intimidated me. One morning, either in June or July 1949, Adam failed to show up at the editorial office. When I called him at home his landlady, highly agitated, told me that Adam had been taken away in the middle of the night by men from the secret police (AVH). They had identified themselves and produced a search warrant but volunteered no further explanation.

Some weeks later a secret policeman turned up at the editorial office and questioned me and other colleagues about our boss. All I could tell him was that the only thing that might be considered unusual was that occasionally he would send us out of the office when he made a phone call. But then we would do the same when we wanted to talk to our girlfriends or lovers. Adam disappeared behind prison walls together with 200 former Spanish Civil War veterans, Western émigrés and Communists with contacts to the Yugoslav partisans and French resistance fighters.

Nothing was heard from Adam for years. His trial, at which he together with other Communists who had returned from Western emigration received life sentences, was held behind closed doors. Not until the October 1956 uprising did he reappear, at which time, as one of the leading intellectuals, he even headed a revolutionary committee. After the Soviet intervention he was again arrested. When he was finally released after some years, he was a broken man. Adam would tell his fellow-prisoners calmly and dispassionately that the years in prison under the Kádár regime, despite their harshness, were nothing compared to the torture and total isolation during the heyday of Stalinism. The imprisoned revolutionaries refused to believe him. 'Communist fairy tales' they called it, and once even beat him up.

The Adam case was naturally only one of many which in this summer of 1949 shook up the world of politics and the media, the Party and government apparatus. On 15 May 1949, the unity list of the People's Front, which now also comprised the bourgeois rump parties, had celebrated a triumphant 'electoral victory', gathering 95.6 percent of all the votes. At the mass demonstration the next day the main speaker was the General Secretary of the People's Front, and Number Four on the list of candidates, Foreign Minister László Rajk. He castigated the betrayal by the Titoist 'running dogs of imperialism', praised the brilliant strategy of the great leader of the peace camp, I.V. Stalin, and the wise leadership of Stalin's best Hungarian pupil, beloved Comrade Rákosi. On 29 May Rajk was invited to lunch by Rákosi. The next evening he was arrested. Two weeks later a brief communiqué was issued announcing that Rajk, Dr Tibor Szönyi, the head of the key personal section of the Party, Pál Justus, at the time a member of the Central Committee and Vice President of the Broadcasting Corporation, together with 17 other people whose names were not made public, had been arrested for conducting 'espionage on behalf of foreign powers'. Within 48 hours *Szabad Nep* reported the receipt of hundreds of telegrams in which workers at protest meetings demanded severe punishment of the 'Rajk gang', of the traitors to the Party and the people, of the 'Trotskyite agents of imperialism'. At the trial in September the accused admitted their guilt in having infiltrated the Party as agents of the American, British, French and Yugoslav secret services and having plotted the overthrow of the new people's democracy.

After a week-long trial in September broadcast twice a day by Radio Budapest, the 'People's Court' sentenced Rajk, Szönyi and his deputy, András Szalai, to death, while Justus and a Yugoslav diplomat to life imprisonment. In a parallel trial the former chief of military counter-intelligence, General György Pálffy, and another high-ranking officer were also sentenced to death. They were executed on 15 October.

The Rajk trial was the opening act in the witch-hunts throughout the entire Soviet bloc, in the unmasking of 'Titoists' and 'agents of imperialism posing as Communists', in the rooting out of 'enemies carrying membership cards in their pockets'. With Stalin's proclaimed 'intensification of the class struggle' as their launching pad, the prosecutors mercilessly moved not only against 'class enemies' in the classic sense, but also, or rather primarily, against particularly dangerous alleged enemies within the ranks of the Party. The script for the memorised confessions, witness testimonies, accusations and sentences had been written in Moscow. Soviet 'specialists' were the central control officers who deployed the most cunning and brutal physical and psychological torture methods. However, Rákosi and his right-hand-man, the Defence Minister and Party overseer of the secret service, Mihály Farkas, together with the Chief of Police, Gábor Péter, were far more enthusiastic tools of repression than their counterparts in the other satellite states. Thus the Poles and Romanians managed to prevent a blood-bath of the Party leadership while the Czechs did not stage their 'anti-Zionist' Slansky trial until 1952, under direct pressure from Stalin.

The most important factors underlying the great purges were the first major events of the Cold War (the test of the Soviet atomic bomb, the creation of NATO, the Berlin blockade and the American airlift) and above all Tito's resistance to the Soviet claim to absolute dominance, which raised the paranoid mistrust of the aging Stalin to unprecedented heights. Today we know that the charges against Rajk and his fellow-defendants were personally approved of by Stalin and that the interrogations by 40 Soviet 'specialists' were prepared and carried out under the direct supervision of General Fjedor Bjelkin, the chief of the Soviet secret police in South-eastern Europe.

Why had the puppet-masters selected Rajk for the role of chief culprit? Obviously because of his involvement in the Spanish Civil War, his subsequent internment in a French camp, his role in the Communist underground in Hungary, and because after his arrest during the war he was deported to Germany instead of being executed thanks to the intervention of his brother, the wartime State Secretary for Domestic Affairs in the Szálasi-Arrow Cross government. All these factors were incontrovertible evidence for a 'connection' both to his former Yugoslav comrades-in-arms and the 'American secret service'. In view of his popularity particularly among the younger Communists as a so-called 'homegrown Communist' and 'hero of the Spanish Civil War', this slender, tall man, one of the few top leaders not of Jewish descent, was doubtless a potentially dangerous rival of the fat, unattractive, balding Rákosi. Fear of competition intensified by a profound inferiority complex may have played a role in the hate-filled persecution of handsome and personable former colleagues like Rajk and later Kádár. As a matter of fact a bizarre passage in a speech Rákosi delivered at a meeting of the Politburo on 21 April 1951, seems to bear this out:

> I once told Rajk jokingly he ought to read Shakespeare's *Julius Caesar*. When Caesar goes to the Forum where he is murdered he says to Brutus 'I don't like this Cassius, such a lean, tormented man who doesn't sleep at night. I prefer fat, bald people; they are more light-hearted, in a better

mood.' That's how it is with you. You're here. We've won. You are a leading personality and haggard. Something's eating you.

He apparently didn't want to quote the key phrases of Caesar's and probably his own reflections because they might have been too revealing:

Such men as he be never at heart's ease
Whiles they behold a greater than themselves
And therefore are they very dangerous.

With his allusion to Cassius, Rákosi referred to still another passage in this scene, which fitted Rajk as well as Kádár later:

Yon Cassius has a lean and hungry look
He thinks too much: such men are dangerous.

Rákosi, this gifted, educated and at the same time diabolical figure heading the Hungarian CP was undoubtedly the only Communist chief in power since Lenin who could quote Shakespeare.

However, at the time Rajk certainly was not a man with an individual political profile, let alone a conscious 'national Communist' or 'revisionist'. According to all available information Rajk as Minister of the Interior was a dyed-in-the-wool Stalinist, a pitiless liquidator of opposition parties, and the architect of the repellent show trial of Cardinal Mindszenty. He played his role in his own trial with the same sort of discipline up to the tragic end.

As to the Rajk trial, there Stalin's classic method of the so-called amalgam, the linking of entirely different factors, was put into play. The purges were directed against native Communists but also against those who had lived or worked abroad, above all against veterans of the Spanish Civil War and against Jews. Men with entirely different pasts were tried together. Rajk, the lifelong Communist who, of all the Communist leaders, had had more fights with the Social Democrats (and with Justus as well); then Justus himself, the perfect example of Stalin's model of a villain, not only a left-wing Social Democrat who because of his independent position had acquired the reputation of being a 'Trotskyite', but also as an intellectual who had spent some time in the West as an émigré; General Pálffy, a former professional officer and one of the few real resistance fighters; and Dr Szönyi, the leader of the Communist emigrés in Switzerland, who with the help of the Americans and Tito partisans in the turbulent postwar days soon returned to Hungary.

Justus's arrest took place on 18 June, a day before the public revelation of the 'conspiracy'. Some months or perhaps even weeks earlier I had spoken to him for the first time since our ideological falling-out in early 1948. On orders of the district Party committee he had come to audit a seminar I was conducting. Since the session was held in the conference room used by both the MTI and the radio station and since his vice presidential chamber was close by, I walked him back to his office. When I said good-bye I mumbled a few words to the effect that I personally was sorry about the step I had taken back then but that it in no way affected my personal opinion of him. Justus accepted my embarrassed brief explanation with a friendly smile and a firm handshake but said nothing.

By then we were already living in an atmosphere of total isolation from reality. We knew that during the summer months numerous renowned public figures had disappeared without a trace. On 18 June Justus, on the way to an end-of-school celebration of his nine-year-old daughter, Eva, was surrounded by the black limousines of the secret police and arrested then and there. The news spread like wildfire. My first instinctive reaction was sheer terror. Were we former Justus students now going to be harassed, fired or perhaps even arrested immediately?

It was the summer of the World Youth Festival in Budapest. Tens of thousands of young men and women from all over the world were, according to the Communist script, supposed to sing the praises of peace and socialism. The well-oiled campaign against the Titoist plotters was carried out by Communists from the West and well-known fellow-travellers. Thus during the very days when Rajk annd the other 'conspirators' were being tortured, the meeting of the World Peace Congress was taking place in Budapest. Famous poets like Paul Eluard of Paris and the Brazilian novelist Jorge Amado heaped effusive praise on the peace policies of the great Stalin and of the Socialist camp led by him.

Decades later the well-known foremost Communist journalist Miklós Vásárhelyi (later President of the Soros Foundation in Hungary) described the mood of many Party members candidly and aptly:

> I was terribly afraid, but I was in agreement with the campaign against Tito and the Rajk trial out of discipline, belief and opportunism... I later lived in permanent fear, but I didn't dare tell anyone, not even my wife. If I had admitted my fear to her and possibly been arrested then she might have had doubts about me because I was afraid. In a Socialist system a person whose conscience is clear could have no reason for being afraid, so went the slogan at the time.

Two characteristic episodes from those days show that not even people who were closely linked to the events dared ask questions. In the case of Party members their arrests were generally belatedly documented or 'cooked' with dossiers in the files of the Control Commission of the Party. Karoly Kiss, its president, was a prewar Communist but not a Muscovite. His deputy was assigned the job of answering the requests of the secret police and making the required archival documents available. Once, while in the process of assembling papers requested by the police, he was summoned to the Rákosi Secretariat. He took the files with him and was arrested in Rákosi's outer office. Kiss, this top Party functionary, noticed the disappearance of his most important colleague only because he had failed to return to his office. But in this atmosphere of intimidation even Kiss did not dare ask why his deputy had been locked up.

Even more scurrilous was the behaviour of Justus's boss, a man named Sándor Barcs, a bourgeois fellow-traveller *par excellence*. Before the war he had written articles against National Socialism and belonged to the left, crypto-Communist wing of the infiltrated and subsequently smashed Smallholders Party. He was rewarded after 1945 by being named General Director of the MTI and Broadcasting Corporation as well as president of the soccer league. Barcs filled both these posts for more than three decades, skillfully surviving all upheavals.

In an interview in 1985 he asserted, to my utter astonishment, 'I read the communiqué in the paper and didn't want to believe my eyes. In this way I lost one of my deputies, because Pál Justus at the time was Vice President of broadcasting and the MTI. He worked in the office next to mine.' The interviewer then asked whether Barcs, as Justus's boss, had been contacted by the secret service: 'Certainly not. Later I was surprised to learn that they were looking for me. Gábor Péter sent word that I was to come to his office. There I was told that I had been appointed a lay judge in the Rajk trial and that I had to accept this offer. 'The conversation was 'extraordinarily friendly,' said Barcs. In answer to his question of what he was supposed to do there they told him, 'Absolutely nothing'. All he had to do was sit on the podium (together with three other people's judges, two workers and a peasant); he would not be allowed to talk nor ask any questions. He was a mere onlooker. In the final analysis he had no doubts about the genuineness of the confessions and simply noted the sentence handed down by the presiding judge without consultation with the panel. Thus Justus's boss casually sentenced his own deputy together with the other accused – probably unique in the history of jurisprudence – and his reflections 36 years later give no hint of catharsis.

If in the course of this sort of trial even a panelist of the so-called People's Court thought that everything seemed to flow smoothly, when all the accused 'fluently' (according to Barcs) testified against themselves, how could we who heard only the voices over the radio arrive at a different conclusion? I will never forget how I, late in the afternoon of 15 September 1949, a Friday, heard the familiar, calm voice of Justus: like all the others on trial he too, marionette-like, recited the concocted confession.

Today we know that neither the AVH directors nor the Soviet 'advisers' initially had any idea how the 'partial confessions' wrung from this left-wing Socialist could be brought into line with the overall plan of the show trial, whose primary purpose was to 'unmask' Tito and to discredit the National Communist trend. The most reliable method lay in the 'political reordering' of the interrogation records. Arrests in the days when left-wing activism had been illegal became espionage on behalf of the Horthy police. Professional or documented contacts with Communist functionaries who now themselves were in prison as well as with Yugoslav or French diplomats became participation in the Titoist-imperialist conspiracy. As Georg Hodos, who survived his trial, tells us in his memoirs, in the course of the interrogation through a perverse sort of 'logic' every past political act was turned into a crime, and the victims, being completely isolated from the outside world, had no way of defending themselves. It was only after the publication of the memoirs and interviews of the survivors that the world found out why they confessed and how sadistic torture turned them into their own accusers and into liars accusing their comrades. Since then we have also learned from those who pulled the wires behind the scenes or 'concretised' the Moscow instructions how they would insert invented cross-connections between people who hardly knew one another into the interrogation records, and how all of this would be seized upon by the torturers and their bosses.

The intrigues and vicious power struggles of the torturers and their superiors in Budapest and Moscow, which in turn depended on the mood and psychosis of Stalin and his Hungarian servant Rákosi all fall within this framework. The partial access to the archives, the publication of memoirs and interviews, including the self-justifications and protests of the top leaders who have since fallen into disfavour, have opened up a breathtaking panorama of evil. Its description alone could fill a book. Therefore I will concentrate here only on the fate of Justus and on details that impinged on my life.

The key role in all of this belongs to a particularly repulsive person, a certain Vladimir Farkas, a security officer who grew up in Moscow. His special position and his direct access to Gábor Péter, the chief of Security, can easily be explained. Vladi (as his bosses called him) was the son of Mihály Farkas, the Defence Minister, head of the secret police and member of the troika (with Rákosi and the NKVD man and Economics Minister Ernö Gerö) in charge of guarding the 'purity of the Party'. Vladi, who had been promoted to lieutenant-colonel and department chief, together with a certain Major Kremniov-Kamenkovic of the Soviet secret service, conducted the interrogations of Justus and the two unhappy women who had to appear as 'witnesses' in the show trial. That however did not prevent the Farkases, father and son, from also eventually becoming caught in the cogs of the purge machinery or in the factional fights. To whitewash his past, Vladimir Farkas in the 1980s decided, with the help of a journalist, to tell the story of his life; in this account he reports – naturally from his vantage point – on the Justus affair. According to Farkas, General Bjelkin and his 'team' stayed in Hungary throughout the entire Rajk trial and played a crucial role in the interrogations and the drafting of the 'confessions' elicited through torture. Moreover, they personally tortured the victims and gave detailed instructions for the staging of the show trial.

When the two torturers, Farkas and Kremniov-Kamenkovic, demanded that Justus admit that he had been a police spy of the Horthy regime since his early youth and been blackmailed into becoming a French agent, and more importantly been recruited into the Yugoslav espionage apparatus, he rejected this absurd accusation, where-upon he was personally tortured by the Soviet major in a chamber expressly designed for this purpose. What this meant in practice has been described by Béla Szász, one of the survivors:

> Somebody would sit on the man's backside and lift up his legs, and another one would hit him with a rubber truncheon with all his might. That treatment consisted of 25 strokes on each leg. I was subjected to this more than thirty times. My soles looked like raw meat, the skin split yet I had to stand on them. Once it happened that I had to stand for nine days without out a break, without water, without being able to wash, without food, standing day and night.

When Justus, despite torture and humiliation, didn't agree to play the role assigned to him, he was forced to a public confession by other means. They threatened to kill his wife, Edith, and his friends in front of his eyes.

Depending on the character and stamina of the victims yet another psychological method was brought into play. After a period of sleeplessness, hunger and cold, after the brutal wielding of rubber truncheons and gun barrels, a new interrogator would appear who spoke about a 'fatal error' or an 'unfortunate involvement' of the victim in the conspiracy and tried to establish fresh contact with the tortured prisoner. Lieutenant Colonel Farkas has denied that he threatened Justus with murdering his wife. The turning point at the Justus interrogations occurred when General Bjelkin spoke with Justus 'privately' (all interrogations were of course recorded) and held out the prospect of a 'normal life' once the trial was over.

That was a popular method. All prisoners as well as the witnesses were assured by the interrogator that they would not be executed or sentenced to long prison terms. After providing this 'ultimate service' to the Party in the 'worldwide battle against imperialism and its Titoist accomplices' (i.e. confessing to non-existent crimes) they would soon be able to begin a new life with their families in some lovely secluded resort, possibly in the Crimea.

We knew none of this in those glum September days in Budapest. What we heard were Justus's fantastic self-accusations of having become a right-wing police agent in 1932 in Hungary as well as France, of having made state secrets available to the Yugoslav Embassy and later 'directly' to the Yugoslav Minister of the Interior Rankovic and the press attaché of the French Embassy, François Gachot, and of having been engaged in systematic, anti-democratic educational activities. In his closing statement Justus summarised the purpose of his 'insidious undermining of Hungarian democracy' in these words, 'It was my role, in line with the instructions of Rankovic, to gather together the Trotskyite and other anti-democratic forces and at the crucial moment make them available to Rajk and his conspiratorial organisation'. Justus and the other conspirators were allegedly to have carried out an armed *putsch*, murder the members of the ruling troika (Rákosi, Gerö, Farkas) and with the help of any and all right-wing Social Democratic and chauvinist clerical elements, set up a 'fascist-type government'.

I and the other former Justus acolytes were alarmed above all by the following passage in the indictment: 'Justus organised persons close to him in a Trotskyite seminar, trained them to oppose democracy, and kept them under his constant control. His group affiliated itself directly with the Yugoslav Minister of the Interior Rankovic.'

What terrified me even more was Györgyi Vándori's testimony. She was a young journalist who together with us regularly attended the Saturday meetings of the so-called Justus Seminar. She confirmed that at Justus's order she had organised an illegal group so that he could build his Trotskyite cadre within the Social Democratic Party. She had organized a group of about 20 people. In his lectures, so she said, Justus sought to convince his audience that the Hungarian people's democracy must be despised and opposed. This illegal group was active from spring 1948 to May 1949. And then a passage from her personal diary was cited: 'It would be treason not to fight against this system,' and 'I had to establish connections to the free Europeans, which I understood to mean the Western powers and Tito'. Justus confirmed this: 'The testimony of the witness on the whole conforms to the truth'.

The witness had been beaten for four days and interrogated by that infernal pair, Farkas and Kremniov-Kamenkovic, and deprived of sleep and food. The pages with the compromising passages had been inserted into her diary. She too had been forced to memorise her confession, and she too was promised that she would be driven home after the trial. Györgyi was to spend more than six years in prison, two-thirds in solitary confinement. They sentenced her to ten years for having engaged in espionage during her emigration in France and for the Americans, even though at the time she was a high-school student and had never been out of the country.

Ica Fleischer, Justus's secretary, was also abducted, beaten, and threatened if she refused to testify against her boss following an invented script. She remained steadfast until she was shown Justus's confession. Only then was she prepared to deliver her testimony at the public trial. Before the trial alll accused were given decent food and new clothes. Ica Fleischer had to memorise the catalogue of lies they handed her and recite it several times a day. They recorded run-throughs, corrected her delivery, and before the actual trial had a sort of dress rehearsal. Hairdressers and cosmeticians tended to the victims to remove any traces of torture and to make sure that the witnesses looked like ordinary people.

All the witnesses, and in crucial cases even their close relatives, were kept in prison. Thus Mrs Fleischer, who was not accused of anything, had to spend six-and-a-half years of her eight-year sentence in prison. Of the 93 people directly involved in the Rajk trial and in follow-up proceedings, 15 were executed and 11 did not survive their incarceration.

What happened to Justus? In numerous poems he recalled the almost five years spent in solitary confinement: every day taking 13,000 steps in the 12 square metres of the cell, and later 2,000 steps all by himself in the prison yard. In the last phase of his imprisonment he was allowed to work on translations and write. His wife, a journalist employed at the trade union paper *Nepszava*, was interned at Kistarcsa four months after her husband's arrest, and only four years later, in the course of the amnesty proclaimed by the first Nagy Government, was she released. Their daughter, Eva, nine years of age, was put in the care of an aunt, and was the only one allowed to visit her mother after 1950 for brief periods.

Only years later, when I had the chance to listen to a taped interview with former Justus colleagues and talk to Györgyi Vándori who was living in Vienna, did I find out that in fact there was a group of about 12 to 15 friends who met once a month in the apartment of the well-known actress Margit Ladomersky. The secret police apparently knew all along about these harmless gatherings. J.M., the wife of a well-known director and later a journalist in her own right (and a former girlfriend of Justus's) reported to the police. Another woman was also pressured to keep the AVH informed about what they discussed at these gatherings. She was, however, loyal, and kept the husband of the actress, a composer and Justus himself informed about her reports, and occasionally they made changes in her notes. In addition the police allegedly had yet a third informant in that small group where discussions ranged far and wide; the only topic never touched upon was the 'fight against democracy'.

As can be seen from this account I had not been part of Justus's inner circle. Yet my contacts with them was enough to get me and many others arrested months or years later and to destroy my livelihood. Justus himself was not released until late November 1955, but even before his release he was sentenced to an additional seven years, in part because of the testimony of the wife of the well-known director. His complete political and legal rehabilitation and compensation for the years in prison had to wait until September 1956.

In the course of time those who were arrested and sentenced as early as 1949 became – together with additional reports of informers – an inexhaustible source of supply for later waves of arrests.

Who now can visualise the atmosphere of that time? Among the Communist leadership corps a psychology evolved out of their conviction of being the 'victors of history'. The political assignment given the state security service was to be the 'shield and sword of the Party' and the 'hard fist of the dictatorship of the proletariat'. Under the direct instruction of the troika of Rákosi, Farkas and Gerö, and the subservient secret police chief, Gábor Péter, all of whom were blinded by the autocratic control of the mechanisms of power, potential critics were depicted as conscious enemies or unreliable and thus hostile elements. At the height of the purges Defence Minister Farkas sent General Peter or one of his deputies a note simply reading: 'X is an imperialist (or British or Yugoslav) spy. Carry out. Farkas.' That sufficed to remove that person from public life and extract the desired confession. It was sheer lunacy. But in all of this there was an inner logic. The purges spread from those arrested to those with whom they were in touch and to friends. As in the Soviet Union in the thirties, the permanent purge developed its own law as an instrument of power.

But were there not people who knew exactly what was taking place because they at one time, while in camps and prisons in their Soviet exile, had gone through this themselves? Of course the hundred or so émigrés who returned to Hungary between 1945 and 1947 knew this, including my editor-in-chief, Comrade Kenyeres. But all of them kept silent and told us nothing. 'If I say anything they'll come for me again,' was their understandable self-justification. And it was many of these former émigrés who became passionately involved in the 'building of socialism,' in the persecution of dissenters or suspects.

Other factors also affected the mood within the Party itself as well as of sympathizers and fellow-travellers. Enormous influence was exerted by those Western contemporaries who were seduced by Stalin's personality or by the Soviet Union as the champion of the fight against fascism or National Socialism. The American Ambassador to the Soviet Union, Joseph E. Davies, who served there at the time of the great show trials in Moscow, wrote a book giving invaluable support to the dictator and his regime. In Davies's eyes Stalin was a man of great intellectual force, balance and wisdom. Davies thought that Stalin's eyes were so kind and mild that a child would enjoy sitting on his lap and a dog would cuddle up to him. And his views about the trials of 1938 had a similarly positive tone.

The Labour Party ideologue, Harold Laski, who in 1935, writing about a conversation with the feared chief prosecutor of the show trials, Andrei Vyshinsky, asserted that he basically saw no difference between the general conduct of a trial in the Soviet Union and Great

Britain and that he considered Vyshinsky a man passionately interested in judicial reform.

And Leon Feuchtwanger, the German novelist, had this to say about Stalin in 1937: 'The people have the need to express their gratitude, their boundless admiration'. Not, mind you, that Stalin wanted so much adulation: 'He is very reticent... Stalin obviously finds it very annoying to be thus deified.' In connection with the trials Feuchtwanger said it is impossible to believe that so brilliant and thoughtful a man could do something so monumentally stupid as to stage such a crude comedy with the help of countless accomplices.

6

Terror and Grim Humour

It was the 'rule of accomplices'. As a foreign policy specialist I was in the fortunate situation of being at least spared domestic political dirty work. Many who later fought in the front lines against the dictatorship generally and against Rákosi and his gang in particular tried to suppress their past. And it was not just Party hacks and Communist writers who trod this path. Respectable bourgeois and populist writers were among the 34 who contributed to a collection celebrating Rákosi's sixtieth birthday.

I too was not reluctant to lash out against 'Titoist Yugoslavia' or 'international Zionism'. Later, deeply ashamed about engaging in these attacks, I wanted the earth to swallow me up. What I find particularly offensive now is that back then I was so full of myself. After all I was a young journalist but already published in the Party's main theoretical organ.

When I think back to those days when tens of thousands were caught up in the rotating purge machinery, when the economy continued to plummet, and instead of the promised 50 percent rise, real wages declined by 20 percent (between 1949 and 1952), when as news editor and commentator I contributed to the edifice of lies, I can find no excuse and even now cringe in shame. This passage from Evgenya Ginsburgh's memoirs, one that applies to all conformists in every dictatorship really sums it up for me:

> In sleepless nights it is no sop to one's conscience that one did not directly participate in murder and betrayal. Because responsibility lies not only with the one who bludgeoned but also with those who tolerated evil in whatever fashion – through the thoughtless repetition of dangerous theories, the wordless raising of the right hand, the half-hearted writing of half-truths.

After 1957, working in Vienna, I became a passionate champion of independent Yugoslavia against the pressure of the Eastern bloc, and then in the late eighties just as energetically I came out against the hegemonic claim of Greater Serbia on the one hand and the chauvinistic aberrations in Croatia on the other. These positions were undoubtedly a sort of subconscious compensation for my part in the dissemination of concocted anti-Yugoslav fantasies between 1949 and 1953. Similarly, my warnings against harbouring illusions about a rapid change in Eastern and Southeastern Europe and my near-obsession with about the now almost trite-sounding 'demons of the past' – racism, anti-semitism and intolerance – may be due to my continuing feelings of guilt for having failed as a journalist back in the Stalinist period of 1949 to 1952.

Hand in hand with the merciless persecution of the middle class and Church, of free and later collectivised peasants, came the unparalleled exploitation of workers by the hated system of production norms. Nonetheless the Rákosi camp continued to fantasise about the 'country of iron and steel' and held out the prospect of doubling industrial production in a mere four years.

Given Stalin's relentless push to prepare for a Third World War, the regime deferred to military considerations in its planning, with particular emphasis on the development of heavy industry. Small businesses and trade were practically liquidated. The campaign against the 'rich' peasants, the so-called kulaks, and for the collectivisation of agriculture led to the reintroduction of food rationing. Accelerated industrialisation after 1951 and the expansion of military spending, together with the steadily deteriorating food situation and the socialisation of private housing led to increasing dissatisfaction among industrial workers and peasants. In the 1950s nine percent of arable land lay fallow, and the region that had once been the granary of central Europe had to import food to satisfy domestic needs. The occasionally candid head of planning, Zoltán Vas, in a confidential talk with a journalist said, 'If we had imported rolled steel wrapped in tin foil it would still have been cheaper than producing it in Hungary'.

The readjustment of foreign trade to dependence on Soviet raw materials and energy led to ominous faulty decisions in economic and industrial policy whose consequences reverberate to this day. Instead of receiving 'fraternal aid' Hungary, like the other satellite states, was exploited by an unfair price policy dictated by Moscow. Yet despite all of this, the economically backward Soviet Union remained the official model. And in addition there was the permanent campaign to display and intensify the 'love' for the 'great Soviet Union' and its 'inspired leader', Stalin. What made the atmosphere so unbearable for so many was the fact that the Party leadership ordered not only subjugation and obedience but also boundless permanent enthusiasm for the Soviet Union and Socialism. That the chasm between dreary reality and the grandiose visions conjured up by the planners produced only resigned opportunism and icy cynicism could be felt time and time again.

The only thing that flourishes in dictatorships of this kind is of course political humour. So: 'What's the difference between existing and functioning Socialism?' 'I don't know.' 'Existing Socialism doesn't function, and functioning Socialism doesn't exist.' There were any number of variations on this classic joke. As for relations with the Soviet Union a joke making the rounds in the early fifties was parti-cularly telling. Two monuments are being put up in Budapest for two Russians – one for Chudakov and one for Budakov. 'Who was this Chudakov?' asks a passer-by. 'Don't you know? Among other things Chudakov invented television, space ships, tape recorders and peni-cillin.' 'Oh,' said the passer-by, 'And who was Budakov?' 'Budakov was the inventor of Chudakov.'

Numerous versions of jokes about the food shortages and Party meetings circulated in which the protagonists are named Cohn and Green, not particularly unusual in cosmopolitan Jewish humour. 'Comrade Cohn, why didn't you respond to the speaker? Don't you have an opinion?' 'Yes, I do, but I don't agree with it.'

Another topic for jokes was deeply rooted in fear: at a Party meeting in the early fifties Cohn gets up to speak: 'Comrades. I'm not asking what happened to the goose liver and the salami. I only ask where is the bread, where is the milk?' A few months later, at another Party meeting Green gets up to speak: 'Comrades. I'm not asking what hap-pened to the bread and the milk. I only want to know 'Where is Comrade Cohn?'

This popular joke reflected harsh reality. In stark contrast to the propaganda about the 'great successes' in the building of Socialism, retail trade in 1952 declined by 57 percent compared to 1951. Despite declining production figures, wildcat strikes in some enterprises and spreading food shortages, there was no loosening of the reins. Between 1951 and May 1953 alone around 850,000 police fines were passed, and between 1950 and the first quarter of 1953, 650,000 people were brought to trial, of whom 387,000 were sentenced. In addition, 5,000 people were interned, and in May and June 1951 about 22,000 'bourgeois' and potentially 'unreliable elements' were relocated, primarily from the capital to remote settlements and communities where they had to do agricultural labour under extremely onerous conditions. Black humour had it that the population was divided into two camps: those who were already in custody and those who would soon find themselves behind bars.

These figures give a hint of the extent of the pervasive oppression, with the omnipresent state security service running a network of 100,000 informants. But the official reports and historical accounts, the songs, poems, novels and plays championing 'optimistic art', 'socialist realism' and the 'duty to the Party' merely covered up the sense of insecurity, unease and fear. Ordinary people had to bear the burden of daily life in silence. Even within families there were many grades between perpetrators and victims. The way people handled the situation was to put other people's trials and other victims out of their mind. Only when friends and political allies disappeared did one prick up one's ears. The trials against middle-class politicians who were sentenced as conspirators to long prison terms, the show trial of Cardinal Mindszenty and two years later of Archbishop Grosz (sentenced to life and 15 years respectively), the so-called MAORT and Standard Oil trials of managers and specialists were crucial building blocks in the increasingly harsh terror rule of totalitarian Hungary. Even though the persecution of the Catholic Church, the nationalisation of the clerical educational system and the dismantling of cloisters and religious orders directly affected my cousin and indirectly his parents, I nonchalantly accepted all of this, as so much else. But then in the spring of 1951 the news of the arrest of the leading Social Democrats hit like a bolt of lightning. Almost all top leaders, beginning with Árpád Szakasits, the Head of State from August 1948 to April 1850 and chairman of the MDP, the united party of Communists and Social Democrats, were arrested and charged with being pre-war and wartime police spies and agents of imperialism. Their sentences handed down in secret trials ranged from 15 years to life. According to a Hungarian researcher, after 1949 180 leading Social Democratic politicians in 20 trials received prison sentences, and this does not even include the many Social Democrats in the internment camps of Kistarcsa and Recsk.

The in part rather naive memoirs of Klari Szakasits, the President's daughter and wife of the crypto-Communist Social Democratic functionary Pál Schiffer, give an unvarnished picture of the mixture of underhandedness and contempt with which the so recently courted left-wing Socialists were treated by Rákosi and his people. At the time, before the birth of the united party, the men and women sporting the Social Democratic emblem on their lapel, the worker carrying a red hammer, were flattered, because they were urgently needed as the grave-diggers of the Social Democratic Party. Szakasits and his wife had even been invited for dinner by the Party chief on the evening of their arrest. Following the dinner Rákosi had Szakasits, who was still the nominal head of state, arrested on the spot based on crudely forged documents about his alleged espionage activities on behalf of the Horthy police and had him held for a few days in the basement of his villa before handing him over to the investigative prison.

All who a year earlier had wordlessly accepted (or rather had been forced to accept) the reports on the Rajk trial at the sessions of the Politburo and the Central Committee now themselves were caught up in the machinery of the purges, including the most zealous fellow-traveller of the Communists, Politburo member György Marosán. At the same time the AVH also arrested the most respected opponents of unification, like Anna Kéthly. The Social Democrats were accused of espionage.

The poet György Faludy, the former president of our Social Democratic high-school circle, tells in his memoirs that he named 'Captain' Edgar Allan Poe and 'Major' Walt Whitman as his contacts at the OSS, the wartime American intelligence agency, and that the AVH officer simply entered the names of these famous dead poets into the interrogation file. Faludy did this to call the attention of foreign journalists to the absurdity of the procedure in case he was ever tried.

Together with Faludy the secret police also arrested a number of former students of Justus and Social Democratic journalists. They were taken to the internment camp Recsk, and two years later some of them were questioned about my activities in the Social Democratic youth movement.

It was a cruel irony of fate that almost all the renowned Social Democrats who had remained in the country now suffered the same fate – whether formerly left or right-wing. The members of the former right -wing opposition in the SDP, those who had worked against the merger of the two parties, had little sympathy for the old political enemies in their own ranks. Even in the prison yard the 'Rightists' did not talk to the 'Leftists'. And during the October Revolution of 1956 any participation of the former left-wing Socialists in the short-lived revival of the Social Democratic Party was passionately rejected.

The wave of arrests sent a shock-wave through the ranks of those former Social Democrats who were still at liberty, though of course they hid their concern behind a wall of silence. Vigilance repeatedly required the submission of new resumes. If the Party had no enemies it had to invent them, since a potential opposition could not be tolerated.

Quite incidentally we learned that summer that even generals and other high-ranking officers had been arrested. All had been active in the resistance, and after that had loyally served in the new army. Seven generals, including the Chief of Staff, László Solyom, were executed. The interchangeability of victim and perpetrator was writ in blood: eight months before his own execution, General Kalman Revay, head of the military academy, had commanded the squad that executed his friend and comrade General György Pálffy in the courtyard of the military prison.

The Social Democratic politician and jurist Adolf Arndt some years ago described the criteria for the selection of the elite during the Nazi regime. He called it 'objective compromising'. Compromising did not demand proof of guilty conduct; ocupying a noteworthy position or function in a system of injustice was all that was needed. In short, the 'objective compromising' of leading functionaries within no time at all turned them into victims of the system which they themselves had kept going so vigorously.

Thus in the spring of 1951 the majority of prominent so-called 'home Communists' were arrested. These were the individuals who had risked their freedom, even their lives for the Party within Hungary in the battle against the Arrow Cross regime. János Kádár, the Party's Deputy Secretary General who a year-and-half earlier in his role as Minister of the Interior on Rákosi's order had tried to persuade his friend Rajk to 'confess' was himself brought to trial for 'hostile' activities, together with Foreign Minister Gyula Kállai and other leading politicians. Kádár's successor as Minister of the Interior, Sándor Zöld, also a 'home Communist', was criticised for his work by the Politburo. He drove home and shot his wife, his mother, his two young children and himself. He knew what degradation and torture awaited him.

The 'Muscovites' and the 'young cadres' newly installed by them, together with a few surviving fellow-travellers, got rid of potentially dangerous rivals, and could thus politically embark on the suicidal course adopted by the second Party Congress in February 1951 to turn Hungary into a modern 'country of iron and steel' within four years. All of us – old and young, functionaries, journalists, managers, artists and scientists, luminaries and lesser figures, not only the claques at the parades and the booers at the trials – looked for a compromise with this devilish system in order to survive, without protesting but not without fear.

Sometime in 1951 I must have begun to arouse suspicion. My girl-friend was a trade union secretary in a popular science publishing house. She was studying at an evening course and worked full time as an editor. In recognition of her good work as a functionary she, together with other deserving activists, was sent on vacation to the Romanian Black Sea resort of Mamaia. I too wanted to go to Mamaia, particularly since I had never been outside the country and had never seen the sea. And naturally I wanted to spend those ten days with her. This plan had grave consequences and took up the time of many high officials. I asked the MTI director general, Sándor Barcs, for permission to leave. But this man, whose survival was the result of his prudence, asked all relevant departments in our offices, in the Party's central office and the Ministry of Education for a decision. Ultimately my request to visit a Socialist fraternal country was reject-ed without explanation. After asking Barcs for a reason he told me that Vice Minister Ferenc Janosi considered the matter 'suspicious'. My repeated telephone inquiries had called attention to me. 'Didn't you tell them that I simply wanted to be with my girlfriend?' I asked him. 'I didn't explain it to them in detail,' Barcs admitted.

This aborted trip at a time of general isolation was undoubtedly one of the reasons that 'they' – the cadre office of the MTI and most likely the Party department in charge of us – decided that I needed to be disciplined. It is quite possible that I had already then become a suspicious 'target person' for the snoopers of the secret police.

How can anyone today visualise the kind of closed society in which we young people were then living? As a high-school student I dreamed that one day I would bicycle through Austria and the neighbouring countries. My father's stories about the time of the 'great peace' before

World War I, when without a passport or ID one could go to Vienna for a weekend to see a play, had made a deep impression on me at least subconsciously despite my political blind-spots. I did not consider the politically innocent request to visit the Romanian seaside a risky initiative. However, back then anything that went beyond the routine of Communist daily life aroused suspicion.

Whatever the reasons both Party officials and guardians of dogma henceforth considered me a 'suspicious figure'. And my friendships were not exactly a signpost for faithful adherence to the party line. The foreign editor of Radio Budapest was considered 'too Western' in demeanor and dress, and because of this he had earlier had to leave the official Party paper where he had been my immediate superior. At the time I didn't know that he was even suspected of being a British spy. My colleague at the MTI news agency was suspected of spying for France. Moreover, I was taking French lessons from his attractive wife who was also the step-daughter of the former cultural attaché of the French Embassy, François Gachot, the very man who according to Justus's testimony had maintained espionage contacts with him. And if that had not been sufficient reason for making me suspect the apartment that I visited regularly was in the building in which the Turkish Embassy was housed on elegant Benczur Street. In addition I was sharply criticized for my open intercession on behalf of a colleague whose parents were scheduled to be deported from the capital.

Moreover, as a former Social Democratic youth functionary it was natural that I be considered 'genetically' disposed toward political opposition; I could count on being arrested sooner or later. But if memory serves me rightly I behaved completely openly, even self-confidently, and probably also extremely conceitedly. It would be wrong to assume that the political oppression and terrorist methods of the secret police moulded all aspects of our lives. Certainly not. Many historians and writers have pointed out that the theatres and concert halls were filled and that the outstanding feats of the 'golden soccer team' with Puskás, Bozsik and Hidegkuti imbued Hungarian society with incredible national pride. The great successes at the 1948 Olympics in London were topped in 1952 in Helsinki where Hungary won 16 gold medals.

Our lives were based on the simple fact that we were unapologetically young. Thus I reacted with pity or indifference to the pessimism of my father, who for professional reasons had formed a lawyers' collective in our house (which incidentally still exists after the passage of 45 years). Nonetheless from time to time dark clouds managed to affect my self-conscious and self-righteous attitude.

In the autumn of 1951 an unexpected blow like a bolt from the blue struck home: I was not routinely excused from military service as I had been in the past. I had to serve for two years. The head of personnel and, as I recall, the Party secretary told me: 'The Party (on occasions like that it was invoked like a supernatural power) believes that military service would be useful for your future'. Any objection on my part would not only have been senseless but also suspicious. I just had to accept it.

Some weeks later, on the 2 November 1951, I had to appear before the local military review commission. For my family that vast building next door to our house was a place rich with tradition. It was the same barracks where my father reported to cadet corps in World War I. After the doctor found me fit for service, the chairman of the commission asked me whether I had a preference for any particular branch of the service. 'Yes,' I answered firmly, 'the Danube fleet'. I had already conferred with a friend and he thought that being a sun worshiper I would feel more comfortable on those small Danube vessels. Moreover, the Danube was bound to be more interesting than a barracks. My answer aroused general amusement. The chairman then announced the unanimous decision of the commission. As a journalist and long-standing Party member and activist, I would be assigned to an elite unit, the so-called 'internal militia'. As in every Communist country these units, together with the border police, were armed formations under the control of the Ministry of the Interior.

7

My Friend
the Informer

After a few days I was shipped off to Szombathely, a town near the Austrian border. The difference between the militia and the army lay in stricter Party control and far tougher three-month basic training. Military service was then two years. On the train I met a colleague from radio, a certain V.P. He was younger than I, friendly, interested and polite. We were to serve in the same unit and I was glad to find an intelligent journalist among the young recruits, mostly workers and farmers.

In addition to the exhausting field exercises, as a Party member I had to prepare and conduct the usual seminars. By nightfall I was ready to collapse. I was never able to make my bed properly nor store my belongings, including food my mother sent me, in an orderly fashion. But to my surprise I was one of the good marksmen.

After finishing basic training our unit was moved to the attractive old bishopric of Veszprem below a castle near the picturesque Bakony woods. A munitions depot was located there and our militia unit was assigned to guard duty at the facility. Occasionally a branch of our company would be sent there. We had 24-hour tours of duty: four hours of guard duty, four hours of rest, followed by four hours in the woods, and so forth, followed by two days of rest which we spent reading and doing light exercises.

What made the assignment so difficult for the man on guard duty was the silence in the darkness of night. Even though I was armed I would break out into sweat if I heard a rustling in the leaves. Was it an animal, a control officer or 'the enemy?' We had been instructed to be especially alert in the early days of March lest the enemy decided to launch an attack on the Party and the Socialist fatherland during the preparations for the sixtieth birthday celebration of the beloved leader of the Party and the people, the best Hungarian acolyte of the great Stalin, Mátyás Rákosi.

Occasionally one of the guards would lose his nerve and fire blindly into the darkness. That never happened to me but never again in my life did I feel as afraid as I did during my night shifts in Bakony.

At the time we were almost unaware of the beauty of the still unspoiled landscape. Guard duty, regular drills, the close quarters in the barracks and the extra time I spent on the basically senseless yet unavoidable work as propagandist in the Party committee of the unit transported me into a closed world. Everything else seemed far away. Even the continuous birthday festivities in honour of Rákosi seemed unreal. Universities and the biggest steel mill, under the directorship of Rákosi's brother who called himself Biro, were named after the bald-headed dictator, and an enormous exhibition depicting his life was organised. At a gala opera performance the great man, sitting under a gigantic picture of himself, flanked on one side by an equally huge portrait of Stalin and on the other one of Lenin, modestly acknowledged the homage being paid him.

This was the high point of the 15,000 gatherings held throughout the country attended by 500,000 non-affiliated workers. In addition the agitprop section of the Party reported that half a million members had participated in evening courses devoted to the life of Rákosi. Needless to say, the curriculum vitae of this son of a merchant (whose name prior to 1904 was Rosenfeld and who had been engaged in shipping train loads of fruit to Vienna) had been trimmed to fit a true son of the proletariat.

During the frenetic preparations for the day of great celebration an annoying blemish threatening to mar Rákosi's personality cult popped up. There was no photo of Stalin with his most loyal Hungarian follower in fraternal embrace. But eventually a true artist of photo-montage was found. And as if by magic a new picture of the signing of the Soviet-Hungarian friendship pact of 13 February 1948 suddenly materialised. Now we can see Stalin and Rákosi appeared together, engaged in intimate conversation.

These months are almost like blank pages in my memory except that they hang in the shadow of my experiences with V.P., the fellow-journalist who was conscripted at the same time as I.

During the fifties the build-up of the so-called Hungarian People's Army was in full swing. Against the background of the Stalin-inspired psychotic fear of a Third World War the leadership spared no expense to turn Hungary into a 'reliable bastion' of the Socialist camp. Between 1950 and 1954 the number of soldiers and members of paramilitary units rose from 100,000 to 160,000: in other words more than 1.5 percent of the population was under arms. With 60,000 men and women already in prison or internment camps or forcibly resettled, the economic as well as political consequences of this plunge into slavish devotion to the Soviet world view were enormous.

Because everything had to be modelled on Soviet practice, the institution of a political commissar, 'Politruk', was introduced to the military. Thus a political officer was put alongside every company or unit commander and the political education of the recruits became paramount, with special emphasis on the elite units of the militia and border police. We recruits of the internal militia wore blue caps; the soldiers of the border police green ones. Of course the political and above all secret police control of members of the militia was stricter than that of ordinary soldiers. These outfits probably also had more NCOs than other units. The rest of the militia soldiers were ordinary recruits, even if carefully screened politically, who had to serve their normal term. As in the armies in the rest of the world only those soldiers who had completed a course for NCOs or who had been promoted to political officers after ideological training at a military or Party academy were eligible for a military career.

I was delighted to be serving with V.P. during my guard duties at the munitions depot. The two of us after all were able to talk about books and the world. One day a friendly sergeant by the name of Monori said he wanted to tell me something in confidence. During a walk in the woods he stopped, stroked his moustache and eventually came out with it. He wanted to warn me against V.P., my best friend. V.P. had informed him as his military superior that he had been assigned to watch me and to report everything he learned about me to counter-intelligence. V.P. had asked the sergeant to take note of this and keep him informed of anything that appeared to be relevant. Sgt Monori ended our brief talk muttering that he didn't like informers, particularly those who pretended to be good friends. I was not to share this information with anyone. He merely wanted to warn me.

I was thunderstruck and shaken. I will never understand what I did after that. I did in fact not share this sensitive bit of information with anybody else – except with the protagonist himself, that is with V.P. I have since asked myself time and again how I could have been so stupid. I cannot reconstruct today what went through my mind at the time. At any rate I told V.P. about the 'nonsense' Monori had spouted. V.P. did not lose his composure for even a fraction of a second. He said I was right, that Monori was a fool who had somehow miscon-strued a joking remark. With that the matter was finished as far as I was concerned. We continued serving in the same unit.

During my interrogations later, the secret police officer casually mentioned that they 'had taken care of that Monori'. I never found out what had happened to him and have never forgiven myself. V.P., on the other hand, had no problems. On the contrary, he quickly advanced as editor with the rank of political officer at the militia and border police's weekly paper. I don't know what rank he finally attained, but he did manage to get himself transferred to the Party paper, and as an indisputable indication of his reliability during the worst times, he became the paper's Moscow and later Washington correspondent.

This unsavoury story is still not over. After my release at the end of 1953 I agreed to meet with V.P. when he called me up. I was very care-ful, did not level any recriminaitons – he would have denied the betrayal anyway – but merely told him that I would fight for my rehabilitation.

Seven years later, now having settled in Austria, came a second blow. In December 1960 the official Party paper, *Nepszabadsag*, carried a long article about Hungarian refugees in Austria, their machinations as speculators and thieves and hate-mongering propa-gandists against the Hungarian People's Republic.

The author, one István Mohacsi, attacked my friend Stephan Vajda and me by name in the vilest manner. It was alleged that Vajda, even though a Jew, was a regular contributor to pro-Nazi, anti-semitic émigré papers in Munich and that I had supported myself for months as a gigolo living off old women, and then as a used-car salesman. Only after that did I become a journalist and so-called Eastern Europe expert in Vienna. Not only did the paper give the two pseudonyms under which I wrote but also my private address. I had never heard of this István Mohacsi and was baffled by the virulence of his piece. But in Budapest journalistic circles it soon became known, and we in Vienna found out within days, that this Mohacsi was in fact none other than my old friend V.P.

V.P. never said why, without provocation or pressure, he had tried to harm me for the second time in ten years. But harm me he certainly did. My father, still living in Budapest, became highly agitated about this first attack on me by name since my defection, and suffered a fatal heart attack.

Meanwhile V.P.'s career prospered with the times. After the collapse of the Communist system V.P. once again managed to arrange things for himself. He became news editor for his paper, which acquired links to a German media giant, and frequently even appeared as an interviewer of top politicians.

To get back to the year 1952, in which the Monori/V.P. case was not yet over. As an excellent marksman I was given a brief special leave which I used to marry my old girlfriend. While still on the train – I don't know why – a young blonde woman caught my eye. When I said good-bye to my parents in front of their building I again saw a woman across the street who looked like the one I'd seen on the train. I walked towards the centre of the city, crossed the courtyard of the university, and at a distance again caught sight of the woman. So I turned around, walked toward her and asked her to identify herself. 'What on earth are you doing? Why are you following me?' I asked. The woman was startled, mumbled something, and disappeared.

What I didn't know then and discovered only 40 years later in the files about me, was that the matter of the 'Lendvai case', 'the right-wing Social Democrat and Trotskyite' – how the case was described – was already in full swing in 1952. A secret policeman had interrogated Pál Justus on 21 June, while he was serving the fourth year of his life sentence. That same day some inmates of the Recsk internment camp were brought to Budapest, where they gave their interrogator whatever proof was needed about the Trotskyite plots I had been hatching on the orders of Justus. At the time in question I had reached the mature age of seventeen. Even in retrospect I cannot blame any of these people. They had already spent years behind bars for doing the interrogator's bidding, having levelled similarly absurd accusations against themselves. However, while it was possible to muster some sympathy for hapless informers, the denouncers were altogether different. There was an enormous difference between informers and denouncers.

Let me digress a little to explain the concept 'Trotskyite' to today's readers. All historians agree that it was Leon Trotsky, and certainly not Stalin, who played a decisive role in the preparation and execution of the 1917 October Revolution. As the first People's Commissar for

Foreign Affairs he headed the Russian delegation at the Brest-Litovsk conference. As People's Commissar of Defence he founded and organised the Red Army in 1918. Lenin regarded Trotsky as the most gifted man among the leaders. But he was not a good politician. By 1925 he had already lost his power struggle with Stalin; in 1929 he was expelled from the Soviet Union and was designated the chief enemy of Communism.

During the big Moscow show trials in the thirties, Trotsky was called the 'driving force and chief organiser of this gang of murderers and spies', 'the most despicable lackey and agent of the German and Japanese fascists'. This scum, it was charged, had already since the first days of the October Revolution been part of a conspiracy against Lenin, the Party and the Soviet state in the service of bourgeois espionage services. After Stalin the vitriol was moderated, but the label 'Trotskyite' was still applied to opposition tendencies in the international Communist movement. But from 1948 to 1953 this was one of the most serious accusation that could be levelled against individuals and groups.

As for me, I was still free and, as my confrontation with the blonde secret policewoman showed, not particularly afraid that anything dreadful would happen to me. After all, I had not done anything.

In retrospect I am astonished at my relaxed, self-confident attitude. I do not even remember whether I had told my wife or our marriage witnesses, two well-known journalists, about V.P.'s spying or the episode with the blonde agent. Be that as it may, in the autumn of 1952 I was transferred from Veszprem to Budapest – together with V.P., my shadow. By that time numerous witness depositions against me were already on file, of which I of course knew nothing. The transfer was probably the prelude to my arrest. My assignment at the barracks and office complex of the militia in a Budapest suburb was to edit the brochures and manuscripts in the agitprop section of the political education department. V.P. was of course in the same room or next door. What was most important as far as I was concerned was that I was allowed to sleep at home and to write foreign policy commentaries for the papers and radio.

In late autumn and winter Stalin's persecution mania reached new heights. The notorious Slansky trial in Prague was one omen of the looming danger, above all for functionaries of Jewish descent. Of the 14 accused, headed by the CP General Secretary Rudolf Slansky, 11, as was trumpeted over and over again, were 'Zionists, cosmopolites, Jewish bourgeois nationalists'. All, including the non-Jewish Foreign Minister Vladimir Clementis, were accused of being 'Trotskyites,

Titoist-bourgeois nationalist traitors and enemies of the Czechoslovak people', and organisers of an espionage centre for Tito's Yugoslavia, Israel and imperialism. Slansky, Clementis and four other leading politicians were executed on 3 December. Even though the Prague CP leadership included relatively few Jews, the trial was held amidst an atmosphere of wide anti-semitic abuse. We now know that the purges that had begun a year earlier ware launched at the express order of Stalin and under the direct instruction of 26 Soviet 'experts' culminated in a bloodbath of executions. Subsequently seven more trials with 60 defendants were staged in Czechoslovakia.

Five weeks after the executions in Prague, on 13 January 1953, a brief communique in *Pravda* informed the world about the newly-discovered plot of the 'murderers in white aprons'. Nine renowned Soviet scientists, six of them Jews, were accused of having poisoned or of having murdered through wrong treatment top Soviet leaders, and of being involved in the planning of new crimes. The instigators? The British and American espionage agencies and the American Joint Distribution Committee. The latter had already been cited in the Slansky trial, together with the governments of the United States, Israel, Yugoslavia, and France, as the organisers of the plot. President Klement Gottwald allegedly was to have been liquidated with the help of a physician 'known to be a Freemason'.

All this sounded the alarm in the minds of the three Jewish members of the all-powerful Hungarian troika – Rákosi, Gerö and Farkas. If a man like Slansky, who had spent the war years in the Soviet Union and was considered a Muscovite, could fall victim to the anti-semitic persecution mania of Stalin, then *all* CP leaders of Jewish descent were in jeopardy.

To prove his reliability and indispensability to Moscow, Rákosi lost no time and ordered the arrest of prominent Jewish Communists, men like István Szirmai, a member of the Central Committee and head of the Broadcasting Corporation, as well as a number of prominent Jewish medical doctors.

Today we know from secret letters and protocols, once hidden in Kádár's locked steel cabinets and in inaccessible Party archives, of the hatred and zeal with which old accounts between the torturers fighting for their own survival were being settled. The months-long campaign vigilance and the upheavals within the secret police resulted in an even greater tightening of the screws of repression.

It was against this background that I, to my utter surprise, was caught in the web. Despite my Jewish descent, the issue of Zionism or the alleged plot from abroad never came up in my interrogations. I had never had any contact with Zionist groups. In my case it was the 'Trotskyite' aspect, that is my Social Democratic past, which was paramount. To this day I still do not know what triggered my arrest. Was it yet another informer's report? Additional serious charges by V.P.? Or was it the internal dynamics of the police bureaucracy which simply wanted to close the open Lendvai files?

What is certain is that I, like so many others, was caught up in a net of terror being spread by a paranoid unpredictable tyrant in Moscow and the machinations of his Hungarian acolytes now scuttling about, desperately worried about their own survival. What is equally obvious, however, is that the death of the dictator and the subsequent structural upheavals in the Hungarian apparatus saved me from an even worse fate. Despite the devil-may-care attitude and inexperience of my youth, in the final analysis I was humiliated and psychologically damaged by the dictatorship I had served. The Serbian-Jewish writer, Danilo Kiš is after all right when he says that it is better to belong to the persecuted than the persecutors.

On the whole I am thought to be temperamental, irritable and quick to anger. Therefore I was astonished and amused to read in my secret police dossier, which I was sent in early summer of 1995, that in his report on me at the time of my arrest, Lieutenant J.F. described me as being 'phlegmatic'.

Still, the description of my reaction to arrest seems to have been accurate. Just as I had seen the sudden appearance of the five secret policeman as through a fog, my response in the apartment followed by my transfer to the interrogation centre must have signaled indifference rather than protest, and certainly not rebelliousness. Why? Simply because – as mentioned earlier – I was suffering from a dreadful cold, was running a fever, and had medicated myself with a great deal of rum. In short, I was groggy. That is why I didn't feel the shock of my arrest. It was not until the next day when I woke up in the cell that I felt it.

The events were Kafkaesque in a profound sense. On the one hand I had been arrested without being told the reason; nor of course could I contact a lawyer. Until my release I would be a non-person, would not exist as far as the outside world was concerned. On the other hand, the police with painful punctiliousness, listing everything I had with me, all of which I had to hand over: socks, three handkerchiefs, a belt, a wallet, a shirt, underwear, a hat, a comb, a scarf, a tie, a sweater, my journalist's ID, No 893, and my Party membership card,

No 326,539. I had to sign this list. As I learned later everything that was confiscated in our and my parents' apartment was also punctiliously documented.

Once the formalities of my booking were over I was given a coarse prison shirt, and my shoes were returned to me without, of course, laces. I was not fingerprinted right then, nor were pictures of me taken. Then two guards took me to a cell, unlocked the iron door with a bunch of big keys, and with a little push shoved me into the cell in which a weak light kept burning day and night. The three unshaven men sitting on narrow wooden bunks in the cell measuring seven square metres frightened me. With their hollow cheeks and long, stringy hair they looked like criminals.

During my detention I got to know a unique cross-section of Hungarian society. But apart from war criminals and their accomplices I never met a single anti-state plotter, saboteur or spy in the pay of a Western country among all the Social Democrats, conservatives or liberals, not to mention casual detainees, among my fellow-prisoners.

The first cautious conversations with my cell-mates reassured me relatively quickly. Tall Gyuri F., who had been in prison the longest, had been an officer under Horthy, and after the war a colonel in the new Communist-controlled army. The short, stocky Pista S. was a Jew who had spent the war in a labour batallion on the Eastern Front wearing the yellow arm band and after 1945 joined the military intelligence service, where he rose to the rank of lieutenant colonel. The third cell-mate was a young army officer. Later still another prisoner joined us in our cell. His name was Feri and like me was an ordinary soldier.

Newcomers were welcome in prison if for no other reason that they brought news from the outside. And there was actually another, even more important, reason. The newcomer was relatively well nourished so that after tasting the disgusting prison fare he would give it to a fellow-inmates who, with an embarrassed smile, cleaned out the bowl in no time.

And there I sat, waiting. While the others were taken away for interrogation I kept on reliving the last four or five years in my mind, yet found nothing that would explain my arrest. Naturally I also thought of my contacts with Justus, who had been arrested more than three years ago, but to me that was all in the past. After all we had broken with him five years earlier. And as recently as a week ago I was still reading foreign policy commentaries over the air without anyone voicing objections. My life record seemed politically clean. I kept on thinking that I would be able to clear up any possible misunderstanding without much difficulty or that this might be my last day in detention.

After five days I was finally brought in for interrogation at 10pm. The young lieutenant in charge of my 'case' asked me whether I had thought about why I had been arrested. After listening to my protestation of innocence and my saying that perhaps a mistake had been made he broke out into hearty, intimidating laughter. There in the files in front of him lay the incriminating testimonies. 'We know everything about you and your activities against the Party and the People's Republic. Don't play any games with me. Here, have a cigarette and write down a truthful account of your life and a confession'. I was taken to a room with a comfortable chair and a desk. After days and nights in the tiny cell, where of course we got on each others' nerves, spending a few hours in an ordinary room with an adjoining toilet was a relief.

I handed my account – I do not remember how many pages – to the guard and I was brought back to the cell. That is when the exhausting wait really began, a favourite tactic of the secret police, which tortured the prisoners not only with beatings and physical mistreatment. Once a detainee had gone about as far as his interrogator could take him, another official would appear, either friendly or a brute. Some of my fellow-inmates had already gone through this routine. During this period none of us was physically tortured. Only once did we hear cries interspersed by loud sobs from another cell. One of the crudest practices was to make us stand for hours; another was not giving us anything to drink. At any rate the four of us were never hit in the cell; nor was I beaten in the internment camp. But the psychological pressures coupled with the total isolation from family and the outside certainly made up for the lack of physical beatings.

The fact that I was a mere twenty-three years of age and in good health undoubtedly helped. I once witnessed the extreme suffering of a sixty-year-old fellow-prisoner with poor bladder control. We were taken to the toilet twice a day. That excursion was torture in itself. Someone who has never been locked in a tiny toilet with four others, having to wait for the others to finish, cannot possibly imagine what an older prisoner with bladder disease goes through under such conditions. Our older cell-mate had worked in the code department of the army and had been arrested together with ten of his colleagues. 'An entire soccer team,' we joked. An informer claimed that they had planned to organise an 'opposition government'. Their crime, in fact, was that they were having drinks in a bar and joked about their hidden talents, inventing all sorts of ministerial posts for themselves. This tomfoolery was turned into a plot to overthrow the government. During my time in prison I never heard anything more absurd. Anyway, our comrade had an accident. He had to empty his bladder in the cell between the two official toilet visits because the guard responded too late to his call. He was sent for that same day and I never saw him again.

Our usual day in prison was strictly organised. We were awakened at five and taken to the toilet. After that we got what passed for breakfast, a thin, dry piece of bread and tepid bowl of *ersatz* coffee. Then came the seemingly endless wait for the much-anticipated midday meal, which was truly awful: disgusting-looking and even-worse-tasting turnips, beans or lentils, sometimes sometimes embellished with a little tasteless lump of leather which passed for meat. I often shared my ration with the always hungry Feri or Col. Gyuri.

The most unpleasant experience apart from the trip to the lavatory was the 'barber'. Once a week all the inmates on our floor were shaved by a prison guard. But since he apparently had only a single used razor blade for all of us it was torture. We were not given any work, nor did we receive permission to take a walk outside the cell. We had no books, no cigarettes, no contact with other prisoners. We were completely cut off from the outside world. No letters, no parcels, no visitors. Even though he was a lawyer and military defence counsel, my father first found out that I was alive and in prison when Feri asked to have my father assigned to him as his defence lawyer.

Our fate as prisoners always hung in the balance, and after every interrogation our mood changed. We prisoners were united by a basic sense of solidarity, regardless of status, rank and background. For me this period was a completely new experience. And in this harshest test of my life to date, my relationship to my cell-mates stiffened my spine against the interrogators and their cat-and-mouse game with me.

The interval between the first and second interrogation lasted a full 17 tension-filled, debilitating days. On 19 February my case officer and his supervisors drew up the so-called interrogation schedule, and the next day I was questioned again, followed by seven more interrogations in February and March. In mid-April 'my' lieutenant submitted a final report, and on 20 May a lieutenant colonel, the chief of the investigative department, arrived at the verdict: internment because of 'Trotskyite activities'. Six days later I had to confirm that decision by signing it. My signature was a mere formality.

But what lay hidden behind these findings? According to the documents from the Hungarian Ministry of the Interior that have since come into my possession I was arrested because of two assumptions that formed the basis of the original 'investigation plan'. The first was a grave suspicion of treason because of my close ties to two journalists, Endre Gömöri, Chief of the Foreign Department of Radio Budapest, and Lajos Korolovszky, Senior Editor of the news agency MTI. My interrogator initially told me that my 'co-conspirators' had already confessed to their crimes. Later he changed his line of attack and said my arrest was merely a preventive measure to forestall the efforts of my colleagues who had already been arrested as spies to recruit me. Their trials were about to get under way, and they were being held in the adjoining cells. Gömöri was said to have spied for Britain, and Korolovszky given his family contacts, for France.

This self-evident nonsense did not succeed in making me confess to espionage. There was nothing they could do to shake me. Of course in the protocols my anti-government jokes or conversations with journalists about mistakes in the press or industrial policies were labeled 'dissemination of anti-democratic ideas'. The only thing an anonymous informant's report could confirm was that I was friendly with the two journalists in question, particularly Gömöri. That was all.

While the really serious charges were quietly dropped, the secret police insisted on my 'documented' Trotskyite activities as by my lectures. And at the ripe old age of seventeen I had been an 'active enemy' of the unification of the Social Democratic and Communist youth movements. So whenever my political activities in the youth movement were mentioned, the label 'Trotskyite' was tagged on. For example, I had told them that prior to the founding of the Ady Circle at the end of 1946 a conference with about 25 to 30 participants was held at the Social Democratic Youth centre. This was recorded as a meeting dealing with the 'Trotskyite education of the youth'. And according to the testimony of a former activist and Justus acolyte I had been sent there to deliver Trotskyite lectures which had pleased Justus and the others.

But why then did I sign these nonsensical documents? Well, the fight over specific expressions, dates and descriptions of persons was part of the established routine of the secret police to undermine the resistance of an accused. Their constant reference to testimony in my files that was so incriminating that I could spend long years in prison did succeed in intimidating me. With the sword of Damocles apparently hanging over me, the 'Trotskyite' charge concerning my time in the youth movement was not nearly as grave. That and a profound fear of harsher methods must explain my signing. At any rate my file was closed on Page 143 on 15 June.

At the end of May three of us were taken out of our small cell and transferred to the notorious Kistarcsa internment camp, about 15 kilometres outside Budapest. It was somewhat of an improvement because there our cell was bigger and we were allowed daily outdoor walks. The disadvantage was that these internments had no fixed time limit.

Kistarcsa had been an infamous camp even back in the Horthy era. Also, the SS and their Hungarian henchmen had used the barracks as a concentration camp for Jews who, without Horthy's knowledge, were shipped to Auschwitz in July 1944. After the war, Arrow Cross members and other compromised right-wingers were held there, followed by alleged speculators and then those political prisoners and their relatives who for various reasons could not be tried in court. It was one of the bizarre aspects of this supposedly Socialist order that because of their years of experience and 'service', imprisoned supporters of Hitler and Szálasi held positions of trust in prisons and camps. Thus, for example, the trustee in charge of one of the women's barrack in Kistarcsa, the one housing Edith, Justus's wife, was the widow of the executed Arrow Cross leader Ferenc Szálasi, a fascist prisoner supervising a socialist inmate in a socialist order.

Now I found myself in Kistarcsa as an accused Trotskyite without ever having read Trotsky. Exactly 25 years later I went to Trotsky's villa in Coyocan, on the outskirts of Mexico City, to look at the room in which an agent of Stalin assassinated the founder of the Red Army on 20 August 1940, and to see his final resting place. I felt no more of a Trotskyite then than I had done 25 years earlier in Kistarcsa.

In the camp I met many people: the janitor who had denounced and been denounced and who, even though toothless, gobbled up his food within seconds and then looked so pleadingly at those who had not finished theirs; the chess grand master who had defected during a tournament in West Berlin and in a moment of weakness let himself be talked into returning; the Arrow Cross's chief ideologue; the historian Odon Malnasi, whom the Social Democratic Minister of Justice had greeted during a camp inspection in 1949 before the minister himself was arrested a year later and tortured to death; the driver of the British Embassy who distributed the programmes of the Embassy's weekly movie evenings at various institutions; Count Festetics, the former Fascist deputy whose distant relatives had become prominent in Austria; the Jewish doctor who during the recently launched 'anti-Zionist' campaign was freed and then rearrested; the boxer and former secret police officer who was now suspected of stealing bread from his fellow-inmates; and many more.

Life in the prisons and camps was a world unto itself. Both the secret police personnel and the prisoners had their own class system. Maria Strasser, the widow of the Austrian Socialist Deputy Peter Strasser, who spent almost six years in Hungarian detention, in 1956 drew up a 'hierarchic table' of the conditions of internment during the Stalin era:

1 Cell without plank and blanket
2 Cell with plank and blanket
3 Basement cell with plank and blanket
4 Prison room on ground floor with mattress, table, and chairs
5 Office with bed linen, stove, and furniture (there I wrote my biography)
6 Room furnished for the prisoner, opportunity to work, car and escort as needed (in the case of renowned experts and scientists)
7 Apartment in a hospital with bathroom and sanatorium care (for ex-President Árpád Szakasits), or with personnel and electric stove (for Cardinal József Mindszenty)
8 Housing in a well-equipped villa but completely isolated from the outside world (for ex-President Zoltán Tildy, and up to 1951 for Györgyi Tarisznyas, the crown witness in the Rajk trial. For a year after the public trial she was forced to attend the opera and go to restaurants accompanied by secret police agents as proof that she had *not* been arrested).

My conditions ranged in the lower-middle categories of this list, between the intolerable and the better-than-average. During my relatively brief detention, a period of about eight months, I saw many changes in the conditions of confinement because of the political turbulence on the 'outside'. And what happened to my family during this period? The searches of the two apartments yielded considerable spoils. However, the zeal of the secret police created unexpected complications. According to the inventory of the AVH they confiscated 129 foreign-language books, 120 foreign-language periodicals, 110 notebooks, 80 photographs and three files containing foreign and one containing domestic materials at my house, and at my parents' house dozens of books and periodicals, Hungarian Social Democratic publications, as well as notebooks, jottings and photos. My father insisted on a handwritten addendum to the list of confiscated materials that the map they had taken was part of his personal collection from the

First World War. He apparently was concerned that they would claim that the Russian map of 1912 or 1914 was part of my master plan to attack the Soviet Union...

During my interrogation they were very sceptical when they came across suspicious names and notations in my address books. 'What does "Wild Rose" mean? Or "Snow White" and all those other things? They're obviously codes for your secret contacts.' They were the names of child-care centres we had looked at for my wife's little daughter from her first marriage. That I had saved autographed pictures of a couple of movie stars was, in the eyes of the interrogating officers, an indication of my 'lack of ideological steadfastness'.

But the most serious complications arose out of some of the books and files. On 3 May and again on 8 May my wife, and on 13 May her boss, the head of the publishing house, insistently demanded that the head of the AVH return seven books on that list without delay; they had been borrowed from the parliament's library. Should they not be returned the publishing house would not be given any more books from the library. In addition, the Party publishing house Szikra also asked for a manuscript about the 'struggle of the Arabic peoples' which had been sent to me for my opinion.

On 22 May came a breakthrough: the secret police returned the borrowed books and the manuscript about the Arabic peoples to my wife. But nothing happened in my case. On the contrary, I was interned.

While my position and those of the thousands of others incarcerated seemed static and stagnant with nothing seeming to happen, in fact a great deal was going on, not in Budapest but in Moscow. The result was that I and thousands of others faced the prospect of conditional freedom much sooner than expected.

While we were still waiting in our holding cell for our transport to the camp at Kistarcsa the dictatorship was celebrating the overwhelming victory of the unity list in the so-called parliamentary elections. With 98 percent of the eligible voters exercising their right, 98.2 percent cast their ballots for the unity list. Rákosi, who had been Party leader and Prime Minister since 1952, seemed at the peak of his power. However, after Stalin's death in 1953 the leadership in Moscow began to shift course. Thus the anti-semitic witch-hunt ceased; the doctors were rehabilitated, and top officials of the Soviet Ministry of the Interior were arrested or fired. And most important of all, prisoners were amnestied. The situation in the satellite states was re-examined, and Hungary was deemed to be the potentially most dangerous crisis spot. The Moscow leadership decided unanimously that Rákosi was to hand over the Premiership to Imre Nagy, the then 57-year-old Deputy Prime Minister and member of the Politburo. In mid-June a Hungarian Party and Government delegation was forced to go to Moscow, where Stalin's heirs in two stormy sessions attacked their hitherto trusted Hungarian vassal with unprecedented severity and biting irony and sharply criticised the country's political and economic policies. The fact that on 17 June 1953, only a day after the order to Rákosi had been issued, unrest broke out in Berlin, was an additional factor for the Kremlin's decision to engineer a political change of course in Hungary, before things got out of hand.

The agrarian expert Imre Nagy, who had been demoted in 1949 because of his opposition to the unbridled collectivisation of agriculture and who had spent 15 years in emigration in the Soviet Union, now relied on the support of his Soviet protectors, and was ready to embark on a 'new course'.

At a closed session of the Central Committee of the Party Imre Nagy, on 27 June 1953, as the designated Premier, delivered a sensational speech. Nagy held Rákosi as well as the other three members of the 'quartet' (Farkas for the violation of laws, Gerö for the adventurous economic policy and Révai for the conditions in the educational and cultural sphere) responsible for the existing situation. He spoke of 'intolerable conditions characteristic of a police state'. Rákosi in his address before the utterly dumbfounded Central Committee indulged in political and personal self-criticism. But he could not stop the resolution which was accepted – a devastating indictment of the Rákosi clique – declaring: 'It was wrong for Comrade Rákosi to have issued direct instructions to the AVH as to how they were to conduct investigations, and it was wrong that he ordered physical mistreatment of prisoners, which is forbidden by law'. But despite Imre Nagy's good intentions and despite the changes in the top leadership, control of the Party apparatus remained in the hands of Rákosi and his people. The fact that another notorious Muscovite, Gerö, was made Minister of the Interior was not exactly designed to strengthen confidence in 'socialist legality'.

Still, the speech Imre Nagy delivered as the new head of government before the parliament on 4 July 1953, was a bombshell. The promise to end arbitrary police action, to close the internment camps, to proclaim amnesty, and to appoint a supreme public prosecutor for the protection of 'Socialist legality' enabled tens of thousands, including myself, to return to a near-normal life. Economic and agricultural policy measures also brought relief. But the decisive measure with far-reaching effects was the shift to a position *against* oppression. As early as 25 July, prisoners sentenced to less than two years for political offenses were pardoned; the next day it was announced that internment camps were to be closed and that deportations would cease.

In Kistarcsa rumours about a 'new course', although still vague and contradictory, began to circulate. Without explanation inmates were shifted around to different barracks, and the obviously changed attitude of at least of some guards gave added stimulus to our speculations about the future.

Like so many other completely innocent men and women, I had learned to accept my fate. I had counted on having to spend years and years in the camp and hoped that after my release I would be able to make a living as a translator. The first ray of hope came on 8 July at a new interrogation about my past. The officer in charge was friendly, and the interrogation protocol concluded that back then, in 1947, I had not understood the destructive nature of my actions and had not been aware of my 'harmful, incorrect views'. There no longer was any mention of 'anti-democratic' conversations among a small circle and of contacts with colleagues suspected of espionage. Despite this new, friendlier interrogation I remained in custody, still without any contacts with the outside world. In August the first internees I was acquainted with were released, and I could send messages through two or three of them to my wife and parents. But another seven weeks were to pass after my last interrogation before I was summoned to the office of the camp commander and handed my release papers dated 1 September. Before I could leave the yellow hut at the camp gate I had to sign a 'pledge' acknowledging that everything that had to do with the camp and the persons detained there was a 'state secret'. And any violation of this state secret was subject to a penalty of ten years imprisonment.

Never before had I signed as many documents as during my eight-month odyssey of pretrial detention and internment in Kistarcsa. Every single page of the investigative protocols had to be signed.

At my release from the camp I was given the personal effects that had been taken from me at my arrest as well as a big suitcase filled with books and papers the secret police had taken from the apartment. And then I stood in front of the camp with two or three other former inmates. I turned around to take a last look at the iron gate. The local train to Budapest stopped only a few hundred yards away. But as I began to walk toward the station the handle of the suitcase broke and the huge bag crashed to the ground. Angry and desperate I was ready to cry. What was I to do, standing here in front of the hated camp? At that moment my two friends turned around and helped me lug my father's huge worn suitcase to the train. The passengers looked at us without saying a word. They knew that we were released internees, and we knew that they knew. We arrived in Budapest on a brilliant, sunny day, and I shared a taxi with an older comrade to my home in the inner city. My friend and the driver helped me carry the suitcase up the stairs to the first floor. We wished each other good luck for the future, and with my heart in my throat I rang the doorbell.

The door was opened by my ailing, weary mother-in-law. Looking slightly embarrassed she told me that my wife was on vacation at Lake Balaton, but eagerly awaiting my return, had left a telephone number at which she could be reached. Jotted down on the slip with the number were these words: 'Don't speak to E.G. under any circumstances; he is a bastard'. Confused and tired but happy to be free, I called her up. I managed to convince her that in my condition I couldn't possibly join her. 'Well, all right, I'll take the next train back,' she said cheerfully. I learned from her that my best friend, who had been charged with spying for Britain and who I thought was in the cell next to mine had never been arrested, nor had the two or three who I thought had fallen foul of the regime. Strange. My best friend was free and not sentenced to a long prison term as my interrogating officer had claimed?

Deep in thought I took the streetcar to my parents' house.

8

The Lost Years of a Non-person

M y father was the first one to tell me about Imre Nagy's solemn announcement of the 'New Course' and his promise to restore so-called Socialist legality and put an end to police arbitrariness. Piles of newspapers my parents had saved were awaiting me. I was stunned by the frank tone and the promise of a new beginning. This was something worth fighting for.

I was 24 and yet again believed that I was standing on the threshold of a new life. But I soon found out that we, 5,057 internees and approximately 16,000 prisoners who had been sentenced to less than two years and hence were amnestied, had merely returned to the gigantic, invisible prison of a Communist system still almost completely unchanged. Within a few days of Imre Nagy's seminal speech, the apparatus embarked on a 'mobilization campaign'. Rákosi, still in office as head of the Party, personally launched a counter-attack before a meeting of Budapest Party activists.

Initially this affected me only slightly. Since I had been arrested and interned while serving my regular military tour of duty I had to report to my last post, the Budapest militia garrison, upon my release. I was promptly given leave, and at the end of my tour of duty I was discharged; discharge papers in hand I went to the MTI news agency where I resumed my work as department head.

Formally everything seemed in order, but from the very first day I felt isolated. I was given a large room but no work. I sat there all alone, and other than read the papers, I did nothing. Sándor Barcs, the General Manager of MTI, that lofty 'non-card-carrying' fellow-traveller was not ready to receive me or even talk to me over the phone. The treatment by my colleagues was not much better. There were the malicious types who who enjoyed seeing the humbling of a young talent they considered too clever for his own good, the opportunists who acknowledged me when no-one else was present but didn't know me when in public, and finally a handful of well-wishers who whispered an occasional word to me over the house phone.

The much-vaunted 'Socialist legality' meant that even though I was free I continued to be looked upon as highly suspect. Exactly four weeks after my re-employment, the minimum legitimate period between my military discharge and my return to my job, I received a brief note from the General Manager and the head of personnel informing me of my dismissal as of 9 December 1953. Nor was I given any work during the remaining two weeks. The reason: 'You are not suited for this job'.

Because of information from the State Prosecutor's office that I had been released from internment because no charges against me were pending, I sued the MTI. Taking advantage of my wife's experience and contacts as former trade union secretary I carried my suit to the highest labour court, but of course without success. Under this regime appearance and reality were two separate matters. A mere telephone call from Party headquarters was all it took to seal my fate. A party official in charge of the radio at the agitprop department simply phoned Director General Barcs to tell him that I was still considered politically unreliable. Barcs passed on this information – again only by phone – to the judge, and that is how my professional life as a journalist was destroyed. For the Hungarian media, and for everybody, I was henceforth a non-person.

In plain language that meant that even though I was free I had no rights, no job, no future. I sent a five-page letter together with a six-page curriculum vitae to the newly-installed attorney general's office. I got no reply.

Back then, in the early fifties, all my efforts for rehabilitation – literally to regain my reputation and my rights – were in vain. I continued to point out both in writing and orally that I had not committed any crime, that my friends suspected of espionage were still occupying their positions of trust, that the charges at the hearings were linked to my political activities at the age of 17 and 18, not to mention that they were irrelevant to the reason for my arrest, something that had been indirectly admitted by the interrogator. In addition I gave the names of 16 persons who could prove that, despite my ideological 'aberrations' and errors as a Justus student I had not been a 'right-wing Social Democrat' nor a 'Trotskyite' (whatever that might mean), but a stalwart leftist and conscientious journalist. Of course, in conformity with the existing yardsticks of political 'credibility' I did not fail to point out that my wife came of a working-class family, had been a member of the Party since 1945, and for a time even Party secretary at her publishing house. However, all my efforts not only proved unavailing but had devastating consequences.

So how was a 'politically unreliable' unemployed journalist in a totalitarian society to make a living? Such a non-person could not work at any newspaper, publishing house or library. During that period of utter despair help came from an entirely unexpected quarter. After I was arrested the head of the publishing house Muvelt Nep, where my wife worked as an editor, asked the 'contact person' with the AVH whether my wife had to be fired. When the answer came back negative, not only did my wife keep her job but her boss even let me do proof-reading and later translations as well, but of course under a pseudonym.

Never before nor since did this overwhelming feeling of not belonging hurt me so much as in these first weeks after I had been sacked by the MTI. Today I am still bitter when I remember running into colleagues on the street who did not want to recognise me, or turned away or, looking disgusted, even crossed the street. The ones who had been amnestied earlier kept silent. As we had promised we did not tell anybody, including close friends, about what we had experienced, heard and seen. Only after the zealots and opportunists at the newspapers had to acknowledge the truth they had not wanted to know, did they deign to greet us again.

Shortly before my twenty-fifth birthday my morale was at an all-time low. Four of us – my wife, my nine-year-old stepdaughter, my mother-in-law, and I – were living in a one-room apartment with borrowed furniture. And it was not even the crowding that troubled me so much as the overall oppressive political and personal climate. Meanwhile friends hinted to me that my wife had become involved with one of her colleagues while I was in camp, or perhaps even earlier while I was on military duty. People who had been arrested were then considered out of circulation for years. The day after my release I profusely thanked her boyfriend for his 'care', something I later came to think of as a miserable act of self-abasement. Despite my wife's tearful protestations, I was not able to stay in the relationship. I returned to my parents' flat.

My 64-year-old father and my mother received me with affectionate warmth and open arms. A street-level office housed the so-called lawyers' co-operative which my father and some colleagues had founded in the early fifties to enable them to continue to work in that era of imposed, all-encompassing collectivism. For freelancers life was precarious, and the earning potential of lawyers more than modest. Before my military service I had still been able to help my parents financially. Now things were reversed. After my years of military service, internment, and unemployment I did not even own decent clothes. Our tailor altered two of my father's suits for me.

While I was occupied trying to rebuild my private life, trench warfare broke out between the new Prime Minister, Imre Nagy, who in a departure from Stalin's model was gradually introducing major reforms within the framework of the Communist system, and the Stalinists around Rákosi, who put a brake on and sabotaged Nagy wherever possible. Although the increasing pressure of the people was a contributing factor, the great crisis of 1956 was in fact unleashed by a general disintegration within the ruling Party. Hungary was the only one of the satellites where a mere four months after Stalin's death – of course at the initiative of a worried Kremlin – Stalinism was openly castigated and a new course proclaimed; only here did two factions fight for more than three years about the future course while control of the apparatus – the approximately 24,000 functionaries, 7,000 of whom were fully paid Party professionals – remained in the hands of the Stalinists until the very end.

Without underestimating the historical importance of the Hungarian Revolution, it would be wrong to ignore either the pioneering role of the optimistic new beginning attempted by Imre Nagy between June 1953 and November 1954, or the crucial turning point in early 1955. The people's revolution became possible only when the Party, above all its leadership cadre, split so decisively on the question of de-Stalinisation that it lost the ability to assert itself.

What some Western observers see as a power struggle between Communists, as a personal rivalry between Nagy and Rákosi, was in fact a conflict between two basically different concepts and methods.

The main points of contention were: the investigation of the secret trials and purges; priorities of economic policy; and the revitalisation of the People's Front as a true expression of popular will rather than as a tool of CP rule.

This conflict was not about abstract ideological debates but rather about the freedom, well-being and future of hundreds of thousands of oppressed, disenfranchised and in part still imprisoned people. Despite my bitterness about my delayed rehabilitation I was very lucky. In 1953 about 400 internees were still brought to trial and sentenced to long prison terms. Thousands of political prisoners remained behind bars up to the summer of 1956, even as late as the October Revolution.

The battle for de-Stalinisation was protracted, not without danger and initially very unequal. In Hungary it was the surviving victims of the trials, the writers, journalists and artists, primarily those Communist or left-wing intellectuals who, feeling betrayed by the Rákosi clique, were undergoing a crisis of conscience. They were the ones who flocked to Imre Nagy, isolated as he was in the leadership, and dictated the tempo of the reform movement. But Rákosi and his accomplices in the Politburo and the secret police, despite tactical concessions, continued to keep a firm grip on the Party apparatus and secret police.

Nonetheless, Nagy and his supporters were able gradually to expand their room for manoeuvre not only for themselves, but also for the disenfranchised collectivised peasants and the workers slaving away to meet the ever-higher production norms. In some respects a new era began for journalists with the opening of an information bureau under the direct control of Zoltán Szanto, an old-time Communist who had been sent out of the country, and his deputy, the dynamic publicist Miklós Vásárhelyi. I and probably other journalists on the internal blacklist felt that the creation of this agency gave us the impetus to continue our fight for rehabilitation and the hope of at least finding someone to turn to outside the impenetrable labyrinth of the Party and police apparatus.

In the days leading up to that Central Committee meeting at which the new course and its spokesmen won a seemingly overwhelming victory, the mood was one of renewal. And that is probably why I felt emboldened to send another letter to the State Prosecutor on 30 September 1954 in which I repeated my request for complete rehabilitation and named 18 persons who could testify to my past and my claims.

This time justice seemed to prevail. The head of the Main Department for Special Affairs, Pál Bakos, asked for my file, V 103,500, and was sent four dossiers. I do not know what Bakos's instructions were, but I was asked to appear for questioning at the notorious investigating office – which was also the state security prison – on December 7.

Even though the minutes of my interrogation covered six pages, only a single incident sticks in my mind. During the interview a man I knew well came in, the same security officer who had interrogated me two years previously and had forced me to sign that distorted document fabricating my links to Trotskyism. He seemingly was only looking for something in the filing cabinet, but I suspect that this scene was staged to intimidate me. Even though my replies this time were recorded correctly, I left the dark building mistrustful and depressed. I did not hear from the prosecutor's office for another 20 months.

Forty years later I was able to take a look at my files. I learned that my case, without my knowledge, had been treated relatively expeditiously and thoroughly. Ten days after my interrogation, Pál Justus, and later seven other persons who during their first testimony between the summer of 1952 and spring of 1953 had levelled at me the serious charge of Trotskyism, being an enemy of unification, or harboring hostile intentions, were now again questioned. At this hearing all of them, including Justus, in their own handwriting or in documents signed by them, stated that even though I had been ambitious or even a careerist I had never harboured 'Trotskyite and other hostile views'.

Even the vindictive Julia Poll, my middle-aged boss who had seduced me, retracted her testimony that 'Lendvai in his work displayed right-wing Social Democratic tendencies and tried to insert imperialist propaganda into his work'. Now she merely spoke of 'character flaws' and 'omissions' in my work, and 'she couldn't say whether that was done with hostile intent'. However, she angrily rejected the implication that she had incriminated me in her previous testimony out of jealousy for being spurned as my girlfriend.

The technique for incrimination by and testimony from former associates in the youth movement became crystal clear from the testimony of a 'witness' called to clarify the record. When G.J. retracted his testimony of 21 July 1952 – namely that Justus had organised Trotskyite seminars and 'Lendvai as student functionary had accordingly delivered those kinds of speeches' – the officer working on the re-examination of my case asked, 'Why did you ever say those things?'

1. *(right)* My father, Dr Andor Lendvai, served in the Austro-Hungarian army during World War I, as a loyal subject of Kaiser Franz Josef. He considered himself more a Magyar than a Jew.

2. *(below left)* My mother, Edith Lendvai, was a religious woman, who, in her later life, never overcame the loss of her family in the Holocaust.

3. *(below right)* As a child, I displayed much of the curiosity, not to say inquisitiveness, which was to stand me in good stead in my later life.

4. *(above)* My great uncle, Dr David Leimdörfer, was above all a Jew rather than a Hungarian. He left old Hungary to become Chief Rabbi of Hamburg, where he died before the Nazis came to power.

5. *(above)* My cousin Zsolt Rajna, born a Christian after his mother's conversion from Judaism, became a Catholic priest.

6. *(below)* Family on my father's side. My cousin Gyuri (extreme left) was killed in Auschwitz

7. *(above)* Family on my mother's side. My grandparents, their two grandchildren (seated on their knee), my uncle (standing left) and his wife (standing centre) were all gassed in Auschwitz.

8. *(below)* My father, unlike his teenage son of the 1940s, was sceptical about politics and politicians.

9. *(right)* Adolf Eichmann has the dubious distinction of achieving the most efficient rate of genocide during the Nazi era. Under his direction, some 437,402 Hungarian Jews were processed for the death camps in a brief three month period (15 May–7 July, 1944). He is seen here in 1943, enjoying the Austrian mountain air.

10. *(below)* Carl Lutz, the Swiss consul in Budapest, provided Swiss documents to thousands of Jews, thus saving them from transportation to death camps. Though less well known than Raoul Wallenberg, Lutz deserves much the same sort of credit.

11. *(left)* Pal Justus, the left-wing Social Democrat, was my mentor and inspiration in my early activist days. He later received a life sentence in the Rajk show-trial as a Trotskyist and a spy.

12. *(left)* Laszlo Rajk was the Communist Foreign Minister of Hungary, who later confessed to being an 'imperialist Titoist spy' at his 1949 show-trial. He was executed but later rehabilitated in 1956.

13. *(above)* Matyas Rakosi, the Hungarian Communist dictator, always strove to curry favour with Stalin and his successors in Moscow. He was removed from power in July 1956 and died in his bed in 1971 during his Soviet exile.

14. *(below)* Ernö Gerö succeeded Rakosi as Communist Party chief but fled to Moscow during the 1956 Uprising. It was he who urged the Soviets to intervene with troops.

15. *(left)* Imre Nagy was a respected though ineffective Prime Minister between 1953 and 1955. But he came into his own during the 1956 uprising as national leader. Shown here during his secret trial, after the Soviet crackdown, he was executed in June 1958 but rehabilitated in the dying days of the Communist regime in 1989.

16. *(left)* Janos Kadar, a victim of Rakosi's Stalinism, was deemed a safe pair of hands by the Soviets in 1956. Reviled for his collaboration with the Soviets and for the execution of Imre Nagy and many other revolutionaries, this wily politician nevertheless ushered in Eastern Europe's most liberal Communist regime.

17. *(right)* Bruno Kreisky, Austrian Chancellor from 1970 to 1983, was a consummate politician and diplomat, whose understanding of the media helped him to propel Austria – or at least the Austrian Chancellor – onto the world stage.

18. *(right)* Kurt Waldheim became President of Austria in 1986, following a respectable career as a diplomat and UN Secretary General. Revelations about his opportunism during the Nazi era also propelled Austria onto the world stage but in a wholly unwanted manner.

The reply was stunning: 'Well, I knew from my own long investigation that an already recorded protocol could not be changed. So when the officer claimed that Justus had been a Trotskyite, I coudn't contradict it. That Lendvai in his statements at the seminar agreed with Justus seemed clear, and so the officer questioning me drew the conclusion that if Justus's speech was Trotskyite and Lendvai had commented on it approvingly, then he too must have been a Trotskyite.' This witness by his own testimony had not seen me since the spring of 1948, when I was 18. Yet four years later the questions he was asked about me were so manipulative that his words very easily made him a hostile witness against me.

The revised testimonies and the detailed record of my interrogation did at least change the situation. On 17 January 1955, a four-man special commission consisting of a state prosecutor, a department head of the investigating commission and two officers who had worked on my case found that my internment had been unwarranted. The four signatories proposed that the rehabilitation committee of the Council of Ministers and the central control committee of the Party take up my case.

But that is not what happened. The chief of the state security service and Deputy Minister of the Interior, Major General István Dekany, who incidentally was married to Rákosi's favorite niece, turned down the report and demanded, in a crude and confused note, that 'additional inquiries' about my two friends (Gömöri and Korolovszky) be made. Furthermore, he requested that Dept IV look into what positions I had taken since my release.

Some weeks later the lieutenant working on my case was able to mollify his suspicious superior. My two friends had been under surveillance by two agents and that operation failed to produce proof of any 'concrete hostile activity'.

Consequently the rehabilitation proposal of the four-man commission was resubmitted to the Deputy Minister on 24 February 1955, and this time he signed it. Everything seemed in order. But four weeks later the head of the investigative department drafted a new, carefully worded 'report', and attached to the first page of this 'highly confidential' paper dated 25 March 1955, was a handwritten note by an apparantly still higher Party official saying, 'We do not concern ourselves with his case'.

That put a sudden end to the four-month-old re-examination and the correspondence between the State Prosecutor and the Interior Ministry. And yet I remained a political outcast for another eighteen months. I had been caught up in the bureaucratic web of dictatorship. I had been someone who had actually not rebelled against the regime but who had became enmeshed in the system by accident.

I did not find out until much later why my rehabilitation was stopped in its tracks just as it was about to be completed after such a promising start. The seven witnesses testifying for the second time had to sign a statement that they would not talk to anybody about the hearing. And they certainly took pains not to tell me about it. In retrospect it was probably much better for my state of mind that I did not have an inkling of how my case was being handled and that I did not get a look at the files for 40 years.

Today the explanation is obvious: between the autumn of 1954 and the following spring the pendulum of Imre Nagy's New Course swung over completely. And in Moscow the climate had also changed.

A rebellion of the editors of *Szabad Nep*, a sensational move given the climate of the times, took place at a three-day conference, where 80 percent of the Party members present came out for the Nagy course and against the economic and media policies of the top functionaries Ernö Gerö and Mihály Farkas. The 100-page record of the conference was sent to the leadership as well as to the editorial boards of other publications and the directors of some important institutions. It hit like a bombshell.

Encouraged by Rákosi's intrigues in the course of a startlingly long convalescent stay in the Soviet Union and alarmed by what it considered nationalistic tendencies, Moscow began to reverse its position. Nagy refused to voice self-criticism. In early March the same Central Committee which only a few months earlier, in October, had unanimously supported his course now, just as unanimously castigated him as a 'rightist deviationist'. On 14 April 1955, the Central Committee voted to expel Imre Nagy, and four days later he was ousted from the Premiership.

In late autumn 1955 the Stalinists took their revenge. Nagy was expelled from the party. With the help of the apparatus loyal to him, Rákosi managed to have dozens of journalists and writers, government employees and Party officials whom he considered suspect or obstacles either replaced or banished to the provinces or transferred. Thus, of 35 journalists on the daily *Magyar Nemzet*, 21 lost their posts. Books and periodicals were shredded, theatre productions banned, and those who weren't prepared to go along with the degrading charade of self-criticism and the renunciation of their personal 'erroneous' opinions had to count on the loss of their jobs and privileges.

In retrospect the seemingly incomprehensible shifts in my personal, utterly insignificant case must also be seen against this background.

Sectarian considerations were not the only concern of the apparatchiks: real privileges were at stake. The high-ranking government and Party officials lived in villas or spacious apartments, isolated from the people, had official cars, were able to shop cheaply at secret special stores, spent their vacations in exclusive resorts and hotels in places like Lake Balaton where armed militia troops protected them from ordinary mortals. Special hospitals and sanatoriums tended to the health of upper echelon comrades. In his memoirs András Hegedüs, speaking of a time when as a 'mere' Vice Premier he headed an official delegation to China during the preparations for the overthrow of Nagy, describes how his hosts protected him. His car was preceded and followed by two security vehicles. But when he asked to visit a department store in Shanghai the Chinese panicked. In no time at all the ten-story building was cleared of all people. Escorted by 40 guards this small figure was able to walk through the completely empty building looking at the merchandise on display.

Part of the new purge was the dismantling of the institutions, so carefully set up by Nagy, that now posed a threat to the monopoly position of the Party. Consequently the information office of the Ministerial Council which had so valiantly fought for the rehabilitation of the freed prisoners and the release of those still in prison was abolished.

During the three years I was not allowed to work, my youth naturally was my greatest strength. But what could an unemployed journalist and writer do? I tried to improve my English and French and began to study Russian. My teacher was an elderly lady from St Petersburg who had escaped to Belgrade before the Russian Revolution and ended up in Budapest. I read all of Balzac and borrowed books by Arthur Koestler and George Orwell from friends, but I spent most of my time in coffee houses. Even then it was possible to sit for hours nursing a cup of coffee and a glass of water and read. But in contrast to the past, there were no foreign dailies available. And the legendary headwaiters who used to let journalists and writers run up tabs or lent them small sums were no longer there. Nonetheless between 1954 and 1956 the coffee house was still the centre of the literary, and increasingly also of political, life. Tradition mattered! We journalists, writers, and artists would meet regularly at 'our' tables at Café Hungaria, the ornately decorated, gilded extravaganza opened in 1894 in a palatial building. Plaques and caricatures of Hungarian writers and artists who frequented it throughout its existence still decorate its walls. There we could sit for hours, loudly discussing the international situation and local political gossip. All of us assumed we were being followed and watched, but as time went on our small circle grew less and less concerned.

For those of us who had experienced and taken part in the campaign against 'Tito, the running dog of imperialism', the political bombshell which exploded in Belgrade on 26 May 1955, was another clear sign of the dawn of a new era. That day the public apology of the Soviet Party leader Khrushchev and his reconciliation with Tito, that heretic of world Communism demolished the very basis of the Rajk trial, which had so blatantly labelled its victims imperialist agents and Titoist traitors. The whole basis of the attacks on Tito and Titoists was suddenly discredited by Khrushchev as 'lying, dirty provocations'. All of us realised that on this day an irrevocable process with far-reaching importance was being set in motion that would affect all our lives. Rákosi and his clique were finally going to be called to account.

Within a couple of days, while the Soviet delegation was still in Yugoslavia, three friends of mine – Miklós Gimes, Miklós Vásárhelyi and György Fazekas – made a daring move at a Party meeting of the state publishing house in the building which housed Café Hungaria. They demanded that the Party leadership normalise Yugoslav-Hungarian relations and as a basic precondition move toward reopening the Rajk trial. The news spread like wildfire in the cafés, in editorial offices and institutions, and among writers and artists. The charge of 'violation of Socialist legality' was the Achilles heel of the Rákosi regime.

The Party leadership hit back hard. Gimes and Fazekas were immediately expelled from the Party. Vásárhelyi was heavily fined by the Party as a 'last warning' and demoted to librarian at the Muvelt Nep publishing house, where my wife worked. But the reverberations of the Austrian State Treaty signed on 15 May 1955, which restored independence free of Soviet influence to Hungary's neighbour, together with the reconciliation between Moscow and Belgrade could not be contained. Sympathisers and supporters began to form around the isolated Imre Nagy. The role of the writers began to take on increasing importance in this emerging anti-Stalinist movement.

We knew that Rákosi was a skilled operator who would not shy away from any desperate measures to protect himself. Arrests of writers continued and when rumours began to spread of lists being prepared of people marked for 'termination'. I was filled with dread.

However, we did not anticipate the huge storm gathering momentum in Moscow which in the end was going to sweep out Rákosi himself.

Khrushchev's secret speech of the crimes of Stalin at the 20th Party Congress of the CPSU on 25 February 1956, released piecemeal, was a veritable bomb shell. Yet the dams the Party apparatus had erected against the reformers did not give way until the complete text of Khrushchev's speech was made available at closed Party meetings. Rákosi was called to account by various Communists and non-Communists alike. Even Marshall Tito waded in. He demanded Rákosi's resignation, the public rehabilitation of Rajk and the retraction of anti-Yugoslav charges as the price for normalising relations with Hungary. On 23 March the omnipotent Party chief had to listen to an unprecedented challenge. The historian György Litván told Rákosi to his face at a Party meeting that he had lost the confidence of the people and called on him to resign.

Even though the nascent opposition had no media outlets except for the publication of the writers union, *Irodalmi Ujsag*, important developments and news spread rapidly and filtered down to all levels of the public. More and more politicians, including members of the Central Committee, sought to make contact with Imre Nagy and other reformers.

We lived through a year of upheaval, and sensed that an unstoppable force was moving toward reform and toward the resignation of Rákosi's people. In early June Nagy celebrated his sixtieth birthday. More than 60 prominent public figures, including two Central Committee members, paid a visit to the outcast in his home – an impressive demonstration of support.

Public meetings and rallies proliferated. Marxist thinker Georg Lukács drew over a thousand listeners with his lecture on politics and philosophy. An emotional high point was reached when Party veterans and former political prisoners staged a public event with students and young writers. Here Julia Rajk, the widow of the executed Foreign Minister, appeared for the first time in public to demand the complete rehabilitation of her husband.

The prelude to the overthrow of Rákosi was a so-called press debate in the auditorium at the Officers Club of the People's Army. By the early afternoon the hallways and rooms were filled to overflowing. Estimates put the number of listeners at between 6,000 and 7,000. Despite the overcrowding I was able to find a relatively good seat in the central hall and stayed along with the majority of the crowd until 2.30am. In sharply worded statements Communist journalists settled accounts with the system they had so fervently served. For many of us the absolute high point of that evening was the long, brilliant address by the writer Tibor Déry. This speech, never published in his lifetime, called the lack of individual freedom a spiritual, intellectual, social and economic cancer. When I left the big building at dawn with my friends we were tired, but enthusiastic and optimistic. It was only a question of time, we thought, before Imre Nagy would be rehabilitated and Rákosi toppled.

However, things did not turn out that way. On 28 June, i.e. the very next day, thousands of workers took to the streets in Poznan, Poland, demonstrating against the raised production norms and the intolerably low wages. After bloody clashes with the police and army, 70 workers were dead and 300 wounded. The clashes sent shock-waves through the Eastern bloc and gave the hardliners a new lease, even if only for a brief period.

Rákosi and his people were determined to use the tragedy in Poznan against the opposition. A sharply-worded Central Committee resolution attacked Imre Nagy and the Petöfi Circle, under whose aegis so many anti-Rákosi meetings had taken place. Protest meetings were held throughout the country and resolutions passed. Rákosi was preparing for the 'complete liquidation of the Nagy conspiracy'.

That summer my friends at various papers became noticeably bolder in their dealings with 'compromised' or not yet rehabilitated colleagues. And so I was able to place some articles on foreign policy themes in a number of dailies and weeklies. While we were pre-occupied with events in Hungary, further afield the Suez Crisis in the Middle East was gaining pace as President Nasser squared up to the British and French interests in the region. So on July 18 I visited the editorial offices of the weekly *Beke es Szabadsag*, which was becoming the mouthpiece of the anti-Stalinists, to deliver an article about the history of the Suez Canal. In the office of the editor's secretary excite-ment reigned; a short while before a friendly member of the Central Committee had called up one of the spokesmen of the opposition to tell him that 'Baldie', i.e. Rákosi, was out. Considering his decade-long rule and the bizarre personality cult surrounding him, this news was a political earthquake.

Forty years passed before it became public knowledge that Anastas Mikoyan, a member of the Soviet Presidium, had spent a week in Buda-pest in July 1956, cabled long reports to Moscow about the intrigues as well as the insecurity of the Hungarian top leadership, and played a major role in engineering a changing of the guard in Budapest.

Rákosi would occasionally give himself away not only when quoting Shakespeare, but also when talking to people close to him. In her memoirs, his favourite niece, Eva Kardos, reports once complaining to Uncle Matyi about the stupidity of Interior Ministry officials where she was working. Her uncle's answer startled her: 'It's not good to surround oneself with smart people; smart people are dangerous'. This explains why the distrustful Party leader preferred to put relatively young people loyal to him into key positions. That they were incompetent did not bother him. When faced with his first true crisis, in October 1956, this cost them all dearly. The incompetence of the Rákosi favourites may have contributed more to the collapse of the regime than the drama-laden battle of the freedom fighters whose number probably never exceeded 15,000-20,000.

It was no wonder that neither Mikoyan nor Soviet Ambassador Yuri Andropov were convinced of the competence of the new leaders. We guessed at the time that their overthrow took place with the express support of Mikoyan and Andropov, but the actual extent of Soviet involvement became known only in 1993 with the publication of secret documents from the Soviet Party and State archives which President Boris Yeltsin had presented to his Hungarian hosts as a symbolic gesture during his state visit to Budapest in November 1992.

The public was thrilled to learn that Rákosi was resigning 'for reasons of health' and going to Moscow immediately after the Central Committee meeting. But the bad news soon followed: Rákosi was replaced by another old Kremlin confidant, Ernö Gerö. Even more disappointing was the failure to resolve the 'Nagy affair'. But as a consolation, two political figures who had been jailed for several years, János Kádár and the former Social Democrat György Marosán were made members of the Politburo. They at least would accelerate the rehabilitation of the arrested Communists and former Social Democrats.

These developments also cleared the last obstacles to my rehabilitation. I now found myself carrying on a strange personal correspondence with Mrs Kádár, who had become head of the personnel department of MTI, my former employer. She wrote to me on 15 August 1956 asking me to come to see her at her office with my Party membership card and all documents that supported my rehabilitation. Once I furnished these: 'We would like to revise the information about your person that has been given to various agencies and which is no longer pertinent'.

On 12 September 1956, the State Prosecutor, that is to say the same department head, Pál Bakos, who had been given my file almost two years before, confirmed my innocence and added that I was not to suffer any material or moral damage because of my unwarranted arrest and internment. Now things began to move rapidly. A week later I was summoned to the Central Control Commission and formally reinstated as Party member. My new Party registration bore the same number as before my arrest. Although as a 'youthful SDP functionary I had committed ideological errors' my internment nonetheless was held to be unwarranted. Since I was a 'talented journalist' and the agitprop section had supported me, the Control Commission restored my Party membership. Finally on 24 September I was also formally rehabilitated by a Special Committee of the journalists' association chaired by Géza Losonczy, a future member of the Nagy Government who was later to die in prison. The journalists' association came out in favour of my claim for compensation by the MTI and proposed that my request to work for the paper *Esti Budapest* be granted.

After 15 months of military service, eight months incarceration, and three years of not being allowed to work, a total of five long (and lost) years, I, as a completely rehabilitated journalist, was again permitted to work. Why then did I, as so many others, like Gimes who was later to be sentenced and executed during the Nagy trial, like Haraszti and Vásárhelyi, accept reinstatement into the Party? Under a one-Party system there was no political life outside the official Party, and membership was simply the precondition for any political activity. For a journalist in particular the Party membership card was the 'admission ticket' to a career. The handful of non-party older fellow-travellers were simply window-dressing; in fact, as I have pointed out, although they did not carry membership cards they were the most faithful supporters of whatever faction was in power.

Beyond that we, all of us who supported Nagy and the reforms he embodied, hoped for a democratic remoulding of the socialist model. What fascinated us most were the changes in Poland and, above all in Yugoslavia, the only Eastern European Communist country that had withdrawn from the Soviet sphere of influence and through constant experimentation had sought to create a new type of Communist society. 'We', that is to say at least all the people I knew, were reformers, not revolutionaries.

For me September 1956, the month of my complete rehabilitation, marked the beginning of a new life.

That I did not return to the MTI news agency but rather went to work for the evening paper *Esti Budapest* was only in part connected with unpleasant personal memories. I had already begun to contribute to *Esti Budapest*. The paper's new editor-in-chief, István Szirmai, had been arrested at the same time as I – he was at the time chief of Radio Budapest – as a 'Zionist-imperialist agent'. After his release this pre-war Communist from Transylvania had also had to wait a long time for his rehabilitation, working as a pawn-broker among other jobs. Our shared fate was a bond, and Szirmai had already offered me freelance assignments back in the summer of 1956. Following my complete rehabilitation by the journalists' union, he held out the prospect a chief columnist's role for me. After five years of senseless interruptions I was to resume professional career in October.

9

From Crescendo to Furioso – October to December 1956

In *The Old Regime and the Revolution* Alexis de Tocqueville said that the most perilous moment for a bad regime occurs when it seeks to mend its ways. He added in his *Recollections*, that the real reason why leaders lose political power is because they 'become unworthy to exercise it'. This exactly describes the situation in which Hungary found itself 100 years after de Tocqueville's analysis.

The prelude to the armed uprising in Budapest was the public burial of the now-rehabilitated victims of the first big show trial. Julia Rajk, László Rajk's widow, who herself had spent five-and-a-half-years in prison, brought continuing pressure on the party apparatus and won her request for a public commemoration. After all, since a show trial had been held should not there also be a show burial? A popular Hungarian saying has it that what Hungary is good at is burying people. In order to lend the funeral the requisite dignity and the proper place in history, 6 October was the date chosen for this

ceremony. On that day the 13 generals of the revolutionary army executed in 1849 in Arad by the Hapsburgs are commemorated. In 1956,
6 October fell on a Saturday, a bitterly cold, rainy, windy day. Two
hundred thousand people braved the awful weather to pay tribute to
the memory of László Rajk, Tibor Szönyi, András Szalai and General
György Pálffy. They followed the funeral procession and stayed to
listen to the eulogies. Silent, dignified, without umbrellas, bareheaded,
the people paid their respect to the dead for more than three hours.
There was a sense of mourning but also one of menacing determination.

Gerö, Kádár and other top leaders were accidentally, or perhaps
intentionally, visiting Moscow on that day. The only speech that spoke
to us from the heart was delivered by Béla Szász, a fellow-defendant
at Rajk's trial, whom Rajk's widow had asked to deliver a brief eulogy:

> For seven years the bones of the executed László Rajk, the victim of false
> accusations, were lying in an unmarked grave. But his death has become
> a warning symbol for the Hungarian people and the entire world. For the
> hundreds of thousands who are now walking by these coffins not only
> want to pay the dead their last respects; their passionate hope and
> immutable decision is to lay an epoch to rest. Lawlessness, arbitrariness
> and the moral corpses of those shame-filled years must be buried for good,
> and the threat emanating from the Hungarian disciples of the law of might
> and personality cult must be banished for ever.

That day was the turning-point in the progressive disintegration of a
paralysed apparatus whose managers were insecure, incompetent and
above all unteachable. One week after the funeral – on one and the
same day – Imre Nagy was readmitted into the Party; Mihály Farkas,
the former Minister of Defence and Rákosi's right-hand man in the
bloody purges was arrested; five previously disgraced and executed
army generals were reburied with full military honours, and a Party and
government delegation including almost half of the Politburo, men like
Gerö, Kádár and Hegedüs, went to Yugoslavia for a week's visit. While
these dignitaries were celebrating Hungary's reconciliation with Tito,
debating the different roads to Socialism and going hunting, the regime
at home continued to disintegrate from day to day, a process accelerated
by the events in Poland. There, despite Soviet threats, Wladyslaw
Gomulka, who had spent years in prison, had triumph-antly resumed
the leadership of the United Polish Workers Party on 21 October 1956.
These events in Poland lent added weight to the dynamics of rebellion
in Hungary. The apparatus of the discredited regime was in disarray,
but they made matters worse with a series of fatal miscalculations.

The recently published 'top secret' reports of the then Soviet Ambassador Yuri Andropov to the Party Presidium in Moscow about his talks with the members of the warring Budapest factions seem almost eerie. A mere ten days before the explosion, a 'quite nervous and insecure' Gerö, the Party's First Secretary, called the situation 'extremely serious', while the former Mayor of Budapest and chief of planning, Zoltán Vas, a former Muscovite but now a Nagy partisan, quite openly warned Andropov of a 'looming national catastrophe' which 'the Soviet comrades do not see because they are listening to people who do not have the support of the Party or the people'. Even the highly intelligent Andropov, who 25 years later was to become the General Secretary of the CPSU, believed his own propaganda and saw the answer in a 'decisive hardline approach' by the Hungarian Party leadership: 'otherwise we think it entirely possible that Imre Nagy could become the leader of the Party and the country'.

The reformers under Nagy, who was determined to adhere to Party discipline, wanted to repair the political system, not do away with it. None of those close to Nagy nor the thousands pushing for reform, myself included, knew or suspected that in the Hungary of October 1956 repair was tantamount to the abolition of the system. That the almost 900,000-strong 'vanguard of the working class' was a colossus with clay feet, and that the personnel and institutional changes and promises always came too late to ward off the crisis within the framework of the system was borne out by the 13 stormy days of the Revolution.

The spark that ignited the smouldering ashes was the programme of the Budapest Technical University, modelled on the 12-point demands of the 1848 Revolution; it went far beyond the reforms on the table. The core demands were: free elections, i.e. a multiparty system, a free press, the installation of Imre Nagy as Prime Minister and the reinstitution of Hungarian national holidays and state symbols. Late at night on 22 October 1956, at the mass meeting at which the Communist youth functionaries lost control of the impassioned debate, calls for the withdrawal of Soviet troops became the most urgent demand. Encouraged by the news from Poland, the protest movement took on a new character. When the leadership rejected the students' request to broadcast their demands, the students issued a call for a solidarity demonstration with Poland for the next day.

By the morning of 23 October, a Tuesday, the young people began to make their way towards the meeting places at the Technical University in Buda and the Philosophy Faculty at Pest. They moved along in small groups, laughing and excited. It was all a new experience for them. After all, apart from the spontaneous displeasure voiced by disgruntled soccer fans over the Hungarian loss of the world championship match in Switzerland in the summer of 1954, not a single genuine demonstration in the streets of the capital had been seen since the Communist takeover.

That morning the organisers at the universities and other institutions discussed their plan: the students of the Technical University were to stage a silent march, while those at the Philosophy Faculty were to march with flags and posters. The various Communist-dominated youth organisations were soon overwhelmed by this spontaneous 'surge from below'. Despite some reservations and expressions of mild unease in the Petőfi Circle and other groupings, they had to join in whether they wanted to or not lest they lose whatever influence they still had. From the Petőfi Circle to the Writers' Association, from the Lenin Institute to the Petőfi Military Academy for political officers, more and more institutions and groups joined in the preparations. At the meetings and discussion in the various groups tension mounted by the hour.

Everybody experienced this memorable, brilliant autumn day differently. For me it was the second day at my new office at the evening paper *Esti Budapest*, which was in the same building which housed the editorial offices of the official Party paper, *Szabad Nep*. When some of my colleagues decided to try to get an idea of what was going on in the city I went along with them in an office car. Deceptive calm still reigned. But here and there we could already see young people sporting rosettes in the national colors in their lapels. On buildings, walls and trees, improvised mimeographed appeals or small posters sprung up. Officially the public meeting that afternoon was to be nothing more than a solidarity demonstration for the (now victorious) Polish reformers, but every politically knowledgeable Hungarian knew that Hungary's future was at stake.

That morning the Politburo held a crisis meeting. The previously mentioned Party and Government delegation that had gone to Yugoslavia did not return until the morning of 23 October. Reports about the weakness of the leadership and the subsequent panic of the apparatus, and above all the top leadership, spread like wildfire. The Politburo wanted to stop the student demonstration at all costs. 'If need be we'll open fire on them,' two enraged Politburo members, József Révai and György Marosán, asserted before a group of Communist journalists, writers, and youth functionaries who protested about the ban on demonstrations broadcast over the radio at 12.53pm. Soon afterwards the police and security officers told the leadership that they lacked the 'proper means' to halt the demonstration. Then an announcement came over the air at 2.23 that the Ministry of the Interior had cancelled the ban on demonstrations.

Most people only found out through the contradictory announcements over the air that something extraordinary was underway. However, the students themselves had paid no attention to either the ban or its retraction.

Meanwhile two powerful demonstrations were forming, one moving from the university buildings in Pest to the Petőfi monument on the banks of the Danube, the other from the Technical University in Buda to the monument of the legendary Polish General Bem, who in 1849 had led the Hungarian troops to victory against the Hapsburgs and the Czarist intervention forces.

Once our paper with its banner headline on the peaceful victory of the Polish reformers and the Budapest student demonstrations was printed, I, together with some colleagues, tried first by car and then on foot to get to the afternoon demonstration at the Bem monument. Tens of thousands were already on the streets.

At first the students sang the Hungarian national anthem as well as the Marseillaise, the Internationale and revolutionary and folk songs. They carried Hungarian and a few Polish national banners. Wherever the mass demonstration passed by life came to a halt. People waved from open windows; the streets reverberated with slogans.

But the character of the demonstration had changed. More and more young workers and sympathisers from among the onlookers joined the students. Flags appeared with the red star cut out. The slogans had become more and more radical and nationalistic: 'If you're a Hungarian you're with us'; 'Russians, out!' 'Go home and take your Stalin (i.e. the gigantic statue) home with you!'

Nobody was in a position to direct the spontaneous demonstration or to influence its dynamic. There were no loudspeakers that worked. The speech of the chairman of the writers' union, Péter Veres, and the poem 'The Call' by Mihály Vörösmarty recited by the actor Ferenc Bessenyei were drowned out by the noise.

A crowd estimated at 200,000 had been gathering throughout the day in front of the parliament building and the surrounding streets waiting for hours for Imre Nagy. When he appeared they greeted his first word, 'Comrades,' with wolf-whistles. His soothing, uninspired speech disappointed many and angered some. Many people at the parade grounds at the city park were pulling down Stalin's statue and smashing the symbol of the hated system to smithereens. In front of the radio station thousands of demonstrators demanded that student resolutions be broadcast. All these actions were completely spontaneous, unorganised and certainly not part of any long-planned programme.

This was not a calculated revolt targeting the most important power and communication centres like the telephone and cable headquarters, police stations, ministries and Party offices. This was an outburst reflected the wrath of the Hungarian people. It was a revolutionary mass movement, a workers' revolt carried out primarily by young workers. The people first directed their fury against the symbols of the dictatorship and Soviet domination. The conspicuous red stars were taken down from public and Party buildings. Late that night the crowds set fire to books and pictures by and about Marx, Lenin and Stalin.

That day of 23 October 1956 was a day of exhilaration, passions, trucks careering down streets loaded with people and banners – and much talk. No revolution in Central Europe would be complete without restaurants and cafés full of debate, philosophical discourse and cigarettes. Our 1956 revolution was no exception. As I met with my colleagues for dinner at a restaurant, we passionately discussed the volatile political situation. Meanwhile after the demonstration in front of the parliament the key opposition organisers repaired for dinner at the Café Hungaria, practically next door to our restaurant. No doubt their discussions were as passionate as ours. But none of us knew that a revolution was already under way. At any rate I went to bed calmly – and slept through the first dramatic night of this revolution.

In the morning I was awakened by a thunderous rattling of chains outside my window. On Ülloi Street a column of Soviet tanks was slowly moving in the direction of the inner city. Our corner building was situated on a strategic point, separated only by a narrow street from the neighbouring Kilian Barracks. A couple of hundred metres further on, on the other side of the street, the small Corvin Passage led to a building complex built in 1928, and between them there was a big movie theatre. I had spent my childhood moving through these familiar streets and the passageway leading to the barracks. And it was in this neighbourhood, particularly all around the cinema not easily accessible to tanks, that the first resistance groups of the revolutionaries had installed themselves as early as the night of 23 October.

Before I heard the first shots I knew instinctively that a completely new situation had arisen. The appearance of the Soviet tanks and the deployment of Soviet troops at the express request of the panicky Gerö camp turned the revolt against the Stalinist dictatorship into a national battle. During the next four or five days the people living in the vicinity of the fighting were practically cut off from the rest of the world. Getting to my editorial office was out of the question. We had to take refuge in cellars.

The revolutionaries, mostly young workers and apprentices armed only with hand weapons and Molotov cocktails, inflicted substantial losses on the Soviet troops. They came out of workers' and student hostels; among the fighters in our neighbourhood there were only a handful of adults. The young people were in the truest sense of the word guerrilla or partisan fighters who initially in small groups, lacking co-ordinated tactics and without thought-out political objectives, took up arms. Despite the superiority of the Soviets, they enjoyed the moral and frequently practical support of the people.

For us, so close to the huge barracks which were at a centre of the battles, there was no escape. It was a paradoxical situation. We were in the very centre of the dramatic events. Here around the Corvin Passage and the barracks, as well as in some areas on the Buda side of the city, a few thousand young men determined to fight to the death brought about a complete turnabout: first the reinstatement of Imre Nagy as Prime Minister on the night of 24 October and then a change in the entire political situation.

If it had not been for the radio we would not have learned of the collapse of the Party's power monopoly, of the blood-bath inflicted by the special units of the state security service on 25 October in front of the parliament in which hundreds of peaceful demonstrators were killed and wounded. We in the cellar also knew little about the activities of the two Soviet delegates, the Presidium members Mikoyan and Suslov, and the acrimonious tug-of-war in the embattled Party leadership.

Not until 28 October did we feel hope again. Imre Nagy declared a truce and some hours later, at 5.25pm, recognised the Revolution as a 'national democratic movement', announced the withdrawal of the Soviet troops from the capital, the dissolution of the AVH as well as the creation of a national guard, amnesty, and the introduction of the Kossuth coat of arms. Events unfolded at a breakneck pace. Even though on 29 October there was still fighting around the Kilian barracks and 20 people were still to die in clashes in the city, things were beginning to return to normal. Despite the fervent pleas of my parents I could no longer stand watching political events from a distance. I left the house.

Meanwhile Imre Nagy and János Kádár, appointed First Party Secretary of a disintegrating official party, continued to issue a string of new declarations and promises. At 2.30pm on 30 October the historic drum-roll was heard: Imre Nagy announced on the radio the end of the one-party system and the return to the four-party coalition of 1945. The next day a new national guard composed of all armed forces, including the revolutionaries, was set up at the Kilian Barracks.

Given the general revolutionary mood and the turbulent developments, I like many others at first believed in the possibility of peaceful change. On 2 November all fighting throughout the country stopped. Old and new parties were formed, and more than a dozen new papers appeared. Army officers liberated Cardinal Mindszenty, who had been under arrest since 1949, and with the concurrence of the Nagy Government returned him to the palace of the archbishopric. Moreover, 3,300 political and 10,000 ordinary prisoners were set free.

In those hectic days I ran into numerous acquaintances in the press building and journalists' union, from Szirmai to Gimes, who were planning for their publishing and editing future. The paper *Esti Budapest* was no longer appearing, but, as I recall, at a side entrance to the building ransacked by demonstrators, I was handed a month's salary for the first time in five years.

Since we in our district were cut off from events, I myself fortunately did not experience or witness any violence. But the sight of bodies, whether of youthful revolutionaries or Soviet tank crews who had died near the Corvin Passage and the Kilian Barracks, will always stay with me.

There had been excesses by the revolutionaries. In the siege and storming of the headquarters of the Budapest city committee of the Party, its defenders were methodically slaughtered, beginning with Imre Mezo, the Budapest Party Secretary, a reformer and Nagy sympathiser waving the white banner of surrender. Pictures of these lynchings and of the 24 mutilated bodies of NCOs, AVH militia members, army officers and employees who had been holed up in the Party building were seen all over the world. Even though these excesses and other lynchings were condemned by the revolutionary organisations, the free press and the leaders of the uprising, and even though the Revolution, from a historical perspective, cost relatively few lives, its enemies were to make much political capital from the brutalities committed at the Budapest Party headquarters. For decades the brutalities would serve the propaganda purposes of the Kádár regime.

The same holds true of the repeated allegations of anti-semitic excesses in the provinces. In Budapest at any rate there were no such incidents. In fact in a country in which so many top political and secret police officials were of Jewish descent it was astonishing that the October uprising did not contain more serious bouts of anti-semitism. Nonetheless many Jewish friends and acquaintances were worried that now, when everything was out of control and central power was breaking apart, pent up anti-Jewish feelings might explode. In fact, however, nothing like that happened. The number of Jews among the leaders of the Revolution (Tibor Déry, Julius Háy, István Angyal, Otto Szirmai, László Nickelsburg, etc) was considerable. Déry and Háy were sentenced to long prison terms after the defeat of the Revolution, while Angyal, Szirmai and Nickelsburg were executed. In the battles and debates of these weeks, people of Jewish descent were to be found on both sides of the issue.

Anyway, generalising labels – evil Communist functionaries versus passionate freedom fighters – fall short of the mark. True, the nation fighting Soviet rule was remarkably united, but at the same time it was also a coalition of divergent forces, from Communist reformers or Democratic Socialists to elements on the extreme right. After all, Hungary had taken a 180-degree turn within the space of a few days, from a disintegrating terror system to the reinstitution of a multiparty system.

Over the radio we heard that the reformers had pushed through the dissolution of the MDP (Party of the Hungarian Workers), the name of the discredited old Communist Party, and founded a new party, called the Hungarian Socialist Workers Party (MSMP). It was chaired by a committee of seven headed by Kádár, including Nagy as well as five well-known reformers.

Meanwhile there were indications that in the Soviet leadership the champions of tough measures had gained the upper hand. Now we know from published secret papers that the final decision to implement the plan to smash of the Hungarian uprising under the code name 'Whirlwind' had already been reached on 31 October. The person in charge of the operation was Soviet Defence Minister Marshal Zhukov. What we heard at the time were only widespread rumours based on reports of the Hungarian border and railroad control posts that the Soviets, instead of withdrawing as promised, had sent fresh troops across the Hungarian border.

On 1 November Imre Nagy announced that Hungary was leaving the Warsaw Pact and declared the country's neutrality. His government appealed to the United Nations and the four great powers to recognise Hungary's neutrality. This was followed by a tape-recorded address by the State Minister and Secretary of the MSMP, János Kádár, in which he spoke of his pride in the role of the Communist youth and intellectuals in the armed uprising and called on all political forces to defend themselves against a threatened counter-revolution and Soviet intervention. However, while this tape was being broadcast, Kádár and the man who had arranged his defection back to the Soviet fold, the old Communist and Soviet agent Ferenc Münnich, were already on their way to Moscow. They had left the parliament building early that afternoon and gone to the Soviet Embassy.

In retrospect, the Soviet intervention in the face of an uncontrollable uprising which threatened the Soviet colonial empire was unavoidable. Today we know that Moscow's decision had been reached before Hungary's withdrawal from the Warsaw Pact and before the proclamation of neutrality.

When the general attack of the Soviet troops on Budapest began at 4am on 4 November, and the fighters in the Kilian barracks opened fire on the Soviet tanks that had wanted to push through to the inner city, the barracks and thus automatically our corner building became a target of grenade throwers, heavy artillery and tank fire. For five days we could not leave the cellar. More than eleven years after the end of World War II the people living near the centre of the conflict found themselves in a worse and more dangerous situation than in the final days of the war.

When our house was being fired upon by the tanks we fled through connecting cellars and backyards, at times crawling on all fours, to reach a building at the end of our block. When the guns fell silent after a few days we returned to our house and I gingerly approached our apartment. It was a terrible sight. The two rooms whose windows faced the street were burned out. My entire library had been destroyed, as had the lovely furniture and the files in my father's office. By a cruel irony of fate the only books that survived were the collected works of Marx and Lenin which we had put into a laundry closed in the bathroom because we needed the space on the bookshelves, yet did not dare to throw them away. I still have some singed dictionaries and novels, reminders of those November days.

We were homeless. My parents moved in with my aunt who already shared her kitchen and bath with two other families. Later they found temporary shelter in a small apartment in our building whose tenants had fled to the West. It took a while before our apartment was more-or-less habitable, but I and the rest of my family had lost almost all our clothes.

The armed resistance collapsed on 11 or 12 November at the cost of 2,700 officially recorded dead and more then 19,000 wounded, but it took months before mass arrests and threats succeeded in breaking the strikes organised by the workers' councils and the protest actions of the intellectuals and students. Six thousand jail sentences and about 400 death sentences were imposed. It was also a crisis winter for the 'victors'.

The so-called Revolutionary Workers and Peasant Government was installed in Budapest on 7 November under the protective shield of Soviet tanks. The rightful Prime Minister, Imre Nagy, together with five members of the MSMP directorate, had taken refuge in the Yugoslav Embassy and refused to recognise the Kádár-Münnich government. The sixth member, Sándor Kopácsi, the police chief of Budapest, had been arrested in his office by the Soviets.

It was an era of illusions and lies, promises and traps, tragedies and betrayals. Within days people who in the early fifties had been thrown into prison by Rákosi and had shared a cell with each other, or the young leaders of the Petöfi Circle, turned into bitter enemies and later split into victims and victors. Nagy, who early in the morning together with his closest advisers (a total of 43 people including women and children) accepted the asylum offered by the Yugoslav Government and fled to the Yugoslav Embassy, didn't yet know that the deck had been stacked. According to the memoirs of the then Yugoslav Ambassador in Moscow, Veljko Mičunović, the script of the military intervention had been discussed in great detail, even who was going to head the Party and government, by Khrushchev and Tito on the island of Brioni 48 hours before the Soviet attack. But Imre Nagy spoiled their plan by refusing to sign the resignation urgently demanded by Tito. During his stay at the Yugoslav Embassy from 4 November to 22 November in the building surrounded by Soviet tanks and soldiers, Belgrade repeatedly urged him to resign and to recognise the Kádár government.

The Kádár group began from zero. Kádár personally and repeatedly promised free passage to Imre Nagy and his friends as well as to participants in the uprising. The breach of that promise through the abduction of the Nagy group by the Soviets, their deportation to Romania, and finally the secret trial in June 1958, in Budapest and the execution of Nagy, Defence Minister Pál Maléter, the journalist Miklós Gimes and other leading personalities, was to remain an ineradicable moral burden for the Kádár regime and above all for Kádár himself. In November and December 1956 a variety of lies were disseminated. Now we know that not only Hungary, the Soviets and the Romanians were involved, but that Tito and his associates had also played along with them from the very outset. Kádár himself had told the Party leadership in December 1956 that Yugoslavia had been given a written promise that nothing would happen to the Nagy group, but orally they were told that there was no intention of keeping that promise.

The deceptions hold true for the American Government as well. For years the American diplomatic and propaganda apparatus guided by John Foster Dulles, above all the Munich-based Radio Free Europe controlled by Washington, had in word and print waged radical psychological warfare against world Communism in general and Soviet hegemony in Central Europe in particular. I shall never forget the young freedom fighter in our street who full of optimism told me that UN troops were already on the way to the Hungarian-Austrian border. His source? Radio Free Europe. Of course the speakers and commentators of the Hungarian-language broadcasts from Munich had not specifically said that, but they did arouse expectations. Even politically better informed Hungarians also believed that the West would not desert them and would force the Soviets to moderate their policies or at least make concessions.

In retrospect there no longer ought to be any doubt of Washington's hands-off policy. Given relentless American anti-Soviet propaganda, US non-intervention proved a bitter disappointment for the Hungarian people. As pragmatic and cynical a chronicler as Henry Kissinger later criticised the Eisenhower-Dulles Administration for having behaved like a 'spectator without any direct interest' in the outcome of the power struggle in Hungary and for its failure to extract a political or economic price from Moscow. During the Revolution and after the second Soviet intervention nothing was done. No diplomatic notes, no pressure, no offer to mediate came from Washington. In Hungary an internally divided Soviet leadership was in fact given free hand. The moral bankruptcy of liberal Western attitudes became obvious to many of us back in the crisis of winter 1956.

Between November 1956 and January 1957 almost 200,000 Hungarians fled the country, a tenth of them to Yugoslavia, the rest to Austria. Many freedom fighters were among the refugees.

Although friends were kidnapped and arrested I did not feel threatened. After five years of forced unemployment I did not want to leave my homeland despite everything that had happened. Moreover, colleagues with whom I had worked in the past and people who had spent many years in prison were among those who tried to reassure us that a return to the Rákosi era was not on the cards and that the essence of what the Revolution had achieved would be preserved.

At the same time journalists under the leadership of Miklós Gimes issued an underground paper, and a few other writers founded various resistance groups that distributed posters and leaflets. In early November, before the Soviet attack, I had run into Gimes whom I knew from our time at the old Party paper *Szabad Nep* and whom I admired for his courageous stance in the fight against the Rákosi clique. We walked along the banks of the Danube and talked about the future. He told me he had visions of founding a left-wing intellectual weekly, something like the London *New Statesman*, and asked me whether I would consider becoming foreign editor. I agreed enthusiastically. After the invasion Gimes went underground and got involved in hectic activity. Despite Kádár's publicly proclaimed threat, Gimes refused to leave Hungary when that was still possible (his wife and young son had taken refuge in Switzerland). On 5 December this gentle, educated man who suffered pangs of conscience because of his role in past injustices was arrested and 18 months later executed.

The future of the press depended on the tempo of the political consolidation. In December a number of papers reappeared and the political editorial offices of the radio station resumed broadcasting. The centrists and careful reformers around the Kádár group who frequently disagreed with one another sought to win over the journalists and writers and to soften their unified stance of opposition.

István Szirmai, the editor-in-chief of *Esti Budapest*, the paper to which I had begun to contribute shortly before the Revolution, happened to be in Moscow on official business during the Revolution and therefore not compromised in any way. Since he knew many journalists he was considered the ideal contact person between the distrustful journalists and the isolated new leadership. Szirmai invited me and a few other colleagues to discuss the reopening of our paper. Our proposal to rename it *Esti Hirlap* and to call it an independent daily was ultimately accepted.

György Marosán, the erstwhile grave-digger of Social Democracy, who after the smashing of the Revolution became a member of the Kádár cabinet protested against that designation: 'What does it mean, independent? Independent of whom, the Party?' But the new name stayed. And we tried to assemble a team of respectable journalists which did not include any of the blockheads pretending to be journalists.

But independence like respectability is relative. This became clear to me when one day Szirmai called a meeting with myself and a few other journalists to discuss the publication of a 'white book' on the 'Counter-revolutionary Manifestations' (meaning the uprising). My job would be to assemble the foreign press reports. Whether out of cowardice or opportunism, I did not say no. For a few hours I sat down and dutifully assembled all the clippings, arranging them by country and language. But using my workload and an imminent foreign trip as an excuse, I quietly bowed out of this disreputable propaganda project.

10

The Road
to Freedom

So where did I really stand? Even in retrospect I would be lying to myself if I were to say I had discovered my better self and gone over to the revolutionaries and resistance. Yet I certainly was not on the side of the Kádár group. I supported the resolution of the Hungarian Writers' League on 28 December against the 'historical error' of the Soviet invasion as well as the speech of Tibor Déry in which he said that 'the biggest, purest, most unified revolution' in Hungary's history and the Hungarian workers movement 'had been smashed because of the regrettable lack of statesmanlike wisdom'.

Together with many of my friends and colleagues I had hoped that the united resistance of the intelligentsia and the working class, the pressure of world opinion and the Western powers, but also the sympathy of Yugoslavia and Poland perhaps would still open the door to an acceptable compromise and prevent a campaign of vengeance.

Meanwhile I had received an invitation to Warsaw via Polish journalists to report on the Polish parliamentary elections scheduled for 20 January 1957 for *Esti Hirlap*, elections that were also seen as a test of the success of the reform wing under Gomulka. The Polish Party paper *Trybuna Ludu* (at the time controlled by reformers) had agreed to underwrite my trip.

In the meantime I had been made Foreign Editor and member of the editorial committee of my paper. My trip was a political mission arranged by friends of reform, since Poland offered a ray of hope for our defeated, muzzled country. Poland was a land in which, so it seemed to us at the time, the peaceful transition from Stalinism to reform had succeeded.

I was then twenty-seven years old and about to embark on my first foreign trip as a professional. The editorial office applied for a passport to Poland for me, including a transit visa for Czechoslovakia and Austria.

Highly excited, I began my preparations for this great adventure – a trip to Poland and a brief side-trip to Prague and Vienna. Before the Revolution I had once tried to join a river excursion to Vienna but did not get my passport in time, and the two boats filled with genuine and would-be writers and artists left for Vienna without me.

I still have the faded Malev Budapest-Warsaw-Prague-Vienna flight ticket dated 10 January 1957. Two days later, on the twelfth, I was sitting in a small Polish prop. plane. Probably in order to drown my subconscious fear about the first plane trip of my life, and to the obvious disapproval of some stern, formally attired officials among the fellow passengers, I began to flirt outrageously with Eva, the attractive Polish stewardess, and in English to boot.

The next 18 days in Warsaw were to change my life. From the very first minute of my arrival I sensed the solidarity of the Polish journalists and intellectuals with Hungary. My trip had been organised by Polish colleagues, some of whom as guests of Hungarian papers had filed sympathetic reports about the dramatic events in Hungary. In all, ten Polish journalists had spent shorter or longer periods in Budapest in October and November. The traditional friendship of the two countries that at one time had even been ruled by the same king, their similar fate after the Second World War (more than 100,000 Poles fleeing the German-Russian occupation in 1939-40 had found refuge in Hungary), the shared threat to their respective reform movements that had brought Gomulka to power in Warsaw and Imre Nagy in Budapest – all these factors worked to make the feelings for Hungary in Poland stronger than in any other country. That Poland had succeeded in forestalling a Soviet attack and achieving its reforms through peaceful means while Hungary had suffered a tragic fate imparted a new and special intensity to the old friendship.

On two occasions I had the opportunity to make a modest contribution to the cause of the Hungarian Revolution. When on 19 January Julius Háy and five other writers and journalists were arrested and both the writers' and journalists' organisations were banned, I arranged for my Polish friends to lodge a protest at the Hungarian Embassy. And a few days later I tried to persuade the Indian diplomat KPS Menon, whom I had met recently in Budapest and whom I knew to have good contacts in Moscow, to intervene with the Hungarian Government and persuade Indian Prime Minister Nehru to lodge a formal protest in Moscow.

However, it became clear in these weeks that the Kádár regime was not interested in a compromise solution and was determined to take a hard line. Executions were already taking place in Budapest and many journalists, including some of my closest friends, were being fired without notice, investigations being launched against a number of them.

I began hesitantly and reluctantly to think about my own situation. After five difficult years I had finally landed a good job as Foreign Editor of a daily paper and for the first time in my life even had my own small apartment. Since it was obvious that István Szirmai, a close friend of Kádár dating back to their pre-war and wartime underground days, was going to play an important part in the leadership of the Party which by the end of December had only 103,000 members, my career prospects looked good. As a former left-wing Socialist, arrested and persecuted and not 'compromised' during the Revolution, my way up the ladder would not run into any obstacles (in the sixties and up to his death Szirmai was even a member of the Politburo). And finally, my parents, with whom I had never had a serious talk about defecting to the West, were living in Hungary.

As I was wrestling with my options I received a bizarre call in Warsaw: a Hungarian publishing house offered me a contract for a book about Kenya. It was a proposal which did not help me in my choices but it did add a touch of surrealism to my growing dilemma.

The persistence of the upbeat mood in Poland and the admiration which the vast majority of the Poles showed for the Hungarian Revolution even though it had failed filled me with some pride. Nonetheless it was becoming clear that candid, truthful reporting was becoming increasingly difficult even in Warsaw. The fact that after the elections two projected books by Hanka Adamiecka and Wiktor Woroszylski on Hungary were banned showed that Polish censorship was also tightening. Still there was a world of difference in the atmosphere between gagged Hungary and still-hopeful Poland. Of course at the time I saw everything through the special lenses of my idealisation of Poland. That the Polish reforms would peter out in the desert of the Eastern bloc's neo-Stalinism could not then have been anticipated.

Thanks to the hospitality of my Polish friends I was staying at the well-known Hotel Bristol. Many of the more than a hundred foreign correspondents and special reporters from all over the world were living there. I met almost all of them regularly in the press centre, the journalists' club, the restaurants and bars of the various hotels. It is difficult if not impossible today to describe what this window that had suddenly opened up onto the great outside world meant to a journalist coming from a completely isolated country. Suddenly I found myself talking face-to-face talking to people whose reports I had heard over the air or read in confidential MTI bulletins.

One day I was having my first, brief conversation with Sydney Gruson, at the time the Warsaw bureau chief of the *New York Times*, and his wife, Flora Lewis. When I told them that Radio Free Europe had come down hard on Imre Nagy and that President Eisenhower had made a conciliatory statement towards the Soviet Union which we in Budapest found incomprehensible, Gruson sighed and said he had always known that Eisenhower basically was a simpleton. I was thunderstruck. Before me stood the correspondent of the most prestigious American paper quite openly making such an impertinent remark about his head of state, particularly in front of a correspondent of a nominally Communist paper of a Communist-ruled country. I had much to learn.

This remark of Gruson's and the countless all-night sessions with others, like Ernst Halperin, a correspondent of the *Neue Zürcher Zeitung*, with journalists from Vienna, with Ronnie Preston, the Vienna correspondent of the London *Times*, with Seymour Freidin, the international correspondent of a number of major American papers and magazines, to name but a few, slowly but inevitably changed my outlook on life, until I finally arrived at the unshakable decision that I could no longer live a lie.

During the time when I and many others were in prison or internment camps, our friends and colleagues in Hungary could somehow still manage to push things to the back of their minds or lie to themselves. But after 23 October 1956 this was no longer possible, at least not as far as I was concerned. That was my own personal discovery.

None of the handful of Western colleagues to whom I mentioned my slowly-evolving decision encouraged me or offered any hope for concrete help. On the contrary. One of them in whom I confided thought that it would be a shame if Hungary's few liberal journalists still around were to leave – possibly with a view toward a useful contact in Budapest.

When I asked myself later how it came about that I, to the surprise of my parents and friends, failed to return to Budapest, the evolving situation in Hungary must surely have been the major reason. With my hosts footing the bill, I made countless calls to my colleagues in Budapest, to relatives in Bratislava and Tel Aviv. I did not worry much about my future. I was ready to gamble away my newly-won career in Hungary, but at the same time I did not have the faintest idea what my personal future would be. Without illusions but also without fear I began to prepare myself for the world of free choice.

Without well-to-do relatives or friends, without professional training but with a working knowledge of English and German, though not good enough for journalism, at the age of 27 without any hope of ever acquiring an accent-free command of a foreign language, I planned a dive into literally untested waters. But what was the alternative? Could I sit and write about Kenya or Britain's economic situation while friends who had helped to free me were now themselves behind bars, and admired authors who had not done anything illegal were facing the prospect of years in prison? Even before leaving for Prague, the next stop on my journey, I was determined to start a new life.

When I visited the Austrian Embassy to pick up my visa I was received by the chief of mission, and the two of us had a friendly chat during which he as a precautionary measure turned up the volume of the radio. The Ambassador told a mutual friend shortly after his talk with me, 'I was convinced that he wouldn't return to Budapest'. And in fact I had become so sure of this that I had to take care not to betray myself.

On the flight to Prague I again began to think of eyes that had haunted me for weeks. After a meeting in the offices of *Esti Hirlap* I had ridden with Szirmai in his black official limousine to the temporary quarters of my parents, that is to my aunt's apartment. An open lorry carrying four or five workers was driving in front of us. In their eyes I saw hate, sheer hatred of us. They hated us because we obviously were high-ranking bureaucrats of a despised new-old power propped up by foreign troops. I remembered this in Budapest and then also in Warsaw. It felt like a festering sore. I never again wanted to have to look into such eyes. When ten years later I visited Hungary, recently remarried and driving my own car, that hatred no longer was there. The people looked at us amicably, curious, at times perhaps with envy, but never with hatred. They knew that this car was not the alienated product of their labour and sweat, that we were private people, not the representatives of a foreign power.

The days in Prague were brief and not without danger. I had had the daring idea of making a dinner date with Flora Lewis, who was living with her husband in Prague's inner city. Though I did not call her from my hotel but from a public phone, it was a careless thing to do, to have dinner with a prominent American journalist in her apartment. Western journalists were being watched by the secret police. I will always be grateful to her for our frank talk. She gave me a seminar about the West, about the media, but also about the intrigues I should expect to face.

After Prague I took a long train ride to Bratislava to pay a visit to my father's older brother, Uncle Oszkar, whom I had last seen eight years ago in Budapest; I decided to visit him because I knew that many years would pass before I would see him again. After breakfast in his favourite cafe, The Carlton, Oszkar showed me the sights of this former Hungarian city where many Kings were crowned, and then accompanied me with his resolute third (or perhaps fourth) wife, Lona, to the train station. Both of them supported me in my intention to begin a new life in freedom.

Back in Prague I had to get an extension for my visitor's permit because the next flight to Vienna I was able to get did not leave until Monday 4 February. But the Hungarian Embassy was not prepared to engage in talks with such unreliable subjects as journalists and sent me to the Czech aliens police. There I was told that my transit visa was valid only for Warsaw, not Vienna. They advised me to return to Budapest first, and from there go on to Vienna.

At that point I remembered a bitter joke I had been told in Warsaw: the Hungarians in October 1956 had behaved like Poles, the Poles like Czechs, and the Czechs like swine.

During my free time in Prague the Czech girlfriend of a Budapest acquaintance took me to see the Hradcin and the Old Town. She was very pessimistic and told me that her country would gain its freedom only after the other Eastern bloc countries had won theirs and that the police no longer had arms. The miracle in Prague eleven years later proved how meaningless and unfair such casual judgments of nations can be.

On Saturday I phoned in a report about life in Prague to my paper in order not to arouse any suspicion.

On 4 February 1957, I showed up at the airport in Prague with a new suitcase purchased in Prague and with the old one from Budapest, which did not belong to me but to friends. With a now valid Austrian visa in my Hungarian passport I passed the border and customs checkpoint without any trouble. A little more than an hour later I landed at Vienna's airport. With my ankle-length, worn-out blue winter coat and all my new hopes I cleared passport control in Vienna and took the bus into the city.

That same day my future wife arrived in Vienna from Paris by car, but that is another story.

II

Witness
to the
Cold War

11

New Beginning in Vienna

When I arrived in Vienna on that grey morning of 4 February 1957, exactly three months after the Soviet onslaught on the revolutionary government of Imre Nagy, the city was still dealing with the impact of the stream of Hungarian refugees. In November 1956, 113,810 Hungarians had made their way into Austria; in December the number of men and women fleeing their country came to 49,685, and in January 1957, after the border had been tightly sealed another 12,882 to Austria. Thereafter the numer of 'new arrivals' declined precipitously. It was no longer possible to pierce the Iron Curtain so easily. After May 1957, given the growing consolidation of the Kádár regime, only very few were able to leave.

I was one of a handful of people who from the very first day in Austria was able to live privately instead of being put into a camp or hostel. A helpful American colleague lent me money so that for four weeks I was able to take a room in a reasonably-priced hotel and devote my energies to making a new beginning in my profession. The acquaintances and contacts I had made in Warsaw proved of tremendous help. I was determined to steer clear of the Hungarian programmes of Western broadcasting services – most particularly Radio Free

Europe, which was so discredited in Hungary – and of émigré organisations. From the very outset I worked as an international journalist. But what today sounds so simple, so easy, was in fact an adventure with an unpredictable outcome.

To begin with there was the language problem. My command of English and German was adequate for everyday life but by no means good enough for a journalist. My first priority was thus to perfect these essential tools, but I did not have any definite plans or ideas. For us, coming as we did from total isolation, everything in Vienna was so new, so exciting, in many ways beyond comprehension. Years later my Austrian friends would occasionally accuse me of still idealising Austria and the Austrians. For us – especially those of Jewish descent who rather than being hounded out of this city were now being received with open arms – Vienna was not only a show-case of the West but above all a beacon of freedom, tolerance and humaneness.

Austria's treatment of the Hungarian refugees imposed an obligation on us when Austria ran into difficulties in 1986, the year of the 'Waldheim syndrome' to express gratitude on behalf of the hundreds of thousands to whom a helping hand had been extended. In 1986, on the the thirtieth anniversary of the Hungarian Revolution, eight of us, writers, journalists and scientists recalled our experiences in the autumn and winter of 1956. This was the time of the 'Waldheim Affair' when Austria was going through its own difficulties and we felt moved to express our gratitude to our new country, whose people had always been helpful, frindly and anything but xenophobic towards us. The great Austrian writer Heimito von Doderer said it all when he told a young author, 'You're a Hungarian and therefore an Austrian'.

Austria's sympathetic treatment of the Hungarian refugees was a major factor in the decision of about 15,000 of them to remain in Austria rather than move elsewhere. A young journalist said that after his experience under a dictatorship he was allergic to the endless questions foreign consulates ask, while the only thing the official at Austria's agency in charge of foreigners asked him was whether he had eaten, whether he knew where he was going to spend the night, and whether he had been given the identification card that would allow him to ride the street-car free.

Without a doubt the Hungarian Revolution, and its suppression by the Soviets, also marked a political and psychological turning point in Austria's postwar history. That a country after seven years 'Anschluss' to the German Reich and war, after almost twelve years of occupation, and so soon after the departure of the last foreign troops welcomed the Hungarian refugees so openly, fearlessly and warmly helped shape an entire new generation and contributed substantially to the self-esteem of the Austrian Second Republic. What Austria did was unique, beginning with the improvised camps and the spontaneous collection drives to mobilising world opinion.

Perhaps driven by guilt at their abject failure during those crucial November days, many Western countries, from Switzerland to the United States and Canada, opened their borders to admit refugees. By the end of 1956, almost 100,000 refugees had left Austria, and by the end of 1957 almost all who wanted to emigrate had left, a total of 157,000. A mere 8,109 returned to Hungary.

I too was soon faced with a decision, whether or not to emigrate, not once but twice. In both cases the initiative came from the outside. In March, relatives living in Toronto offered me the chance of a fresh start in Canada. They sent me a letter of sponsorship and even a plane ticket. Dutifully but without much enthusiasm I went to the Canadian Consulate. I told them candidly about my turbulent past and my membership of the Communist Party. Quite a number of refugees had been returned to Vienna from the United States and Canada because they had attempted to clean up their records by concealing past Communist affiliations. I did not want to embellish my record, let alone keep secret what I had done or the mistakes I had made. In June 1957 I was informed by the Consulate that I did not meet the Canadian requirements for immigration.

Some time later I had a similar experience with the United States. In this instance the push came from the American press attaché, who had edited a book about Hungary. Two of its chapters (on the media, youth movements, etc), about one-sixth of the text, had come from me. The editor put my name on a preferential immigration list, but the unvarnished story of my past worked even more quickly with the Americans than with the Canadians.

The world press was still interested in Hungary, and so all I had to do was listen every hour to the Hungarian news broadcasts and pass on news about what was going on in Hungary to the correspondents of the *New York Times*, the *United Press*, and the London *Times* to make enough money to keep me afloat.

From my first day in Vienna I tried to work in two languages, English and German. In my contacts with foreign correspondents English was essential. Since I accepted all assignments, from interviews with foreign correspondents to feature articles I made enough money that summer to buy a used car with 100,000 kilometers on the tachometer.

And so on 4 October 1957, the day the first Soviet Sputnik was launched, scaring the West, my friend Stephan Vajda and I embarked on my first foreign trip. We went first to Munich where we tried (unsuccessfully) to sell some short stories and articles about the East to magazines, and then to Switzerland and across the Simplon Pass to Italy. Near Nervi, with tears in my eyes, I saw the sea for the first time in my life.

A Czech colleague at the UPI news agency could not understand our behaviour. 'These Hungarians,' he said to an Austrian editor. 'They have no permanent job, no citizenship, no insurance, and the first thing they do is to buy a car and take a quick trip to Germany and Italy. One can see they're not serious people.'

The birth of György Hollo, Arpad Becs and Paul Landy

At that time in Vienna I lived from day to day. Having escaped the deadly grip of both the brown and red dictatorships and having made the final break with the world of lies, I felt that this unfamiliar state of suspense was the quintessence of freedom.

I did not publish a single word in Hungarian during this time. Through the contacts I had made in Warsaw many doors were opened to me in Vienna. Austria's leading daily, *Die Presse*, published articles by me under the pen name György Hollo. Why, one might ask, did I choose a Hungarian pseudonym rather than a less conspicuous German one? I now no longer know the reason. Possibly both I and the paper wanted to emphasise the special competence (i.e. the Hungarian background) of the paper's new Hungary and Eastern Europe expert. At any rate the revealing pseudonym gave many an agent for the Hungarian secret service something to do as they tried to unmasked this Hollo. It did not take long but that did not prevent Hollo (Hungarian for raven) from being quoted back in Hungary either with or more frequently without attribution, a practice not exactly unknown in journalistic circles throughout the world.

The birth of Arpad Becs, my second identity, took place in the spring of 1958, when the editor of *Zukunft* (*Future*), the theoretical monthly of Austria's Socialist Party, commissioned some essays about the political and economic situation in Eastern Europe. It was his suggestion to choose the pseudonym Arpad Becs (Becs is the Hungarian name of Vienna).

Yet by far the most significant pseudonym was Paul Landy. Under that name I was a regular contributor to *Heute* (*Today*) from 1959 to 1961. *Heute* was a weekly with close links to the Socialist Party (SP) but in many respects an unorthodox, liberal paper whose financial backing was eventually withdrawn by the dogmatic leftists in the SP executive. At that time articles and reports by Paul Landy were also beginning to appear in the German daily *Die Welt* of Hamburg.

My meeting with John MacCormac, the Vienna bureau chief of the *New York Times*, played a vital role in the birth of 'Paul Landy' and in my professional career as an English-language foreign correspondent and political commentator. MacCormac had been stationed in Vienna since the end of the war. His office and living quarters occupied two floors of a building close to Vienna's inner city. Back then *New York Times* correspondents still lived in great style, and not only as far as office and housing were concerned. In addition to a cook, maid and a chauffeur-driven car, Mac Cormac also had special assistants versed in Hungarian and Czech affairs. Yet with all these perks he was an extremely modest and sensitive man. A few days after my arrival in Vienna he invited me for lunch. We had a long talk and I made no secret about my pessimistic view of the Hungarian situation. My imperfect English did not stop Mac Cormac from hiring me as a expert on Hungary for his Vienna office at a very respectable monthly retainer. Until his sudden death in the summer of 1958 he was a trusted friend and adviser. He gave me books and manuals by top *Times* writers about English-style journalism, about how to write leads and about sentence structure and style. He taught me how to differentiate between what is important and what is not. MacCormac was a correspondent of the old school whose devotion to his work, his intimate familiarity with his subject matter and his ceaseless pursuit of the greatest possible objectivity set him apart from many of his colleagues.

In the meantime I had also been hired by the UPI as a Hungarian specialist. Aside from supplying me with such vital tools as telephone, telex, newspapers and typewriters, my early instructors in daily journalism, the Pulitzer Prize winner and chief correspondent, Russell Jones, and his colleagues showed me how 100 lines could be cut to 50 without curtailing information and content, how the gist of a report can be incorporated into the lead sentence so concisely that both the editor and hurried readers would not necessarily have to read the entire article.

My contacts to the highly-regarded political bimonthly *Problems of Communism* were probably established through MacCormac. At any rate, my long article 'Hungary Since the Revolution' under the pseudonym Paul Landy appeared in the September-October 1957 issue. In subsequent years the American bimonthly published six more Landy articles on a variety of topics, among them the social-economic roots of corruption and the effects of Yugoslav economic reforms.

My contribution to this journal served as a valuable visiting card. Thus, beginning in 1959, I was able to place a number of articles in the *Birmingham Post*, in the *Economist*, and some other papers. In addition, between 1958 and 1962 I wrote about 60 articles for the US Information Agency (USIA), the publisher of *Problems of Communism*. These Paul Landy articles were distributed worldwide and reprinted in numerous European, Asian and Latin-American papers, generally without mention of the USIA.

I continued to live in different worlds simultaneously. After so many years of isolation and my consequent ignorance of what had been going on in the world I was determined to catch up, to fill the gaps in my knowledge of post-1945 history and the turbulent events in world Communism as quickly as possible. The collected works of George Orwell and Arthur Koestler, Franz Borkenau and Manes Sperber, but also of Otto Bauer and Karl Renner, Isaac Deutscher and John Gunther, as well as many other books and memoirs became required reading for me. I wasted a great deal of time preparing book projects and corresponding with countless periodicals and newspapers. I even found the time to read Leon Trotsky. After all I had been arrested as a fervent disciple of his, so I might as well see what he had to say. I concluded he had not been worth all that grief.

The *Financial Times* as flagship

The turning point in my career came on a visit to London. After a brief conversation in the foyer of Bracken House, that conspicous red brick building then housing the *Financial Times* near St Paul's Cathedral, the foreign news editor wrote asking me to send him some reports about Austria. The first of these appeared on 4 May 1960, the last one almost 23 years later. Those first articles about Austria's economic recovery and steel production were signed 'By a correspondent'. The third article about the trade prospects between Austria and Great Britain, already carried the by-line 'By our own correspondent'.

The paper became my primer for learning economic terminology in English. I began to clip and file their reports and surveys on sectors such as the paper or chemical industry, breweries, oil refineries and pipe-lines. I filled notebooks with frequently used or difficult technical terms.

At the outset of my work for the *FT* I had my first major interview with Bruno Kreisky, the then Austrian Foreign Minister, about the role of the neutral members of the European Free Trade Association (EFTA), a topic which dominated Austrian foreign and domestic policy for years.

The *FT* became the most important factor in my professional career. I was lucky insofar as my association with it coincided with its internationalisation and later Europeanization. Numerous brief reports and an increasing number of longer articles appeared under the by-line 'Our correspondent in Vienna'. Before 1 June 1970, the paper did not carry any signed contributions, a practice still followed by the *Economist*. Beginning in 1961 I also began to write about Hungary and Yugoslavia, and occasionally about Czechoslovakia and Poland as well. In addition there were the regular special surveys of three to five pages compiled and written largely by me about Austria's economy and politics, and later also about particular points of interest like the city of Vienna, foreign trade, investments and the capital market.

Relatively early in my link to the *FT* I had found out that in Vienna the paper was available only in the reading room of the British Council; not even in the big newspaper kiosks in the centre of the city was it on sale. And so I suggested to London that they ought to do something about marketing in Vienna. When I visited the editorial office Peter Galliner, the head of foreign publicity and advertising asked to see me. He had fled Germany during the Hitler years and his first job with the *FT* was as its librarian. Promoted to the post of foreign manager, Galliner was eminently successful. He was aston-ished that a correspondent would come up with marketing ideas, and after a lengthy conversation wanted to hire me on the spot as his deputy. But I was interested in politics and contemporary history, not in business, so I let it pass.

The Editor of the *FT*, Sir Gordon Newton, was one of the most important and distinguished names in the British press world. A man with an eye for talent, he hired many gifted university graduates and turned them into first-rate journalists for the *FT*. On my second London visit he asked to see me. After polite introductory words I fell silent, and suddenly this introverted, shy man began to talk with great animation about Austrian ski resorts. It was a topic to which I, not being a skier, had absolutely nothing to add. I feigned interest but with no evident success. Sir Gordon soon ended our talk, embarrassed but friendly. I had to discuss the matter of my salary with the equally embarrassed foreign editor, who told me with a deep sigh that all foreign correspondents when they came to London only wanted to talk about higher fees.

My work for the *FT* in the small world of Austrian politics and media did not go unnoticed in other circles. Many years later I came upon the Hungarian Interior Ministry's bizarre *curriculum vitae* of me. It stated among other things that my wife was co-owner of the *FT* and that my association with 'her' paper was her doing. When we got to read this report 30 years later my wife and I were highly amused, and in part regretted the inaccuracy. It would have been nice for my wife to have owned the *FT*.

My marriage indirectly was in fact due to the contacts I had made in Warsaw. Through the *Sunday Times* correspondent Anthony Terry, for whom I had worked for two years as a consultant, I met Boris Kidel, the correspondent of the London *News Chronicle* at a party with his wife, Margaret Pollock. Later we accidentally met again, and continued to meet and fell in love. After her divorce we got married in Vienna in July 1962. The witnesses at our wedding were Eric Bourne, the correspondent of the *Christian Science Monitor*, and Ernst Halperin, the former correspondent of the *Neue Zürcher Zeitung*. During the marriage ceremony in the local town hall Halperin, who was sitting behind me, whispered in my ear, 'Please note under whose portrait you're getting married'. In fact the brief ceremony was taking place under the watchful though not unfriendly eyes of Mayor Karl Lueger, the notorious anti-semitic Viennese politician at the turn of the century, who however qualified his antsemitism with the classic remark, 'It's up to me to decide who is a Jew'.

Margaret may not have been co-owner of the FT, nor was she instrumental in getting me my job there, but certainly without her quiet help, noble restraint and inner strength I with my quick temper, and facing the difficulties of handling a new world, would have been completely at sea without her.

Meanwhile 'Paul Landy' continued to remain active, while the name of the journalist Paul Lendvai never appeared anywhere. I wrote under the name of Landy even for the London economic weekly *Statist*, since 1878 essential source for stock market professionals and investors. And when my freind Ernst Halperin left Vienna for an academic post in Boston, I inherited from him the Zurich daily *Die TAT*, which took on Paul Landy as its Austrian and Eastern European correspondent.

The power of striptease

Newspaper people are not interested only, and often not even primarily in money but in reputation and recognition. Why did I have to put myself through all these hoops of anonymity? Why these pseudonyms if key people already knew who was hiding under these pen names?

Despite my growing professional success and my personal happiness in the West I was suffering from guilt about my parents. After every sad letter from Budapest I reproached myself. I wanted to do everything in my power to avoid more problems for them. Hence my desperate effort to hide behind all these pseudonyms. Moreover, I wanted to help them financially. In 1958 the regime for the second time had had my father's name deleted from the list of licensed lawyers and forced him into retirement. What was at issue was not only the fact that he now received only a very small monthly pension, about a quarter of the average wage at the time. Worse was the fact that going in and out of the apartment he had to pass the office of the legal co-operative he had helped found. It was a real psychological burden for him. In 1960 the Austrian Ministry of the Interior granted my parents immigration visas and permits to settle in Vienna. Now all that was needed were exit visas; but because their son had been declared a non-person, these were refused. The attack on me by V.P. in December 1960 was an unequivocal warning bell. Obviously the unmasking of György Hollo and Paul Landy showed that the use of cover names not only did my parents no good but made me still more suspect.

My parents were an uneven pair as regards, age, education, and temperament. But as their only child I was the centre of their universe. Shortly after being castigated by name in *Nepszabadsag*, the mailman brought them their fifth and sixth negative response to their application to emigrate. A few days later, on 8 February 1961, my father died of a broken heart. I could not even dream of going to Budapest for his funeral.

My mother was left alone. Her seventh and eighth appeals were also turned down. That she was summoned to the Ministry of the Interior in August 1962 and told officially and in writing that her son had been imprisoned unjustly and therefore was not to be discriminated against was almost a mockery of a widow whose nerves could not cope with reality.

Then an unexpected, even absurd, series of events occured. The chief protagonist of this tale was Gyula Ortutay, an ethnologist, former Minister of Culture and rector of Budapest University. The then

52-year-old man was an expert in the art of survival. During the war he was considered an anti-fascist; after 1945 he became a member of the executive of the Smallholders Party, and later a prominent fellow-traveller. I had never met him in Hungary but knew that after the quelling of the Revolution he became Secretary General of the so-called People's Front and member of the Presidential Council.

In September 1962 I was surprised to get a call from an old Hungarian colleague. He was in Vienna on some official business, escorting Ortutay, and he wanted to talk to me. After referring to a mutual friend, he added that what he had to tell me might prove of interest to me. We met in a cafe, and before saying anything he asked me to be discreet about our meeting. He then told me the reason for his call: 'I've been working with Tutus (the nickname by which Ortutay was generally known) as press chief of the Popular Front, and he trusts me completely. He has a secret yen, and he doesn't want the Embassy to hear about it. He would like nothing more than to see a striptease show.' He was almost whispering now.

'So? What do his secret yens have to do with me? I lead a perfectly happy life although I've never been to a striptease bar,' I answered rather dismissively.

'Don't you understand? He's got no money for outings like these, he's married, and I hinted that maybe you might be able to help.' And then he let the cat out of the bag. 'I know that you're trying to get the papers for your mother's emigration. Tutus is a gentleman, and if he gives you his word it's practically a done deal. He is very important for the Party. Believe me, Ortutay can do a lot...'

Sceptical and uncertain I promised to call him that evening. I told my wife about this request; she thought the whole thing was very fishy and insisted on being present when we met the next time. I made a date with my colleague to meet him next evening at a cafe in the centre of the city. When my wife and I arrived the Hungarians were already there. Not only Ortutay and his press spokesman were present but also three other men, none of whom I knew. One was the driver, the second the secretary and the third his bodyguard. Ortutay greeted us warmly and chatted with my wife in English while I whispered to my old friend that I couldn't possibly take half a soccer team along to such an expensive place. He in turn whispered to me not to be so petty, that Tutus had promised to get my mother out, that I should trust him. He was reliable.

Half an hour later the seven of us set out for what I had been told was the most daring striptease performance in town. The girls were top-notch professionals with beautiful bodies. Ortutay and the other men were spellbound, staring at the stage. Meanwhile I was adding up the number of empty champagne bottles. The bill was astronomical for someone in my position. We left the bar after midnight. Ortutay and his companions were in high spirits. I kept looking over to my wife. Ortutay assured me when we were saying good-bye that he wouldn't forget 'my mother's case'. My wife said to me in a low voice and with great self-restraint, 'Now we've got to wait to see whether we've really won the lottery with this man'.

Two months later my mother called me up, and choking back her tears said, 'Imagine, just now the mailman delivered a letter from the passport section stating that I can come and pick up my travel pass. Not an emigration document but an ordinary tourist pass. What should we do now?'

'Nothing,' I answered. 'You go there to pick up your pass and I'll take care of the rest. The main thing is that you can finally come.'

Shortly before Christmas 1962 my mother arrived in Vienna. After being separated for six years we fell into each other's arms. The tab for the striptease was settled. Ortutay had kept his promise.

My mother lived peacefully and happily in Vienna. She was granted Austrian citizenship and received reparation payments from Germany. As long as she was physically able to she periodically visited her sister Relly in Tel Aviv, and after becoming an Austrian citizen relatives in Budapest as well. She made new friends in Austria and died at the age of 87 in Vienna after suffering a stroke.

But my story about Ortutay is not over. About a year-and-half later his press secretary called me up again. 'We're attending a scientific conference at the Hofburg Palace and we'll be here until the weekend. Tutus still remembers the lovely evening you organised for us. What do you say, can we do it again?' I agreed without hesitation because I knew that he could help me in an important matter. I was relieved to hear that this time the 'delegation' consisted of only three people, and also my wife agreed to let me go by myself.

This time I selected a bigger nightclub where, according the papers, the striptease was combined with a trained horse. Tutus was again enthusiastic and got very excited when one of the strippers came very close to him. In the intermission I broached my request. Could he help me normalise my relationship to Hungary so that I could be granted a visa as a newsman. After all, János Kádár had embarked upon a new course under the slogan 'Those who are not against us are with us'. I had already been to Poland, Yugoslavia, Czechoslovakia and even

East Germany. Was it not time for me to visit Hungary? Ortutay did not seem averse. A few months later my visa application was approved.

The Ortutay case was proof that a talented operator can convert a series of dodging and feinting into a successful strategy for survival. His very complicity with injustice on the highest level gave him special elbow room. Yet no dyed-in-the-wool Communist dignitary would have dared to intervene on behalf of a mother of an 'enemy of the state'. But Ortutay, the success-oriented showcase, was able to out-manoeuvre the apparatus by using his direct connection to the Party leader. He was acting on his own and was proud of his success. Nonetheless we had to keep the story secret. That the matter was a purely personal initiative on the part of Ortutay was made evident by the circumstances surrounding it: I was never contacted by a third party or asked for co-operation. However Ortutay's penchant for passion eventually got the better of his survival skills when he lost his grip on power and influence following a widely known affair with a much younger TV announcer.

In the early sixties Kádár and his most sophisticated media and cultural advisers continued to polish the facade and the packaging of the unchanged one-party system. Between 1962 and 1965, that is still before the major economic reforms, the regime went out of its way to polish up its image in the world. It issued exit permits to people like the recently released writer Tibor Déry, and tried to curry favour with famous non-Communist writers like Gyula Illyés and László Németh. Even some of the 'October refugees' were allowed back. Ortutay's initiatives fitted into this framework. They could succeed because they were undertaken at a propitious time.

When my mother took up residence in Vienna I was gradually able to get rid of my pen-names and use my true identity. By the end of 1963 neither the name Hollo nor Landy were to be found in *Die TAT*, the *Presse*, or in the *Statist*. The feeling that my mother was finally safely with me in Vienna and that during my planned visits to the so-called 'Socialist world' I could not be blackmailed was truly liberating.

However, in my travel euphoria during the early sixties I forgot that in the Eastern bloc countries refugees or émigrés, even though citizens of other countries, were still looked on as natives so long as they had not been specifically 'released' from their original citizenships. I ignored or at least underestimated this potential danger. Ironically, when I did finally get round to the petitioning, the Hungarian Presidential Council granted my request to rescind my Hungarian citizenship on 19 March 1965. But I was not informed of their ruling until seven years later. They allegedly did not have my address!

12

New Relations
with the East

I first returned to Hungary in March 1964, seven years after my
defection. It coincided with the political thaw under a consolidated
Kádár regime which was embarking on a cautious economic reform
course.

First return to Budapest

The convention of the Patriotic People's Front, that reinvigorated
transmission belt between the ruling party and the non-Communist or
anti-Communist population was in full swing. Its clever managers had
made sure that during the two days of discussions representatives
from all spheres of public life, from Church dignitaries to renowned
scientists, from the Party leader Kádár to the aged composer Zoltán
Kodály, were given the floor. Kádár's slogan, 'Those who are not
against us are with us,' provided the theme for the show and the sem-
blance of a 'Socialist national unity'.

Even though Kádár was the First Secretary of the Central
Committee of the Hungarian Socialist Workers Party and Chairman
of the 'Revolutionary Workers and Peasant Government', the official
name of the regime installed by the Soviets on 4 November 1956, this
strong man of the reconstituted government was listed only as a guest

speaker. The initially polite attention of the thousand or so delegates soon gave way to alert interest. The speaker departed repeatedly from his prepared text; in place of shop-worn political jargon he used normal language with which everybody could identify. Time and again referring to the breach with the past. Kádár chatted, remonstrated, ridiculed and told anecdotes. Judging by his genuine hold on the convention, this 51-year-old former metal worker knew exactly how to appeal to his audience.

Kádár basically had remained a 'centrist', a man of compromise. A convinced Communist and excellent power-broker, he was a man to whom the rigid dogmatism of Rákosi was as unpalatable as the revolutionary radicalism of the Nagy followers who – 'an unforgivable sin' – during those fateful October days were ready to cede the Party's monopoly of power. A pragmatist who never ignored the complicated interrelation between flexible tactics and unchanging strategic goals, Kádár was a careful reformer who believed in the primacy of the Party yet at the same time knew that it could not operate in a political desert.

The human factor in politics may be incomprehensible, even unpredictable, but without understanding it all historical perspectives are incomplete. Would Hungary's fate have been the same if in November 1956 the Soviets (largely in response to Yugoslav pressure) had not elevated János Kádár to head the Party and Government? Or what would have been the fate of Russia (and Eastern Europe) if the Soviet Central Committee Secretary Fyodor Kulakov had not died suddenly in 1978 and been replaced by the provincial functionary Mikhail Gorbachev who was summoned from Stavropol? The role of accident and of personalities even under bureaucratic single-party rule turned out to be extraordinarily important despite the Soviet hegemony in a small country like Hungary.

From the very outset I did not consider Kádár either the mere agent of Moscow or the liberal father-figure of his country. In fact he was both.

I became involuntarily entangled in the contradictions of the Kádár system sooner than expected. In my reporting I had described the tangible change in Hungary from a quest for freedom to the pursuit of status symbols, the worship of the Golden Calf, the loosening of university admissions requirements, the precedence of professional qualifications over Party membership for positions in the economy and administration, the creation of a more tolerable atmosphere within enterprises and the possibility that a technician could earn some extra money and buy a refrigerator or possibly even take a trip abroad instead of spending his free time at Party courses learning by heart Lenin quotations. And I also stressed the psychologically extremely important possibility of trips to the West. In 1954, 3,040 Hungarians (functionaries, bureaucrats and sportsmen), but a mere 95 private individuals, were allowed to visit a Western country. In 1958 this figure rose to 21,000, in 1962 to 65,000, and in 1963 to more than 120,000. True it was freedom subject to recall, but that trips to the West became at all possible for all those who could afford them provided that one wasn't among the 280,000 unreliable people on whom the Interior Ministry still possessed 'incriminating statements' in 1960. But I always stressed that the Communist system had not undergone any basic changes.

But reporting on Hungary and Eastern Europe had its downside for an émigré. In the eyes of some, both on the left and right, I was too 'naive' and sometimes it was even whispered too 'Communist-friendly' because I always wanted to depict the extent of the changes within the different Communist countries. Or, like so many of my Western colleagues, I became the 'handmaiden of imperialism', of 'world Zionism' or 'German revanchism'.

The roots of this hostility lay, as was to be expected, in my original homeland.

Encounters with the Stasi and other services

In the spring of 1966 I wanted to go to Hungary again. Since I had been to the country five times during the previous two years I considered my request for an entry permit routine. But my application was rejected by the Hungarian consulate. No explanations.

It was only 25 years later that I discovered why. I met Joachim Gauck, who had been placed in charge of Stasi files by the German Government, at a conference in Berlin in autumn 1992. Gauck, a former pastor, who with the help of about 3,000 assistants was sifting through six million files and 35.6 million index cards, described the organisation and work of the invisible Stasi network with its 90,000 regular employees and its 173,000 so-called 'informal assistants', in other words informers and spies.

Since I wanted to find out about the internal workings of the Stasi and what their archives had about me, I asked Gauck for access to my files. We corresponded, and on the way to another conference in Bonn I made the detour to Berlin to spend a few hours in the former Stasi building. A friendly woman in charge of my case brought me to a reading room and handed me two slim files. About 20 people were sitting at separate small tables, in front of some mountains of files. At the exit sat an official posted there to make sure that no-one took any papers out of the room. She handed out an envelope containing pencils as well as a brief description of the organisation of the Ministry for State Security, and a glossary of abbreviations and file code. The relatively small room was oppressively still. It was in this room and two other reading rooms that many of the almost four million applicants first became aware of the actual extent of their surveillance by friends, neighbours or, as in one famous case, a spouse.

The first of my secret files in the Central Archive (3508/72) of the Ministry for State Security contained a handwritten list of the contents covering 16 pages. I was astonished to see that the very first document was a personal telegram (No 1007) to Erich Mielke, the Minister for State Security, of 21 October 1965, from Budapest. The then Hungarian Minister of the Interior, András Benkei, transmitted information about me, about my former Party membership, my defection in 1957, and described my activity as follows:

At this time he is working for the English paper *Financial Times*, the Austrian paper *Die Presse*, and the Swiss *Die TAT*. Lendvai is a qualified journalist. Within a short period of time he became an authority. He is regarded as the best specialist on questions of the Socialist countries of East Europe. In *Die Presse* and other Western papers he published tendentiously hostile articles about the Socialist countries, particularly Hungary. These articles initially appeared under a cover name but now are published under his own name. In content they differ not at all from other articles in the Western press. He writes constantly about the 'split' in the Socialist camp, about the 'disintegration' of the Council for Mutual Economic Aid, about 'national-Communist developments' as well as about contradictions in the Party. Up to now L. has relied on his past experience. But in order to remain a good journalistic expert, it is necessary for him regularly to visit the Socialist countries of Eastern Europe. In consideration of the above information I ask you, esteemed Comrade Minister, to refuse Lendvai an entry permit to your country.

With 'Socialist greetings' Benkei asked the chief of the Stasi to inform him of his decision 'on this matter'.

The offices of the GDR thereupon began to work feverishly, issuing an order for a 'search' of the files of their overblown apparatus. On 3 November a certain Col. Damm, Department X, informed his boss, the acting Minister Gen. Marcus Wolf, that I had been 'registered' by the main Department of Intelligence, and asked with reference to the request of the Hungarian security organisations for 'appropriate measures'. But not until 30 November 1965 did the acting head of Department VII transmit the results of his search to Col. Damm of Department X, which, as was to be expected, said that his people on the basis of the existing materials agreed with the Hungarian security offices about their assessment of me.

Two days later Minister Mielke sent a telegram to his Hungarian colleague thanking him for the information, confirmed the common views held about 'the character of Lendvai', added that I, as Central European Correspondent of the *FT* had visited East Germany in November 1963, and finally reassured Benkei that I would not receive any more entry permits to the GDR.

The obvious aim of these activities was to destroy me professionally. That is probably why the Polish and Czech governments also rejected my visa applications in the second half of the sixties. Once I was turned back without explanation at the Czech-Austrian border when I wanted to use a so-called day visa for visiting my uncle in Bratislava. The Poles also returned my next visa application, and because they alleged that I neglected to affix stamps to my request I even had to pay a hefty sum at the post office.

I learned from my visits to Bulgaria that despite the obvious links between the individual East bloc countries not everything functioned as planned. In the sixties I often visited Bulgaria, once accompanying Foreign Minister Bruno Kreisky. Todor Zhivkov, the Party chief, even granted our small group of Austrian journalists an interview, after the failure of a plot against him. In fact, however, I still visited Bulgaria without any difficulties in 1966-67, wrote a series of articles about the country, and even met with Foreign Minister Iwan Bashev, a capable man who some years later died after a mysterious accident.

But even in Bulgaria my file eventually caught up with me when in 1973 I accompanied the Austrian Foreign Minister (and later President) Rudolf Kirchschläger to Sofia. In Bulgaria we were guests of the Foreign Ministry. We journalists lived in the Hotel Balkan built in the Soviet style of the fifties.

At 9am on the day after our arrival I was not even fully dressed when two security officials in plain clothes appeared in my hotel room. 'You're coming with us,' they declared. I was nonplussed. Not even in Stalin's Soviet Union would they have dared arrest a guest accompanying a foreign statesman. I had to act without delay. To the utter astonishment of the leaden-footed secret policemen I picked up the phone and called the residence of the Foreign Minister where the official talks had just started. The first person I reached there was a confused Bulgarian photo reporter. He immediately grasped the seriousness of the situation and promptly handed the receiver to a Bulgarian diplomat. I indignantly told him what was going on and handed the phone to one of the policemen. There followed a lengthy conversation between the ranking policeman and the officials on the other end of the line. Within minutes the acting chief of protocol of the Foreign Office arrived in my room out of breath. He persuaded the two visitors after a brief exchange of words to leave my room. A few minutes later he reappeared and said that he was sorry, that there must have been a 'misunderstanding'.

Even before we met Kirchschläger for lunch the embarrassed hosts rushed to placate the Foreign Minister: 'They certainly had not wanted to arrest the journalist Lendvai, only to expel him from the country'. I had apparently been on a blacklist for years but the police had not been notified of my arrival in advance.

Nationalism and anti-semitism under Communist rule

I was not one of those who after their flight to the West wanted to shed their entire past by indulging in a one-track, undifferentiated, even blind anti-Communism, a sweeping rejection of Communist reform or Socialist experiments. Of course I was and still am closely tied to the sad history of contemporary Hungary, including the Nazi death-marches and Communist prisons and camps, the cycle of unspeakable degradation and belated rehabilitations. Still the Kádár era, for all its intellectual and political appeal and its openness to economic experimentation, could not have been compared with Yugoslavia in its quest for new approaches within a Communist or Socialist framework to resolve its ethnic social and political problems.

The Yugoslav partisans were, except in the special case of Albania, the only movement (despite the bloody trail left by the settling of old accounts in Croatia and Slovenia, in Vojvodina and Kosovo) that offered resistance to the Axis powers and their vassals and who came to power on their own. The Yugoslav Communists were the only ones who stood up to Stalin and his enormous power and proved that it was possible to remain a Communist without becoming the obedient servant of a foreign power. Therein lay the true dynamic of the Titoist heresy.

Against this background the Titoist experiments with workers' councils, factory self-management, and administrative decentralisation gained a dynamism of its own. As the symbol of the 'third way' these experiments attracted people far beyond the borders of Eastern Europe. In addition, Yugoslavia's foreign policy of non-alignment seemed to stand for something excitingly new. But in fact the Yugoslavia, which for decades had helped shape the attitude of many Western politicians and diplomats, never really existed.

At the same time Yugoslavia was the pivotal country in a region which for a variety of reasons moved into the foreground of American and European geopolitical thinking. Yugoslavia's three Balkan neighbours went their own way. Bulgaria, the great loser of all the Balkan wars, for historical and nationalistic reasons was the ward of Russia and the Soviet Union, yet at the same time remained a threat. In the sixties we experienced the 'Romanian miracle', the strange transition of a silent satellite to a national Communist regime which at first skillfully managed to exploit the Moscow-Peking conflict to enlarge its own room for manoeuver. Then there was little Albania, which went from Yugoslav satellite to Soviet client state and then managed during that time to rid itself of Soviet tutelage as well. It was a special case. For historical reasons the Albanians always interested me. When I was a young child I was fascinated by the pompous wedding of Countess Geraldine Apponyi and the Albanian King Zog. The loneliness of the Albanians, who were as isolated an ethnic group as the Hungarians, and their language, which, unrelated to others, sounds as exotic to the ears of other peoples as Hungarian, stirred my imagination.

On many journeys to Yugoslavia, at Party congresses and in conversations with members of the party bureaucracy and the intelligentsia I could follow the national stirrings and the protagonists of emancipation from Soviet hegemony. The emerging co-operation between Belgrade and Bucharest on the one hand, and the Soviet attempts at intimidation on the other, formed the international framework within which the small and big foreign policy manoeuvers were taking place. Almost simultaneously the Western European states became engaged in an active Eastern Europe policy. French foreign policy under de Gaulle was great on rhetoric, but the many trips of Foreign Minister Couve de Murville yielded no tangible results in Eastern and Southeastern Europe. Things however were entirely different with the Italians and Japanese, the Germans and Austrians, whose companies concluded very successful business deals.

The relationships and conflicts between these states, and the fate of the large Hungarian minorities in Romania and Yugoslavia; the obvious historic, cultural and economic points of contact with Greece as well as modern Turkey as the heir of the Ottoman Empire; and finally the great burning issues surrounding Transylvania and Macedonia, Kosovo and Sandzhak in southern Serbia, Bessarabia and Bucovina between Romania and the Soviets provided material for endless reflection and studies.

But it was the phenomenon of nationalism in its many facets which overshadowed everything and in the final analysis created an entirely new situation. Again and again I learned that the national issue represented a stronger force than ideology when the two clashed.

But this was not a lesson I had yet fully absorbed in the 1960s. The fact remains that I, as so many other observers, overestimated the chances of survival of the Titoist system, its 'unity in diversity'. And I was too optimistic at the time about Romania's journey from national emancipation to democratic reforms.

1968 was the year of youth rebellion from Paris to Berlin to America. The so-called '68 generation today runs the politics, economy and media of Western Europe. Developments in Eastern Europe sadly took a different course. While exuberant protest in the West led to real change, in the East the politics of tanks was able to destroy the 'Socialism with a human face' which the Czech reformers were striving for.

At the same time Wladyslaw Gomulka's regime in Poland not only disappointed the hopes invested in him in October 1956, but also began to indulge in the politics of anti-semitism. In the guise of 'anti-Zionism' Gomulka launched his campaign after the Six Day War of June 1967. It reached its peak between March and September 1968. The official version spoke of a 'dangerous, well-staged conspiracy' and accused 'Zionist elements' of having launched 'an open attack on the social order and its leaders in Poland'. 'Purge the Party of Zionists' was the slogan. The regime used the Jews as whipping boys to distract the people from shortages and from its own failures. The fact that in Poland Hitler's war and his machinery of extermination had wiped out three million Jews did not deter the Communist rulers from using anti-semitism as a political weapon against a handful of Jews who were left in Poland. Playing the anti-semitic card in Poland was always likely to pay off and win popularity.

General Wojciech Jaruzelski, the then Minister of Defence and 20 years later the country's president, wrote in his memoirs: 'I personally saw this period as one of the most dishonourable in our history. This period has left me with a feeling of profound disgust. And I also regret not having taken a firm enough position.' In this overheated atmosphere about 20,000 Jews, 'half Jews' and 'quarter Jews', frequently with their non-Jewish spouses, were ousted from leading positions and driven out of the country. I met many outstanding intellectuals and artists, former functionaries and civil servants in Vienna on their way to the United States and other Western countries as well as Israel. The sight of this latest exodus from Eastern Europe moved me to write a book on the role of Jews in the Communist movement from the October Revolution to the present. With the title *Antisemitism Without Jews*, the American, British and French editions were published and well received.

In Germany on the other hand S. Fischer, the publishers, experienced 'technical problems' which caused repeated postponements in the scheduled date of publication. When I finally got a look at the German manuscript I discovered to my astonishment handwritten notes commenting on the ideological and system-based causes of Soviet-style anti-semitism with a lot of added gratuitous comments. 'And what about Vietnam?' Or 'What about the treatment of blacks in the US?' I now wondered whether the puzzling postponements were due not, as I had assumed, to internal problems. I requested a personal meeting with Peter Härtling, the writer and publisher. When I mentioned the critical marginal notes Härtling told me somewhat embarrassed but mincing no words that a number of his editors – 'One might call them our Left' – were opposed to the publication of the book because they believed that a work about anti-semitism in the Eastern bloc could disturb Bonn's striving for an understanding with the East.

Despite Härtling's assurance that the contract would be honoured, publication dates were repeatedly postponed. Finally I was told that a manuscript that had been delivered in 1969 might *possibly* be published in 1972 after a delay of three years. All this happened in Germany, in a publishing house founded by a Hungarian Jew!

In an exchange of letters with Melvin Lasky, the widely-respected Editor of *Der Monat* in Berlin and later of *Encounter* in London, Härtling then hinted that it would not be 'advisable' to publish a book about Jews and Communism since many Jews were at that very time trying to get out of the Soviet Union. It was a sensitive topic. This argument was factually and morally false, Lasky told him, adding that Jews who wanted to leave *wanted* to have their story told: 'What would the reaction have been if S. Fischer in Amsterdam in 1934 or S. Fischer in Stockholm in 1938 or S. Fischer in New York in 1942 would have refused to publish a book about the fate of Jews in Nazi Germany because Jews in Berlin, Frankfurt and Munich wanted to emigrate?' I withdrew the book from Fischer, and the German version was published a few months later by the Europa-Verlag in Vienna.

I relate this unhappy story because it mirrors the dangerous mixture of hypocrisy, ignorance and cowardice not a rarity in the Germany of the seventies and eighties.

But there is a happy postscript. The book even appeared ten years later in Polish in the form of two slim volumes, printed by an underground publisher. This Polish edition is one of my most treasured mementos.

13

Bruno Kreisky – Orator and Communicator

Thirty years of my life were linked to the 'sun king' and 'journalist chancellor' of Austria, Bruno Kreisky, at times closely, at times loosely, at times visibly, at times behind the scenes, often harmoniously, sometimes in disagreement but never at an indifferent distance. Kreisky was simply not someone about whom one could be indifferent. In the words of a friend of mine, Kreisky was 'the last splendour' of *fin-de-siecle* Vienna. He was 'like a whim of nature... something unfathomably talented – from his wealth of talent half-a-dozen politicians could live comfortably'.

Whether as Foreign Minister (1959-1966), as leader of the Opposition (1967-1970) and as Chancellor (1970-1983), Kreisky's towering intellect, political imagination, tactical skills and sensibility enabled him to recognise contemporary trends early. Coupled with his command of foreign languages, all this made him a more respected figure abroad than at home, and above all more than in his own party. Kreisky had been an active Socialist since his early youth and because of his beliefs was imprisoned first by Austria's authoritarian regime and then by the Nazis. In early 1951 he returned to Austria after 12

years in Sweden. Kreisky was of Jewish descent, hardly the best rec-
ommendation for a political career in post-war Austria.

When I met him he was not only Foreign Minister but already one
of the acting Social Democratic Party chairmen and an influential
member of the reformers' group in the party. The fact that in his youth
as an émigré he had been involved in journalism doubtless helped him
to have a special understanding of the work of foreign correspondents
in Vienna. Having been a correspondent of the London *Tribune*, occasionally of the *Die TAT* of Zürich, and writing under the pen name of
Gustáv Pichler for Swedish papers, he always cultivated his contacts
with journalists.

It must have been at the end of 1961 or in early 1962 that I
received my first invitation for lunch at his house. I was about to take
off on a combined honeymoon and working trip to South Tyrol. For
Kreisky winning the support of the press against Italy over the issue of
South Tyrol – above all the British press – was obviously important.

What was then the 'magic', the 'allure' of Kreisky, terms which
both criitics and admirers of this superb politicans were wont to use?
Kreisky's power-base lay in the written and spoken word; in his inimi-
table ability to fascinate famous journalists like Cyrus L. Sulzberger or
Marion Countess Dönhoff, then the publisher of *Die Zeit*, as well as
young tabloid and TV reporters. Kreisky may have been the only
politician in Europe who spoke with all journalists, even beginners, and
left them the impression or illusion that he was taking them seriously.
He was always open to their questions, and at eight in the morning at
breakfast would answer the questions of local reporters as readily as
of foreign correspondents.

He himself succinctly described his technique with the press:

> I told myself that if I tell the journalists nothing then I shouldn't be sur-
> prised that they don't write anything or the wrong thing. That's why I'm
> always here, that I can be called up, that I can be asked questions… If on
> the other hand I am very cryptic I shouldn't be surprised that the journalists
> don't know what to make of it. They must be told things which may seem
> unpleasant or indiscreet, but for the journalists it must have news value,
> it must make sense for them to write about it, and that's why I am a
> perhaps not always pleasant but indispensable partner.

From the very outset he was not only the architect but also the salesman of his foreign policy ideas. However one feels about his foreign
policy, whether one emphasises the positive (Eastern Europe) or the controversial (Near East) dimension, Kreisky's press and media policy was

a custom-made suit which fitted only him and no-one else. An Austrian journalist once referred to the 'anesthetising effect of the Kreisky myth' criticising the Chancellor's 'international pursuit of recognition'.

Andreas Khol, a conservative opponent of Kreisky, recognised the dividends to Austria which Kreisky's communication skills paid:

> Through the recognition which [Kreisky] received from the outside, Austrians were given confirmation by the outside world that they had achieved something: in the person of [Kreisky] they got confirmation that a country once divided and on the bottom of the heap had become a respectable member of the community of nations, for the first time since the days of the monarchy.

There was an elusive, and for outsiders often incomprehensible, mutual fascination between Kreisky and the media, a constant irritant for many backbenchers in the Opposition and for the many secret enemies in his own party, which could not be explained away with simplistic labels like showman or actor. Whatever it was it undoubtedly explains some of the domestic and foreign policy successes of this unusual politician.

The Austrian poet Hugo von Hofmannsthal once said that politics is magic, and it obeys those who are able to invoke it. Kreisky was indeed a 'magician', relentlessly active, improvising, a man often intoxicated by his own words and passion for talk, but at the same time a politician skilled in keeping a hundred things in play simultaneously.

It was difficult not to be captivated by him. Something he said to me at our first lunch – 'This is confidential', or 'You're the only one I'm telling this to' – also worked with countless other journalists. The occasional addendum 'No, you can't write this', could be figured out only by seasoned Kreiskyologists, for it was by no means certain whether he really meant it or whether he was challenging you to write it. Kreisky never had a staff of full-time or part-time press spokesmen and press secretaries. Aside from one press secretary (who was not an official press spokesman) he always relied on himself, on his ability to feed the media, on his understanding of the job of journalists, including the pressure of deadlines for the first edition of the paper or the TV evening news.

The fact that he did not have an unlisted phone number, that he introduced the institution of the so-called press lobby after the weekly cabinet meeting on Tuesday, at which every young reporter or foreign journalist could ask him direct and unrehearsed questions, were first-class political moves. It exerted a powerful appeal, but it was also a source of profound personal satisfaction for him. I frequently witnessed telephone calls from complete strangers who wanted something from him. He would then interrupt an important conversation, make notes and instruct his secretariat to follow up on whatever hardship case had just come his way.

Max Weber wrote that passion was one of the crucial qualities for a politician, the passionate dedication to a 'cause'. Kreisky since his earliest youth not only wanted power for the sake of power but in Weber's sense saw it as a passionate devotion to a cause, service and responsibility on behalf of that cause. The cause already for the young Kreisky was the Social Democratic movement, an honest belief in the humanitarian goals of his party.

There were a number of reasons why my personal relationship with Kreisky grew closer over time. It was of course based on mutual interests. Kreisky, like all policitians, wanted a 'good press', and the British, German, Swiss and Austrian papers I was writing for were important to an Austrian politician. For me, as for every journalist, access to unfiltered information and to the opinions of one of the best-informed observers and shapers of the European scene were extremely important. That I came from Hungary and despite my past Communist Party deviations still had a Social Democratic touch also helped.

Kreisky was a far more dangerous opponent of the Communist dictatorships than many who touted their anti-Communism to the world, because he was a supporter of an aggressive policy of detente. An early understanding of the nature of change in the Communist world made him an early champion of an imaginative Eastern policy which was always conscious of the limits as well as the possibilities of Western influence.

In a tiny room adjoining his office Kreisky told me in the spring of 1966 over a cup of tea that he was considering becoming a candidate for Party Chairman at the next Social Democratic Party congress. Somewhat hesitantly I touched on the issue that later preoccupied many other people: can, ought and should a Jew, given the anti-semitic prejudices in all parts of the population and even in his own party, become Party Chairman and thus automatically the candidate for the chancellorship?

In this respect too there existed a certain unspoken affinity between the two of us. Both of us were of Jewish descent, but above all we had opted for Socialist internationalism and against Jewish nationalism. We were for liberalism and openness, against prejudice and separatism. And finally both of us were agnostics, people who respect the religious beliefs of others but who do not believe in an Almighty God.

In the event, at the decisive Party congress on 1 February 1967, only about 70 percent of the delegates cast their votes for Kreisky, and in the preceding vote of the executive committee the vote was 33 to 19 for Kreisky. Some of the most important people in the leadership, led by the defeated Party chairman and the trade union leaders' opposed him.

After his election to the chairmanship of the Social Democratic Party Kreisky set an explosive tempo. Thanks to good contacts and mutual personal esteem between him and Cardinal Franz König, a historic reconciliation was effected between the Catholic Church and Social Democrats. The Soviet intervention in Czechoslovakia in August 1968 gave Kreisky the opportunity to deliver a brilliant speech before 3,000 Social Democratic activists, in which he pointed out three lessons to be learned from that tragedy: the hope that a Communist dictatorship could be 'democratised' was illusory; military intervention was an essential component of all dictatorships, and finally cohesion and decisive attitude, not compliance and treading softly, make impressions on dictatorships. A year later came the significant 'Eisenstadt Declaration' against dictatorship and any co-operation with the Communist Party. A year after his victory Kreisky received an overwhelming demonstration of confidence: at the next Party congress he was elected with 97.4 percent of the vote.

On 1 March 1970, the Social Democratic Party won the general elections for the first time and Bruno Kreisky become the first fully-fledged Socialist Chancellor of the Second Republic. Between 1970 and 1979 Kreisky went on to win four elections, each time with growing support – a unique series of victories for Western European socialists.

Victory – but for what? How does one reconcile the contradiction between vision and reality, between Social Democratic goals and the support essential to maintain power among a population hardly inclined towards socialism? After winning his absolute majority Kreisky told me:

> I am firmly convinced that if we can't do more with power than to practice it for a long time we will deserve to lose it again. Our position of power must be morally grounded. We must not want power for its own sake but we must want it to come closer to our goals... I say that there is nothing more alarming than the long rule of a party that becomes rigid in routine and administration.

(After a quarter-century of Social Democratic hegemony in Austria Kreisky's warning is more valid than ever.)

A day after Kreisky's new government took office a political bomb-shell exploded. The new Minister of Agriculture admitted to having been a member of the SS. Kreisky told me that he had known nothing about the man's Nazi past. In the high-pressure atmosphere of forming a government he had relied on the recommendations of his friends from the Carinthian Party organisation since he had never given much thought to this particular post. Nevertheless it was bizarrely ironic that it was a Socialist Prime Minister who for the first time in the history of post-war Austria helped an SS man attain a ministerial post. At a press conference a few days into the affair I asked the Chancellor whether the controversial man would resign, and if so, when? Kreisky, under attack from all sides, was clearly annoyed with me.

But the Minister did resign his post after only a month 'for reasons of health'. Meanwhile, on the eve of the Social Democratic Party congress in June 1970, the Hamburg news magazine *Der Spiegel* revealed in a report based on information by Simon Wiesenthal, the head of the Jewish Documentation Centre in Vienna: in Kreisky's first government no fewer than four of his eleven ministers were former Nazis. At the Party congress a Kreisky loyalist, without denying the truth of the *Spiegel* story, called the Wiesenthal Documentation Centre a 'private secret tribunal', accused it of waging a campaign against Social Democracy and threatened to curtail its activities. The stage was set for a confrontation between two stubborn fighters, both Jews, trying to sort out the balance sheet of the Holocaust, one the moralist the other the pragmatist.

The question of how to deal with the Nazi past, the attitude toward Jewry and Israel, toward the Palestinians and the problems of the Near East frequently led to heated exchanges between Kreisky and myself. Even though I eventually came to accept many of Kreisky's arguments on the Palestinian question and the recognition of their legitimate claims, if not his frequently unnecessarily provocative and offensive style, we had more than one fight about his biting, uncom-promising and overly harsh dismissal of the corporate state under Dollfuss and Schuschnigg and in stark contrast to that, his puzzlingly understanding treatment of the Nazis. On that last point he never tired of pointing out that everybody had a right to make political mistakes.

During an argument with me at a lunch in a resort hotel in Lech in the Tyrol while I was working on his biography Kreisky resorted to one of his favorite arguments: 'After all I lost, as you know, 21 relatives in the Holocaust'. I, out of control because of my own involvement and my own dead, retorted, 'Have you asked the 21 relatives whether you can talk in their name?' Kreisky practically exploded and left the table – we were about to have our coffee – 'How dare you? What impertinence!' I continued to sit there for a while in silence and then went on a long walk toying with the idea of an early return home.

No sooner had I returned to my room than I found a note from Kreisky asking me to come to see him. As if nothing had happened, he then embarked on a long-winded attack on the Communist émigrés in Sweden before the war.

It was this mixture of seemingly uncontrolled eruptions followed by periods of detached indifference, of self-righteous monologues and tolerant friendly discussions, the sudden shifts in behaviour which formed the puzzle of this complex personality. But he was also a gentle, sensitive man who at times knew how to act the part of Chancellor.

A key to his success was his dual aura. 'There are those who smell the Socialist in him, and the others who smell the Liberal' a friend once told me. That Kreisky saw his life also as service in the cause of the working class and enjoyed mixing with the people – factory workers, pensioners, peasants and students – by no means ruled out his penchant for artists, intellectuals, industrialists, bankers and aristocrats. In his house I met musicians like Leonard Bernstein and the singer Hilde Güden, the sculptor Fritz Wotruba, John K. Galbraith and scientists like Viktor Weisskopf, together with journalists and young politicans who felt more at home with him than with apparently more youthful members of the government.

What made Kreisky furious, apart from stupidity, was the disloyalty of close advisers. Of course it was true of him as of other major personalities who had been in power for a long time that in the final analysis he did not trust anyone completely. However, in his case, especially beginning in the mid 1970s, the distrust was more than justified.

Kreisky never succeeded in becoming an all-powerful party leader. He remained the target of inner-party attacks. He, well on the way to being a legend in his lifetime, was basically a lonely man, particularly late in life, sickly, embittered and left in the lurch by his closest Party friends.

I met him a number of times during this period of internal party intrigues. In the course of long walks with one of his two boxers, on Sunday afternoons in his garden, or during trips to Hungary, what dominated these talks was not politics in general or the economic situation but the weight of his personal problems within his party. Kreisky was well aware of similar intrigues and personal animosities in Germany's Social Democratic Party between Willy Brandt, Herbert Wehner, and Helmut Schmidt, but he emphasised that in Austria things were entirely different: 'Willy is at times naive and careless; I find Wehner puzzling and unpredictable; Helmut Schmidt is too curt and too harsh. You know how I've always been able to rely on Willy. Our friendship has never been based on popular appeal.' Except for Torsten Nilsson, an old friend and Swedish Foreign Minister, the only people he spoke of as being true, good friends were Brandt (whom he knew as a fellow émigré in Sweden) and Olof Palme. 'There are not too many people on whom one can rely,' Kreisky was wont to say, sometimes sadly, at other times aggressively. The bruising episode of the Androsch affair in which his young deputy Hannes Androsch, the controversial Finance Minister, was encouraged to mount a challenge to Kreisky's party leadership as well as a range of other party intrigues did little to endear Kreisky's political colleagues to him.

An injury which years later resulted in the complete loss of vision in the right eye, and a lost referendum about the commissioning of an atomic power plant at Zwentendorf gave a powerful fillip to those in his party who wanted to replace Kreisky. To their astonishment Kreisky managed at the general elections in May 1979 to increase the Socialist vote and win more seats for his party.

It must have been some time in the summer of 1980 when the Chancellor called me up one Sunday afternoon and invited me to his house for coffee. 'They're conspiring against me'. I looked sceptical. 'Wouldn't you say it's a plot when half the government or even more people meet behind my back and plan an intrigue against me? They want to defeat me, but won't succeed; the Party, the people are all behind me.' I asked him who was at this meeting which he called a cabal. The angry Chancellor named half of the Cabinet.

Kreisky's kidney ailment as well as his age may explain his unrestrained explosions. They were directed not only at party political foes and rivals. Another target of Kreisky's tenacity and intense emotion was Simon Wiesenthal against whom he displayed an almost biblical hatred. In his uncontrolled public outbursts he even accused Wiesenthal indirectly of cooperation with the Gestapo.

What was the reason for the irrational attacks on Wiesenthal and the emotional basis of his position against Israel, his wounding, explosive language, in contrast to his restrained treatment of the Nazi past? There was and is no proof of his alleged Jewish self-hatred, Jewish anti-semitism or for any hostility toward his parents in general or his mother in particular. His conflict with Wiesenthal involved not only their diametrically opposed positions on Israel and on facing up to the past but also very specific differences: the profound contrast on the one hand between the scion of a fully assimilated, old-established Jewish family who saw himself as an Austrian, a Socialist and a Jew, whose first loyalty was to his homeland and his Socialist movement; and on the other hand the refugee and concentration camp survivor from Galicia, with his life story and his fixed attitude toward the Jewish state, and the prosecution and sentencing of those responsible for the Holocaust.

Added to this was Kreisky's anger over tasteless publicity around his slightly retarded older brother, Paul, who had been living in Israel since the Anschluss. Kreisky had always supported him generously. Some Israeli and German papers published illustrated features about the brother whom the anti-Zionist Chancellor and 'Jew Kreisky' had left in the lurch. All this and alleged attempts to bring his brother to Germany as part of an anti-Kreisky show raised Kreisky's anger to boiling point. The rumour that Wiesenthal was allegedly connected with this whole affair was, according to Kreisky's family, concocted by the Polish secret service.

Kreisky's attitude toward Judaism and the Middle East were central themes up to the very end of his life. It was the Israeli writer and far-left politician Uri Avnery who in May 1995, during a discussion in Vienna's Kreisky Forum, outlined the problem most generously and perceptively:

> His relationship to Israel and to the sister party, the Israeli Workers Party, was always very ambivalent, and that was connected to the fact that Israel had just as ambivalent an attitude toward Kreisky, to put it mildly. The Israeli Zionists could never forgive Kreisky for being a Jew. That means that in Israel people feel that a Jewish politician owes Israel absolute, unconditional and uncritical loyalty. Of course, Kreisky had never done that; he was extremly critical and that made relations so difficult. He felt like an Austrian and consciously he had little to do with Judaism. I think he once said that he only felt like a Jew because it would have been undignified to deny his Jewishness after what had happened. However, I think that's not quite so. His attitude toward Israel was rather the attitude of a rejected suitor. He could never understand why Israel treated him with such hostility. He was deeply hurt.
>
> Kreisky was a wise man, and from a distance he understood Israel's existential problems far better than the Israeli politicians who are involved with them constantly. Therefore he understood quite early on what most Israeli politicians still have trouble understanding, that Israel's main job is to make peace with the world around it, with the Arab Near East.

Avnery is of course not a representative Israeli voice, and Israel's mis-understanding of Kreisky has not been erased by the passage of time. Bruno Kreisky was committed to a breakthrough between Israel and her neigh-bours even when deluded fanatics on both sides sought to block that road.

In Austria itself Kreisky, because he was a Jew, could afford often to be painfully insensitive to the feelings of the victims of anti-semitism, and in his choice of words threw many a sacred cow overboard. Some psycho-logists have claimed that Kreisky even profited from latent anti-semitism, from sublimated guilt complexes among Austrians, and from the fact that broad sectors of the population looked on him as the personification of authority and credibility, particularly because he so obviously lacked the very characteristics that anti-semitic propaganda ascribed to the Jews.

Despite all his fits of rage against Israeli politicians and his Jewish critics he never denied being part of Jewry, bound together by a common fate. At the same time nothing gave him so much inner satisfaction as the irrefutable fact that the Austrian people several times, and with an absolute majority, elected him – a formerly disenfranchised, rejected, persecuted man – to supreme power in their country.

In 1983 Kreisky lost his absolute majority and departed from the political stage. Six years later in 1989 *The Independent* phoned me to write a full-page obituary about the former Chancellor as soon as possible. At the time Kreisky was in his house in Majorca. His health had recently declined dramatically and I understood the need for urgency. I began to sort out my ideas and to check some dates for accuracy. When in my draft I reached his term as foreign minister I picked up the phone and called his house in Mallorca. I wanted to know how he was doing and hoped that someone other than he would answer. No sooner did his phone ring than I heard that so-familiar voice: 'What's new in Vienna?' I could not tell him that I was working on his obituary and stammered something about the usual rows in the coalition government.

When Bruno Kreisky died on 29 July 1990, at the age of 79, a part of our lives and perhaps also of our dreams disappeared irrevocably. Without Bruno Kreisky Austria has become smaller, greyer, more boring.

III

An Epoch
Ends

14

Blacklisted

When his daughters asked Karl Marx in 1865 what his favorite motto was, he answered: *de omnibus dubitandum* (doubt everything). Conscientious journalists have paid obeisance to this principle even though they might never have read Marx or heard of this adage. In the final analysis it is the essence of a free press to reject thought control and to guard against the misuse of the media.

In the seventies and eighties, particularly after the signing of the final Helsinki agreement, the 40,000-page document of the Conference for European Security and Cooperation, on 1 August 1975, by representatives of 33 European countries and the USA and Canada, interest focused on questions of freedom of the press in the Eastern bloc countries and the free flow of information between East and West. The free dissemination of information, including the improvement of working conditions of foreign correspondents and access to international radio and TV broadcasts as well as to foreign publications, became one of the most crucial factors in the great debate about the future of East-West relations.

Alexander Solzhenitsyn's open letter to the Soviet leadership of September 1973, and Vaclav Havel and Charter 77's indictment of the system of lies some years later sensitised worldwide public opinion. What Solzhenitsyn said in 1973 did not apply only to the Soviet Union: 'This universal, obligatory force-feeding with lies is now the most agonising aspect of existence in our country – worse than all our material miseries, worse than any lack of civil liberties'.

Against this background the international radio broadcasts and TV transmissions to the GDR, parts of Hungary, Czechoslovakia and the Baltic states constituted an indispensable lifeline of information for almost 400 million people in Central, Eastern and Southeastern Europe. The costly jamming operations by the different regimes in the region and the frequent, often almost hysterical attacks against the 'espionage centres' and 'subversive instruments of imperialism' were telling proof of the vital role of the Western broadcasts.

In the second half of the 1970s Western radio broadcasts in Russian and 14 other languages were heard on an average by one-third of the population of the Soviet Union. Four out of five Czechs and Slovaks, three out of four Hungarians, Romanians and Poles, and one of every two Bulgarians heard the short-wave programmes in their native languages broadcast by Radio Free Europe, Voice of America, BBC and the German stations.

Apart from Romania and Hungary, where Western transmissions had not been jammed since 1964 and 1963 respectively, all Eastern bloc countries engaged in round-the-clock interference. The cost of these activities amounted to billions of dollars by the mid-seventies. Jiri Pelikan, the former head of Czech television, recalled in his memoirs that the sums spent in the sixties for electronic jamming in Czecho-slovakia would have sufficed to build a modern TV centre, including colour transmission.

In the eyes of the Communist regimes all foreign journalists were carriers of subversive ideas, a potential danger to national security. Instead of being granted the promised visas, qualified journalists reporting on Eastern Europe from their Vienna offices (as for example the correspondents of the Frankfurter *Allgemeine Zeitung* and *Le Monde*) were refused their visas for two or three years by the Czechoslovak authorities.

To understand the war waged against the media one must assume that the Communist functionaries were not only the victims of their own propaganda but also the captives of a psychotic fear of espionage. This applied particularly to the officials of Czechoslovakia's State Security Service and Foreign Ministry. Given the shock effect of August 1968, they were aware of the weakness of their system and at the same time were eager to earn the approbation of their Soviet saviours and protectors for being political and ideological model pupils. Beyond that, Vienna was one of the prime targets of Czechoslovak, Hungarian and East German espionage. After the defection of Czech diplomats and agents in 1968-69, the personal press secretary of

Austria's Minister of the Interior, the head of the code department of the Foreign Ministry, an official of the federal press service as well as employees of the Department of Commerce and of Civil Aviation were all indicted for espionage on behalf of Czechoslovakia and the East Germany. In 1981, a defector from the Romanian Secret Service unmasked the chief of the alien registration office in Vienna as an accomplice of the notorious Securitate of Bucharest; he had been spying for Romania for more than ten years.

Austrian papers estimated that at least 6,000 foreign agents of all persuasions were active in Vienna in the sixties. With the exception of Berlin there probably was no other European city with so many full-time and part-time secret agents, informers and intelligence officers.

Working as a journalist in Vienna it was impossible to be immune from the shadowy world of intelligence. In the early sixties an American who spoke broken Hungarian called me up one evening and asked whether we could meet. He acted very mysteriously and muttered that he was acting on behalf of 'a certain service'. He said he could not be called back since he had not checked in at any hotel. All he wanted was to speak to me briefly in person. During this strange telephone conversation I was thinking that this might be a Russian or Hungarian provocation. He knew my private address and said he would like to come by for a brief visit. I decided with my wife that she should talk to him when he came, made my excuses to him and arrange another appointment with this mysterious caller. He came by and was disappointed not to find me at home, saying he would try again later. My wife said that with his little plaid hat he looked like a character in a spy thriller. Only the pipe was missing.

Since I knew the head of the USIA in Vienna I asked him to check with his colleagues in the CIA whether this was in fact a genuine if somewhat clumsy American agent. I still thought that an Eastern European secret service might be trying to entrap me. A few days later the Press Counsellor at the US Embassy called me up sounding somewhat embarrassed. The man was indeed an American. I felt very relieved, and never heard from him or the CIA again.

Much later, in the mid-seventies, in a very elegant setting at a lunch in a fashionable restaurant in Vienna, a high-ranking Scandinavian diplomat asked me whether I was ready to meet regularly with his 'colleagues' from a particular office. After my polite but immediate 'no' he changed the topic. Even though we met repeatedly at various social functions with our wives he avoided any further references to his proposal.

Aside from these two instances no intelligence service ever contacted me. The strange incident with the Hungarian-speaking CIA man left such an indelible impression of amateurism that I was never really surprised when I read about some of the mishaps and failures of the much-vaunted American secret service. But if the Americans could be amateurish, their level of incompetence was no match for what a journalist would confront in the East. There of course clumsiness and incompetence was spiced by a degree of paranoia which created a culture of watchfulness providing infinite opportunities for absurdity.

The levels of supervision differed from country to country. It involved not only tapped phones and bugged hotel rooms but also (frequently unnoticed) round-the-clock watch by the secret police.

During a trip to Romania in 1976 I noticed the many cars 'escorting' me in various parts of the country. I raised this with the then Vice Foreign Minister, Vasile Gliga: 'You want to catch up with the West,' I said to him, but you employ four to six strong young people and a number of cars and waste valuable gas just finding out which restaurant I stopped for lunch in on the way to an interview arranged by your ministry?' Gliga (later Ambassador in London), unlike his colleagues was a cultivated, cynical diplomat. He did not deny that I was being shadowed. Chuckling, he said to me, 'You see, for something that the West needs only one man we here need six; that too shows how backward we are!'

This Romanian could at least be light-hearted about his country's security japes. But when the Czechs decided to target me they went about it with a vengeance.

Two months later I reported on the Czechoslowak CP congress in Prague and in the following years about the visit of the Soviet leader Leonid Brezhnev, the Austrian President Rudolf Kirchschläger and the British Minister of Trade John Smith as well as about economic matters for the *Financial Times* and for Swiss and Austrian papers. In 1978, after a handful of Austrian journalists and foreign correspondents in Vienna were accredited in Prague they could automatically, generally within 24 hours, get a visa. However, the accreditation had to be renewed every six months, a condition which most of them had difficulty in fulfilling.

At the same time the Helsinki agreements were being flagrantly violated: between August 1975 and August 1978 at least 16 foreign correspondents were harassed. For example, the secret police would confiscate notes the correspondents had taken during visits to Czechoslovak citizens.

In June 1978 I applied for accreditation at the Czech Foreign Ministry and so on my behalf did the *Financial Times* in London. That the officers and agents of the State Security Service of Kafka's native city would engage in fabricating a bizarre story about my person and my metaphysical contacts there and compile two 'top secret' dossiers of 152 pages would not have entered my mind. Friends in Prague (who must of course remain nameless) have recently given me access to these documents, so I can now describe the strange events about which I had no inkling two decades ago.

I had first aroused suspicion when back in February 1976, during a visit to the Planning Commission, I persisted in asking questions about the energy, price and industrialisation policies. A 'serious source' immediately informed the State Security Service that too much had been asked too aggressively. Therefore I was suspected of economic espionage and a file on me was opened. The secret service began to pay serious attention to me only in early 1978. A first lieutenant drew up a five-page-long investigative plan under the code name 'Host' ('Guest') and set up File No 14,346 for Host. Originally this file consisted of 75 reports but 12 were later removed because they apparently dealt with other people.

In a number of action plans the diligent investigators saw to it that all my border crossings were immediately reported to Prague, that in all hotels 'TA 122, TA 211 and TA 144' were activated (i.e., that all my telephone calls were to be monitored, the rooms bugged and regularly searched), that all contacts with Czech citizens as well as with representatives of Austrian, American, and later also British embassies were registered and evaluated, that all addresses at which I called were logged and all telephone calls recorded. After a detailed description of my career and of my 'dyed-in-the-wool anti-Socialist and anti-Communist' articles and my 'slanderous' TV commentaries about Czechoslovakia and above all Poland, I was denied accreditation as the *Financial Times* correspondent in Prague.

One of the oddest reports was made by a certain Lt Col. S.B., the chief of the First Department of the XI Main Department, which was in charge of fighting economic espionage. In the introduction First Lieutenant K.J., the man assigned to my case, stated laconically that Lendvai 'uses citizenships of the GFR, Great Britain, Austria, and the USA,' i.e. that I was the citizen of all four countries, and had 'received special training in the USA and Germany'. Since I had published a book about anti-semitism in Eastern Europe it was noted that I 'published Zionist literature'.

In this report and in numerous other documents a puzzling story is cited and repeats itself throughout the entire dossier. At some time in the late seventies the business cards or addresses of two persons had allegedly been found in my room. Investigations about all facets of their lives were later removed from my dossier for reasons of security. What has remained is the remark of Lt Col. S.B. of 8 May 1980, that one of the two was involved in an action of 'the Vatican's espionage agency to bring clerics out of the country'. The charges against the second person who 'was said to be a contact point of a not identified espionage service' were being investigated. Finally the 'target person', that is me, should be followed in order to observe contacts with Czech citizens. Apparently I was interested in an apartment in Bratislava which was suspected as being used for conspiracies. Another report by an agent stated that I had lived in Levice in Slovakia between 25 June and 12 July 1970, in the house of a certain Jozef Zidovic.

That was quite a revelation. Between 1965 and 1976 I had not even been to Czechoslovakia, let alone lived in the house of Josef Zidovic. I had never heard the names of the two people charged with anti-state activities nor had I even spoken to them. That I was looking for a 'conspiratorial' apartment in Bratislava was also sheer fantasy. I did have a cousin by the name of Tibor Lendvai who had already lived in Bratislava but he had left Czechoslovakia in 1968.

Was all this sheer invention by eager secret service agents who wanted to impress superiors with great successes in the fight against Western class enemies? Or was it a mix-up of business cards and addresses which had been found in the briefcase of another visitor or in another hotel room in Brno years ago? A truly Kafkaesque story.

Despite surveillance and the depressing political climate I must admit that on every one of my visits I succumbed to the magic of Golden Prague. Even though I knew how drab daily life was in the districts that tourists rarely or ever get to see, it was still an indescribable pleasure after the boring, hypocritical official talks to wander through the narrow streets of the Old Town and walk into the churches and synagogues, to stroll around the old Jewish cemetery, to take the old 'royal road' from the Old Town across the Charles Bridge up to the Hradcin. Late at night when I and friends went out to a bar in the Old Town we occasionally talked about the ruling elite's strange fear of the novels and short stories of the long-dead Franz Kafka whose works were not to be found in any bookstore, not even in translation. But had I wanted to I could have bought a Thai-German/German-Thai dictionary at a very reasonable price. Kafka would have enjoyed the irony.

The various operational plans in my dossier made it clear that several secret service agents were engaged to deal with me as a so-called 'target person'. Thus Section 6 of the First Department of the Second Main Department laid down in nine points and with deliciously bureaucratic seriousness the following measures to be carried out in the framework of the action against Host.

To collaborate with Section 1 of the II Main Department of the Security Service with the aim of finding out the contacts of the target person with the officials of the US Embassy in Prague.

Deadline: 30.4.1981

To collaborate with Section 3 of the II Main Department of the Security Service with the aim of finding out the connections with the officials of the British Embassy in Prague.

Deadline: 30.4.1981

On his arrival to control and to describe his contacts with Czechoslovak citizens through the utilisation of the means at the disposal of Section 4 of the II Main Department.

Deadline: continuously

During his stay in Prague assignment of operative agents in the hotels and to organise contacts, meetings and other activities through the operative agents of the IV Main Department in the hotel and immediate vicinity.

Deadline: continuously

Electronic methods should be applied in the hotel (codewords: ZTU Construction and Diagram) in order to control the content of messages and phone calls received and sent with the aim of finding out his range of contacts.

Deadline: continuously

Organisation, protection and implementation of searches in the place of residence of the target person of the action 'Host'. To copy notes, addresses and phonecalls relating to Czechoslovak citizens and to foreigners with permanent residence in Czechoslovakia, to find and to copy suspicious documents, material and technical accessories which indicate an illegal activity in Czechoslovakia.

Deadline: permanently

To check up through the Administration Section of Passports and Visas on his current journalistic activity relating to the Czechoslovak Socialist Republic and the other socialist countries. Depending on the results of the investigations, to remove his name possibly from the index of undesirable persons and to enable him to travel to Czechoslovakia which could be necessary for further investigations against him.

Deadline: 30.4.1981

To enlarge the contact circle of the target person with the aim of finding a suitable person who could be engaged in efficient counter-espionage activities against 'Host'.

Deadline: 30.6.1981

After evaluation and analysis of the above listed countermeasures a decision has to be taken, in which way further efficient investigations should be carried out against the target person of the action 'Host'.

Deadline: 31.10.1981

Already two years earlier, in February 1979 an application for co-operation with 'the friends in Hungary and Poland' (i.e. with the fraternal security services) was completed and a decision was taken 'to pass on the information collected about the target person to the friends in the Soviet Union'. These measures were contained in the first major investigating plan against me.

What then did these massive searches and investigations unearth? The copy of an article by me in the *Bund* of Berne about tensions between Yugoslavia and Czechoslovakia, which the Czech Embassy in Berne had sent on to Prague back in 1976 as proof of my 'deeply ingrained anti-Communist and anti-Socialist position'; a copy of a telex report from me about the Prague visit of the Austrian head of state despatched to the German short-wave service in Cologne which an agent stationed in a hotel had 'cleverly obtained', and the transcript of a tapped telephone conversation between the Austrian Ambassador and the US Minister in Prague in the summer of 1980 in which arrangements for a lunch with me and my wife were discussed. That the report despatched to the German radio was subsequently broadcast by them in many langauges showed the absurdity of going to such lengths to acquire and file a report of an ordinary state visit to a neighbouring country. The fact that in the spring of 1981 I was a guest lecturer at the Santa Barbara campus of the University of California was described as 'special training' for me in the United States.

At any rate my dossier concluded once again that my reports were 'completely non-objective' and that my negative coverage of Czechoslovakia in the Western press was second to none. On the basis of such weighty proofs a group leader, Lt J.D., proposed to put me on the list of undesirable persons, and to bar Host from entering the country for 15 years, a proposal which Lt Col. M.S., the head of the department, approved on 4 August 1981.

That the regime itself would collapse much sooner than that, after eight years, neither the colonel nor his staff nor Host, the dangerous subject of the dossier, could have foreseen.

15

Riling the
Eastern Bloc

I n the summer of 1982, I left the *Financial Times*, and became the head of the newly established Eastern Europe desk of the Austrian TV and Radio network.

Millions of householders in Slovakia, Moravia, Western Hungary, Croatia and Slovenia were able to tune in to our news reports, documentaries, late-night talk-shows and panel discussions. Our programme thus often became political events. In view of the mounting tensions in the various Eastern and Southeastern European countries and the growing divergences within the Eastern bloc, the first explosion was not far off.

In the autumn of 1982 the rulers of Czechoslovakia, after years of tension, sought to improve relations with Austria. We were given permission to shoot a harmless documentary, 'Bohemia in Autumn'. And I was granted an interview with President Gustáv Husák after I sent a cassette of my interview with the Bulgarian Party chief and head of state, Todor Zhivkov, to the officials in Prague. I had of course no idea that I had been placed on the blacklist, barring me from entry to Czechoslovakia for 15 years.

At any rate, on 10 November 1982, on the eve of Husák's first official visit to Vienna, I received permission to visit Prague and film a TV interview with him. As was customary on such official occasions at the Hradcin, dozens of technicians, secretaries, and security officers were scuttling about in attendance. While they were attaching microphones to our jackets before the interview we exchanged a few words in German. I asked him whether the rumour that a Warsaw Pact Summit was soon to be held in Prague was true. Husák said yes but could not give me the exact date. He spoke vaguely about the first half of December. When I asked whether the often ailing Brezhnev would participate he answered unequivocally that 'of course Comrade Brezhnev will come to Prague'.

Next morning in Prague we learned that Brezhnev had been dead for some time.

The Soviet leadership had kept the news of his death from Husák and probably also from the heads of the other 'fraternal parties'. Of course as a journalist could not resist commenting on the symbolism of this extraordinary event.

Husák had to postpone his official visit to Austria for about two weeks because of the funeral ceremonies in Moscow. The interview with him was then broadcast in its original form before his arrival. At a lunch Kreisky gave in his honour I met Husák again. He was extremely unfriendly. *Rude Pravo*, the official Party paper, even criticised me by name in a report from Vienna. The vain, rigid Husák was furious that he had been made to look foolish because of the secrecy surrounding Brezhnev's death.

This incident riled the Czechs so much that other dark clouds appeared on the political horizon of our Eastern Europe department. Our Bohemia documentary was sharply attacked from Prague. Where they were especially indignant that the Austrian film had been shown at an Italian film festival.

Matters escalated on 26 January 1983, when the Soviet government paper *Izvestia* attacked me and my associates in a long, extraordinarily acrimonious article entitled 'Lies on a TV Screen' charging us with 'ideological subversion' with the 'planned expansion of co-operation with Radio Free Europe', with 'abuse of hospitality' and with 'vilest ingratitude'. Finally, the Moscow paper concluded that the activity of our editorial department was incompatible with Austria's neutrality and the state treaty.

On February 6 *Izvestia*, the official Soviet paper, launched another sharp attack against our 'slanderous reports' which 'showed hostility and sowed distrust among peoples', similar to 'the distortions broadcast by the mouthpieces of the CIA in Munich's "Radio Liberty" and "Radio Free Europe" stations' and aimed at deceiving millions of Austrians.

As it became clear in Moscow and other Eastern European capitals that our broadcasts to and on Eastern Europe were serious and here to stay the attacks on us broadened. Thus when years later I was studying my Stasi file I came across a telegram from a General Kratsch dated 6 December in which the chief of Department X informed Hungary's security service that I, as head of the Eastern Europe department and Editor-in-Chief of the Austrian broadcasting service, planned to 'intensify the hostile reporting on the Socialist countries of Eastern Europe'. He added, 'Unofficial information points to the fact that the choice and assignment of these correspondents is guided by secret intelligence considerations'. What seemed particularly suspicious to the general was the fact that Lendvai 'has repeatedly reported about the counter-revolutionary developments in the People's Republic of Poland in 1980 and 1981'. And in Czech documents about me the specter of Poland was also repeatedly raised.

The hostility towards us was not surprising. Our TV and radio journalists were particularly dangerous for the Communist dictatorships because so many of their subjects were able to see film reports or hear broadcasts in a language they could understand, as many Czechs, Hungarians, Slovenes and even Croats still had German as their second tongue. When Austrian TV was able to show the growing freedom of the Hungarians or Slovenes in contrast with the suppression of Solidarity in Poland, or programmes about the legacy of Yalta, the Soviet occupation and the Communist seizure of power, the Soviets reacted hysterically and with some reason. They saw such programmes as a threat to the legitimacy of their regime, which they were, even though they were designed for Austrian viewers.

The fact that our broadcasts turned out to be so politically sensitive in countries like Czechoslovakia was an accident of geography, not a conscious manoeuver on our part to undermine the regimes.

Obviously, playing off the 'good' Eastern bloc states like Hungary against the 'bad' ones like Czechoslovakia was a completely legitimate and highly effective tactic. We certainly saw no reason to let the propaganda chiefs of the Communist countries intimidate us. On the contrary I was determined to exploit the different developments in these states and to break the united front against us by following the Leninist tactic of focusing on the weakest link of the chain, i.e. Hungary. In reports, commentaries and documentaries about Hungary we continued to emphasise the extent and limits of the changes.

That this tactic worked was borne out by an internal memorandum of the Czech Embassy in Vienna which has since come to light (File

No 6681/83). It records a conversation in Russian on 6 September 1983 between the Czech press attaché Jiri Gotz and the Second Secretary of the Soviet Embassy, Nicolai A. Muravliev. When the two talked about 'conduct of the countries of the Socialist community in their relation with the Austrian TV's Eastern Bureau and specifically with P. Lendvai'. The memo states that the 'Soviet friends' are beginning to pay closer attention to our broadcasting activities and that the Embassy would not grant Lendvai a visa. The Soviet Embassy was interested in having all Socialist countries take a unified approach towards us. At issue was a boycott of the Austrian broadcasting corporation. The problem was, however, that the Hungarian People's Republic was proceeding unilaterally so that for Lendvai, even though he was a Hungarian émigré, the road to Hungary remained open. The varying attitudes of the individual Socialist countries would unfortunately lend support to our activities. The Soviet side remained interested in a co-ordinated posture for the countries of the Socialist community in dealing with our operation and in particular with Lendvai. In a five-page supplement this memo provided a detailed analysis of each Warsaw Pact country's attitude towards our broadcasts. The memo went on to say: 'Hungary treats Lendvai like a well-known Western journalist, taking into account good Austrian-Hungarian relations. (In the sixties Lendvai was on the list of people denied entry to Hungary)'.

Exactly one month after this conversation at the Czech Embassy in Vienna (a conversation about which I obviously knew nothing at the time) I applied to visit Czech television and the Foreign Office in Prague. I thought it important to keep up the pressure, so among other items I requested that they cancel the ban on our hapless reporter who had fallen foul of the Czechs because of her 1982 'Bohemia in Autumn' documentary. The Austrian-Czech cultural day then underway seemed to offer a favorable framework for the improvement of our relations. Since I had a so-called service-passport, I did not need a visa. The Czech Embassy in Vienna only had to arrange for my appointments. I flew to Prague on 6 October. Despite my passport and despite officially arranged talks I was turned back at the passport control and I was forced to fly back to Vienna on the same plane that had brought me.

Now I knew for certain that I was on the blacklist. What I did not suspect, however, was the fact that actually I had been on the index of undesirable journalists since August 1981, and that my interview with Husák was an exception. After some hectic telephoning between

Vienna and Prague what threatened to become an international incident was averted when the Czechs finally confirmed an entry permit for me.

After the then Czech Ambassador in Vienna (now director of the Prague branch of a German insurance company) apologised I once more flew to Prague, on 8 October this time, however, with my wife as a guardian angel. The Austrian Ambassador demonstratively came to Prague airport to ensure my safe entry and waited for me at the airport. The secret police equally demonstratively made their presence known. I followed my original appointment calendar. At the Prague Foreign Ministry an official cryptically informed me that I was on the index because of 'personal insults to the President'. It was obvious that neither I nor our reporter would soon again receive entry permits.

The efforts of the Soviets and their Czechoslovak vassals to moderate our coverage of Eastern Europe and to blackball me failed spectacularly four weeks later with Hungary's refusal to join the Soviet-decreed boycott of Austrian broadcasting. On 17 November 1983, an evening talk show 'Club 2' was presented from Budapest for the first time: the lively discussion involving prominent artists and journalists from both countries moderated by me was later shown by the Budapest TV station, although the ticklish passages about October 1956 were edited out. Next year similar programmes were broadcast from Belgrade and Warsaw. These were also shown uncut to the domestic audiences in Yugoslavia and Poland. Obviously detente and the self-interest of individual states combined to isolate the hard-liners in Moscow and Prague.

My relationship with the Czech blacklist was a continuous on-again off-again saga. Despite my Public Enemy Number One status among Austrian journalists I would be let into the country on official business, and on one occasion, when with other journalists I accompanied Austrian Foreign Minister Erwin Lanc to Prague, I was the guest at an official dinner in Prague, where on my right sat the Czech Minister of Culture and on my left the Vice Foreign Minister. This social mingling in high places could not prevent yet another conflict. The journalists who reported on this visit flew to Bratislava, from where we were to return to Vienna by bus barely an hour's drive across the border. But at the frontier we were held up for about an hour and our bags were rudely gone through – not exactly proof of good-neighbourly relations. We all naturally protested. As a result the official in Bratislava in charge of journalists (and also an associate of the security service) reported to his bosses in Prague that I was the instigator and spokesman at the protests.

At any rate, as the files were later to reveal, on 11 July 1983, I was put on the index of undesirable persons for the second time. These files, under the codename 'Pel', ('Pollen') reveal that Captain I.M. declared that Lendvai was a 'strongly anti-Socialist journalist who has crudely attacked the Czechoslowak Republic, the USSR and other countries of the Socialist community'. On the basis of these facts the captain recommended 'for preventive educational reasons' to put the PEL dossier 'in the archive' for five years. The head of Section 6 of the Second Main Department of the Security Service, Major I.J., concurred. Thus first as Host and subsequently as Pollen I was black-listed for a combined period of 20 years.

In the meantime the fact that I had been able to travel wherever I wanted, including the Soviet Union, apparently did not affect Czech attitudes towards the ban on me. Gustáv Husák's personal pique against me was enough to keep the ban alive in Czechoslovakia.

My access to Soviet Union was unhindered after the mid 1980s and in April 1986, we even organised a live round-table TV discussion from Moscow. Valentin Falin, former Soviet Ambassador in Bonn and a clever proponent of the party line of the moment said haughtily that this broadcast would 'of course' also be carried by Moscow TV. Nothing of the kind happened though at least we were able to broadcast our programme, if not live, at least uncut.

But censorship and blacklisting were not the only hazards to navigate in Moscow. In the huge TV centre which employed 22,000 people we could find no standard lamp. And as if to prove that rigidity was not the exclusive domain of Communist bureaucrats, the set designers we had brought over from Vienna demanded a standard lamp for our set. After all we always had to have a standard lamp. So one had to be sent over from a hotel. Shortly before the beginning of the broadcast the carpet in the studio began to smoke; one of the old cables had caught fire. We all pitched in and were able to put it out. When I introduced the programme and the discussion was already in full swing the fire suddenly started up again. All of us remained seated during this second fire-extinguishing exercise acting with such aplomb that the viewers knew nothing about the drama behind the scenes.

Our toughest negotiations about TV reports were in Romania. In the eighties Nicolae Ceausescu, the head of State and the Party, became a favourite target for international criticism. This was hardly surprising given the absurd cult of personality built up around him and his wife Elena. Human rights organisations and the Western media investigating conditions in the country found the violations and political corruption grotesque and made the 'greatest genius of the Carpathians' personally responsible. The intolerable pressure on the population, particularly the large Hungarian and rapidly-dwindling German minorities, completely and irrevocably destroyed the reputation of the 'most beloved son of the Romanian people'. News teams were allowed access only to Party congresses and similar events. They were welcome to record the triumphal appearances of the dictator and the orchestrated enthusiasm of the delegates but could not show the appalling consequences of Ceausescu agricultural and industrial policies on the everyday life of citizens.

In 1985, when I commissioned a documentary about the bizarre Ceausescu cult and the general misery in Romania, we both knew that this film would turn us into dangerous enemies of the 'Conducator'. We produced a rough cut of the film showing Ceausescu, experts, perpetrators and victims, and with extensive cutting achieved very special effects. What was still missing, however, was a shot showing the building of the state palace which had become a symbol of the absurdity of the regime. I therefore took advantage of the opportunity in early December 1985 to accompany Austrian Foreign Minister Leopold Gratz on an official visit to Bucharest. We arrived on a Sunday. On Monday, during the official talks and obligatory sightseeing tours, and escorted by a young Romanian diplomat, we began shooting outdoors. Tuesday was to be the high point of the visit, the scheduled talk with Ceausescu.

We had taken two taxis and were riding around the city seemingly aimlessly. The camera man wanted to shoot the outlines of the notorious White Palace from different angles openly, not surreptitiously. Suddenly a Securitate agent in the guise of a workman carrying a long stick stopped us and demanded that we hand over the video cassettes. In the background stood another group of stern-looking 'workmen'. I refused his request, told him of our 'official status' and showed the agent my blue service passport. He was not particularly impressed and demanded that we accompany him to the 'proper office'. I told him via our diplomat-minder that I would accept no such instructions, and moreover that this 'shameless treatment' would be brought to the attention of President Ceausescu himself.

Two more hours went by. We waited in the bitter cold in our taxis for the young to scuffle back to his office and break the deadlock. Finally, shaking, he came back, and we were allowed to go back to our hotel. In fact once out of the Securitate's clutches we decided not to make a fuss. We did not want to miss the opportunity of filming Ceausescu the following day.

The next morning our young Romanian diplomat-minder, visibly shaken, called on me and asked whether Foreign Minister Gratz was going to mention our embarrassing encounter to the President. Throughout the night the various offices had talked to each other and to him. All – so it seemed – were deadly afraid of the choleric 'Conducator'. As I calmed him, I once again sensed how thin the ice was on which servants of a dictatorship had to skate.

At any rate we had our pictures and our documentary, 'A Latter-Day Caesar', was shown worldwide. A Romanian diplomat warned me that the documentary was 'an insult to our President and the entire Romanian people' but this did not prevent the video cassette of the documentary from becoming a best-seller on the black market in Romania, where in the months preceding Ceausescu's fall it sold for about $100.

Next to Czechoslovakia, East Germany was the most difficult area for our broadcasting activities. In contrast to the Soviet Union and the other Eastern bloc countries East Germany was not prepared to permit the broadcast of a live TV discussion from East Berlin. The Gauck office, which now administers the Stasi files, has allowed me to see the correspondence between the East German Ministry of State Security and the Hungarian Interior Ministry. On 20 September 1984, the Security Ministry sent a telegram (No. 1074/84) to Budapest (and a copy in Russian to Moscow) asking advice about his [i.e. my] political attitude and possibly existing operation-relevant information. On 5 February 1985, General Damm forwarded the result of the investigation 'for your information and operational use'. The Hungarian Interior Ministry informed the East Germans on a 'top secret' basis that a certain Paul Lendvai 'is listed in our files as a hostile person'. On two-and-a-half single-spaced pages they said, among other things, that my activities in Vienna since 1959 had been 'attentively followed', that I, as head of Austrian broadcasting's desk, was engaged 'in a differentiated anti-Communist and anti-Soviet activity' and that our TV reports had an 'anti-Communist' starting point.

All this confirmed the dark suspicion of the fraternal colleagues in the GDR. Our proposal for a live broadcast from East Berlin was politely turned down. In retrospect this should not have come as a surprise, particularly since one of the secret service documents (Report No 011194) of 17 August 1981, said I was a 'person denied entry' and was listed as 'honorary collaborator of a centre of the PID'. With the help of a Stasi dictionary I found the explanation for this puzzling acronym. PID stood for 'political-ideological diversion' and turned out to refer to Radio Free Europe in Munich. This was the centre of PID of which I was named as an 'honorary member (freelance journalist)'.

In a long computer printout in Russian dated 8 September, Berlin forwarded the same information to Moscow. The information about me went to SOUD, the highly centralised system for gathering and collating information about the adversaries of the Eastern bloc from all sources. The Russian acronym stands for an organisation set up in Moscow at the end of 1977 by the Warsaw Pact countries plus Mongolia, Cuba and Vietnam to co-ordinate intelligence data on Western activities perceived to be harmful to the East. SOUD thus registered not only suspected agents but also Western journalists, businessmen, cultural figures and diplomats who were deemed unfriendly.

I had never worked for RFE. So where did this false information come from? It turned out that my friend, the writer Stephan Vajda, had occasionally worked for RFE while trying to make ends meet in his early days as a Hungarian émigré. Thus the astute conclusion that I too must have worked for RFE.

Thus were legends born and disseminated. Today, in retrospect, this sort of nonsense seems absurd and perhaps amusing. But back then such reports by incompetent agents became accepted instruments for arrest and harassment. What gives this and similar information recorded in my file in East Berlin ('Lendvai maintains connections with criminal elements in Hungary') an air of surrealism, even by Communist standards, is that in the early eighties I was conducting interviews with János Kádár and numerous top Hungarian functionaries as well as with intellectuals critical of the regime. But since reports such as these had already made my wife co-owner of the *FT* the level of fiction to be found in them is not surprising.

In May 1983 the then general secretary of Austrian Broadcasting and I set off to Albania, the poorest and most sealed-off country in Europe. Ostensibly we were to draw up an agreement between the broadcasting corporations of our two countries. Our real purpose was of course altogether different. We hoped that such an agreement would open the door to filming a political TV documentary about this isolated land, which for four decades had been in the grip of single-minded and unpredictable Communist dictator Enver Hoxha. Agreements such as the one we were pursuing would often be broken by the Communist regimes but they were still useful because while they were being respected they provided protection for our journalists, and even when broken their breach provided us opportunities to make a fuss about the behaviour of these regimes who, in addition to whatever else, could be justifiably accused of not reporting agreements.

At the time of our visit to Albania there still was no rail link to that country's two neighbours, Greece and Yugoslavia, nor was it possible to reach Albania via passenger ship. Air traffic was limited to Mondays and Thursdays. Between Friday and Monday the only way out of the country was by road.

An Albanian-Austrian broadcast agreement was signed during our visit and it included a paragraph about the projected production of a film about Albania our team. In June 1984 I went to Tirana with a crew. During two four-week-long trips to Albania I covered more than 2,000 miles criss-crossing the country, always in the company of three official and countless unofficial minders. On foot or on bicycle, watchdogs followed in our footsteps of the strangers wherever we went. They never even made the slightest effort to hide who they were. 'Sensitive' situations, such as filming at the old market in Tirana, were personally supervised by the Director General of Albanian TV Marash Hajati. We had to listen to his harangues because we had dared to film an old man riding a donkey, but when I threatened to pack up and leave immediately he agreed to allow us to continue without having to submit daily schedules, as originally demanded.

The hour-long documentary 'From Skanderbeg to Enver Hoxha' was broadcast in August 1984, and subsequently taken up by ten foreign stations. Despite the close control our cameraman managed to capture not only the beauty of the country but also the eerie atmosphere of the final round in the fight for a successor to the ailing Hoxha.

I had meanwhile managed to become a pariah in Albania as well for two reasons. Firstly I had reported with great emphasis on the Hoxha cult, his vengefulness and the removal of the photo of his purged deputy Mehmet Shehu from a picture of the top Albanian leaders, taken when Shehu had still been Number Two. And secondly I had committed the unpardonable sin of filming an interview in Paris with King Zog's old widow, the former Hungarian Countess Geraldine Apponyi. Also present at that interview was her son, the eccentric royal pretender who called himself 'King Leka'.

Since the 'king' normally lived in South Africa in the outskirts of Johannesburg with his Australian wife, I had, after a lengthy correspondence, gone to South Africa to interview him. 'King Leka', however, was not to be found. 'His Majesty had to fly to Paris', I was told by 'Queen Susan' over the phone. Apparently South Africa's then still apartheid government had asked him to leave the country while I was there to ward off any undesirable publicity. Despite the confusion, telephone calls, inconvenience and irritation I was ultimately grateful to 'His Majesty'. By leaving me high and dry in South Africa he had at least given me the opportunity to obtain a peek at a country which in some respects had the police state characteristics I was familiar with from Eastern Europe.

At the time of our Albanian adventure it would never have occurred to me that ten years later my documentary with a new introduction would be shown on Albanian TV, nor that during my visit in September 1993 I would again meet Marash Hajati, the former TV general director, president of the journalists' union and powerful Central Committee member, who back then had put me on the 'permanent index of unwelcome journalists'. Now in 1993 he was the busy proprietor of a small kiosk selling all kinds of wares in a side-street of the capital. Nor would I have thought that during my 1993 visit I would be spending a week at the Hoxha villa at the cost of about $125 per day for the apartment of the now imprisoned Hoxha widow. Eastern Europe and the Balkans never fail to produce something of the theatre of the absurd from their eventful histories.

16

The Waldheim Affair

A ustrian presidential elections are not events which normally capture world headlines over a protracted period. The elections of 1986 were a dramatic exception. The Social Democrats chose Kurt Steyrer, a medical doctor and former Minister of Health. The People's Party nominated Kurt Waldheim, the highly prestigious former Foreign Minister and UN Secretary General. 'A man the world trusts' was the proud slogan on the posters with a picture of Waldheim standing in front of the UN building in New York. But no sooner had the campaign started when Austria's media and the World Jewish Congress in New York were fed copies of Waldheim's army file, with data about his membership in the Nazi student organisation and a SA cavalry unit. The man who for ten years had symbolised the conscience of the world was suddenly linked to Nazi war crimes. What made matters worse was that in his previously published memoirs Waldheim had made no mention of sensitive aspects of his military service in the Balkans, claiming to have spent critical periods invalided out of the military. And Austria was soon in the dock with Waldheim. The rhetoric from around the world was hostile and at times quite shrill. As a result the Austrian population closed ranks against foreign attacks. Unfortunately the anti-semitic side-effects of this soon followed.

Given the name of the 'World Jewish Congress' many Austrians seemed to discover the phantom 'conspiracy of world Jewry' and 'international Zionism' so beloved by the Nazis as well as right-wing and left-wing extremists. In any event, the net result of all this was that Waldheim was elected President with a 54 percent majority in a substantial 87 percent voter turn-out.

I was not involved either directly or indirectly in the debate over Kurt Waldheim's candidacy, but in view of the far-reaching dimensions of the affair I could not remain passive. I was concerned with Austria's reputation, the country in which I had found a new home and which I wanted to support in difficult times.

I had known Waldheim since the early sixties when he was Political Director of the Foreign Ministry. We occasionally met professionally. During his rise from Austria's UN Ambassador to Foreign Minister, and during his two terms as Secretary General of the UN I had on occasion interviewed him. I also knew that Kreisky and Waldheim and their wives were on friendly terms. Kreisky had become personally involved in the efforts to get Waldheim elected and then re-elected to his UN post. But when all is said and done I knew little about his wartime past.

After Kurt Waldheim was elected President of Austria I was convinced that in view of the dramatic deterioration of Austria's image we would have to transcend internal political differences and mobilise whatever talents and resources we could toward a common national interest. I felt that a small commission of distinguished independent individuals should quickly be gathered to recommend what should be done. I canvassed various personages in Vienna with these thoughts (including Chancellor Vranitzky and Cardinal Franz König). The resulting committee came to draft a 13-page 'list of measures to be taken' in dealing with the charges leveled against the country abroad and in working out points to be emphasised for a positive image of Austria.

Between the summer of 1986 and the spring of 1987 the committee met four times; among the participants in some of these sessions were Cardinal König, Simon Wiesenthal, about ten well-known journalists, industrialists, managers and academics. In the meantime, in April 1987, I was appointed Director of Radio Austria International (ROI), the short-wave foreign broadcasting services financed by the government. Needless to say this placed me even more in the forefront of attempts to repair the damage to Austria's image.

Our primary task was to deal with Austria's tainted image in the United States. Thus in the second half of October 1987 I embarked on a two-week lecture and information trip to Los Angeles, Chicago, Boston, New York, and Washington. The fact that Columbia University initially refused to make an auditorium available to me as an Austrian speaker, and that only through the intervention of Professor István Deák was I able to address faculty and students at his Institute on East Central Europe, says everything about the atmosphere at the time.

Austria's image problem was by no means limited to the 'East Coast' or to Jewish organisations. There was no real prospect of altering President Waldheim's image, yet I felt that the inaccurate unfair and one-sided reports about Austria could be countered if we were prepared to accept a measure of self-criticism. There seemed no point in dwelling on the past. But we did have to be unqualified in our rejection of anti-semitism and xenophobia and we did have to immediately condemn any anti-semitic and racist statements made by political functionaries.

The *Washington Post* did publish a lengthy op-ed piece by me entitled 'The Besmirching of Austria'. In it I rejected the undifferentiated, blanket condemnation of the entire Austrian people. I criticised the 'vengeful, poorly prepared and sensational campaign of the World Jewish Congress' and pointed out that 270,000 Jews from the Soviet Union and tens of thousands from other Eastern European countries had emigrated to Israel and the United States via Austria. The reply to my article was not long in coming. As far as the World Jewish Congress was concerned I was merely 'an apologist for Waldheim'.

I was and am convinced, after examining all the available evidence, that it was Simon Wiesenthal who got it right and not the people of the World Jewish Congress. Kurt Waldheim was not guilty in criminal law. Yet there is no denying that his memoirs and other autobiographical writings show astonishing memory lapses. The repression or covering-up of the facts of his war service also made Waldheim's 'defense strategy' difficult to sustain. And Waldheim's dubious declaration, which he himself later corrected, that he had 'only done his duty' cast doubt on the credibility of the whole notion, so crucial to the county's post-war image, that Austria had been the first victim of Hitler's aggression.

But the reasons for the extensive campaign against Austria was not primarily due to Waldheim's personality or past. It had much deeper roots. In part it was a settling of accounts for Kreisky's Middle-East foreign policy, which Waldheim served and symbolised as Secretary General of the UN. And the fact that post-war Austrian governments had treated the restitution settlements of about 100,000 Austrians driven out of the country as merely a legal matter rather than a political and above all a moral problem played a central role. This was not a matter of money but of attitude toward those driven out. Waldheim came to symbolise Austria's ambivalence with regard to National Socialism.

At the same time America's hypocrisy about Austria must also be examined. The US secret services and agencies used former middle- and high-ranking Nazis for their purposes during the Cold War. And the United States as well as the Soviet Union, France and Great Britain had supported Waldheim's two UN candidacies and even his campaign for a third term, an effort that failed only because of China's veto. Were CIA, KGB and MI6 files really devoid of any data on Waldheim's wartime background? Finding out what the Great Powers *really* knew about Waldheim's past would undoubtedly be a revealing task for a historian with access to the secret archives of Washington, Moscow, London and Belgrade.

17

A New Lease of Life

On 1 October 1991 I died. That was what the doctors later told me. I was clinically dead for a couple of minutes following a heart attack in my office in the middle of a hectic day. I lost consciousness at the very moment when I tried to tell the young emergency physician, that I had been experiencing severe chest pains for about 15 minutes. With massive support from the emergency services, including electric shock treatment to the heart, I ended up extremely lucky to be alive today.

I spent about four weeks in the hospital, largely in the intensive care unit, before being sent to a rehabilitation clinic in the country for another four weeks. Gradually my strength came back to me and just as well because I was soon caught up once again in the tragic events in Yugoslavia.

When, toward the end of the eighties, long before the outbreak of armed conflicts first in northern Yugoslavia and later in Bosnia, I sketched out sombre brief scenarios for Yugoslavia and critically examined the inaction and naivete of the West I was criticised by left and left-liberal colleagues. Because I deplored the aggression of the Serbian leadership and criticised Serbian (but also Croatian) intelligentsia for its intolerance and their loudly-proclaimed 'Socialist humanism' and emphasised the national claims of the Croats, Slovenes,

Bosnian Muslims and Albanians, I was accused of deliberate pessimism. I recognised both the sufferings of hundreds of thousands of Serbs and tens of thousands of Jews under the wartime Ante Pavelić's terror regime as well as the evil of bloody vengeance the victorious partisans wreaked on tens of thousands of innocent Croats, Slovenes, Hungarians, Albanians and Muslims. But I warned against using the crimes of a generation as an alibi for crimes against their children and grandchildren.

The tragedy of Yugoslavia is by no means over. This was made amply clear in the spring of 1998 when Kosovo grabbed the world's headlines. It is certain to occupy generations of historians. The consequences of the explosion of historic hatreds, envy and fear for the entire region, even for all of Europe, cannot be ignored. This is why those who have dedicated themselves to the study the Balkan nations must continue to ask questions and criticise the serious developments in the region which demands an approach crying out for compassion, understanding and realistic scepticism, rather than ignorance and arrogance, prejudice and hostility.

In assessing the future in Yugoslavia I am convinced that these people – Croats and Serbs, Moslems and Albanians – cannot be helped by a confrontation of claims, by striking a price for past injustice. The past can never be restored. Because I have got to know so many people over three decades from Zagreb to Ljubljana, from Belgrade to Pristina and Skopje, as a true friend of all the national groups I have always pleaded that politicians and intellectuals should be moved by tolerance rather than hatred, by understanding rather than the settling of old accounts. National narrowmindedness, intolerance and exclusion will always ensure defeat for humane civilian values.

The past is never dead

As a broadcaster and lecturer, observing Eastern Europe's transition from dictatorship to a democracy, from a command to a free-market economy, is still central to my work. During my travels and at meetings with the new democrats I am often reminded of William Faulkner's words that 'the past is never dead, it is not even past'. That holds true for some aspects of the East-West media war and the unbroken power of the secret services who continue to control archives and access to the lies and denunciations of a not-too-distant past.

I share the opinion of Joachim Gauck, the man charged with administering the East German secret police files, that access to and the widest possible utilisation of these files is necessary. Gauck has rightly said that the East Germans must meet the challenge of whether to run away from their history or to show the good together with the bad. With the exception of the Czech Republic most post-Communist states have unfortunately not yet heeded this call.

Thus the heirs of the former regime in Hungary and Romania continue to refuse full access to the archives of the old secret service despite the pleas of international and domestic researchers. They contain nothing about me, I have been repeatedly and personally assured in Budapest. Since the informer who denounced me in 1952 and 1960 has remained a star journalist even after the collapse of the Communist system the reluctance of the authorities is neither surprising nor confidence-inspiring. The overseers of the blacklists have often merely changed their masks. A new 'History Office' has been set up in Hungary and this could mark a change there. But the jury is still out on this gesture.

As in the days of the Cold War, extremists of various sorts seek to silence and discredit critics, particularly if they hail from the country under criticism. With a mixture of lies and threats the men in power attacked and continue to attack the critics of Serbian and Croatian nationalism.

On Belgrade TV for example, along with a list including such names as Hitler and the Croat fascist Pavelić, I have been castigated as a 'former resident of the city of Senta (in Serbia) and a secret agent of Horthy's Hungary'. The fact that I was born in Budapest, grew up there, and at the time of Horthy was a high-school student, and that I have never lived in Senta did not seem to bother the propagandists in Belgrade.

Nationalism, or more accurately national self-assertion, contributed substantially to the collapse of Communism and the Soviet empire. I have written a great deal about the two faces of the phenomenon of nationalism and have always supported the safeguarding and defence of the national identity of small nations. But the return to tribalisation in Eastern and South-eastern Europe endangers the old and new minorities and individual rights to freedom. Karl Popper, in his *Open Society and Its Enemies* wrote prophetically: 'The more we try to return to the heroic age of tribalism the more surely do we arrive at the Inquisition, at the secret police, and at a romanticised gangsterism'.

The uncompromising battle against xenophobia and anti-semitism is of course a part of the necessary task of building a workable civil society with protection of individual and minority rights and freedom of the media. But let us not fool ourselves. The growth of the right-wing extremist National Front in France, the unresolved problem of Northern Ireland, the Basque ETA, the tensions in Belgium and the xenophobic tendencies in Germany and Austria are sufficient warnings that the West ought not feel so smug and superior when the issue of extremist or populist moves in post-Communist states is raised in the various committees of the European Union.

I have condemned the Red and Brown dictatorships alike. For the millions who died it makes no difference whether they perished in Vorkuta or Dachau. The transformation of victims into perpetrators, the expulsion and in many instances the murder of Germans in Poland and Czechoslovakia immediately after World War II were the consequences of Nazi crimes, but it is unacceptable retrospectively to seek justice in vengeance. As far as I am concerned the Holocaust, the annihilation of six million human beings, among them a million and a half children, solely because they were Jews – and despite everything that has happened since in the world – is a unique crime which must remain unique. The thought of vengeance in kind for the injustice would be preposterous. In the same way the notion of vengeance as an option needs to be expunged from the consciousness of all Eastern Europeans.

My life history has been intertwined with Austria for over 40 years, yet I have never erased the Hungarian past from my memory. It has never been my intention to deny my first 27 years and the turbulent history of my intellectual error, the belief in the Marxist claim to exclusive truth.

That I have been allowed to live and work in freedom and relative affluence I consider largely a matter of luck. As memories continue to crowd in on me, I am becoming more and more aware of how much what was a foreign country has emerged as my actual homeland. While Budapest has become for me a close old relative I like to visit and Hungarian is my mother tongue and Hungary the country of my childhood and youth, Austria is the place where I feel really at home: in Vienna – and in Altaussee.

'Altaussee is not a village, but an illness which one can't get rid of', Jacob Wassermann, the noted German-Jewish writer wrote in the 1920s. It is more than a generation since I first fell victim to the magic of Altaussee. On our honeymoon, my wife and I spent a few days in the 'Seehotel'. It must have been at this time in August 1962 that we both became infected by the incurable 'Aussee illness'; on the hotel terrace overlooking the lake and during the first unforgetable five-mile-long walk around the lake.

I have travelled all over the world, from Tokyo and Kyoto to Caracas and Rio de Janeiro, from Cairo and Beirut to New Delhi and Hong Kong, from Helsinki and Stockholm to Aix-en-Provence and Elba – but I have returned here again and again. As I grow older I come back even more often to the Ausseerland, as the entire area is called. Whether in rain, storm or on sunny days, I can only repeat in endless variations what the poet Hugo von Hofmannsthal wrote: '... this is my most favourite place of all, where I am most myself'.

For this reason a few years ago we bought a small flat in the appartment house attached to the Seehotel with a view of the lake, the woods and the Dachstein-Glacier. It is probably the natural isolation of this Styrian valley which explains the magic of the area. In contrast to other beautiful places in the Salzkammergut region, Altaussee is a natural blind alley. There is no road leading from it to anywhere. The Austro-Jewish writer Friedrich Torberg, a 'prisoner' of Altaussee since his childhood, wrote a gripping poem with the title 'Nostalgia for Altaussee' from his American exile in World War II: 'The mountains surround and encircle the lake, they almost form a fortress, in which one feels softly protected,' he wrote. I believe with him that it was and is this feeling of being protected which has lured so many writers and poets here.

That I have been able to write my memoirs here, and perhaps only here, may in a more profound sense be linked to the fate of some of the people who have spent part of their lives here and who have influenced my life. The circle closes for me in and around Aussee, not only because of the checkered fate of so many literary figures and artists but also because of my own memories of the year 1944.

In this fateful year, the Nazi chieftains of the Upper and Lower Danube areas moved into the villas and houses in which some of the illustrious artists and writers, men like Theodor Herzl, von Hofmannsthal, Wasserman and Torberg had once lived. Later they were joined by fascist governments-in-exile forced to leave their Eastern and South-eastern European countries as the Nazi empire began to shrink. Taking along the jewels and works of art they had stolen from their victims, largely from Jews, they together with a host of SS troopers hoped to disappear in this Alpine redoubt. At the same time, however, the area also included resistance fighters and politically active ordinary salt miners who blocked plans to blow up of the salt mines near Aussee. They were thus were able to save the works of art hidden there by the Nazis. It was the resistance fighters who helped an American unit find the road to the mountain retreat of Ernst Kaltenbrunner, the chief of the German security service, the terrorist arm of the Nazi regime.

However, Adolf Eichmann – the man who directed the extermination of the Jewish communities in the countries occupied by Hitler's Germany, and who up to December 1944 did everything in his power in Budapest to kill the last survivors of Hungarian Jewry, including me and my parents – managed to escape from this very place where he had come to hide – Altaussee. His wife and their three children stayed here for seven years before they joined him in Argentina. When I take my walks in the village I pass the house in which the family had lived, and recently I learned that one of his sons has a summer bungalow here.

One of the prosecution witnesses against Eichmann still lives in Altaussee. He is the former SS officer Wilhelm Höttl. At the Nuremberg trials in 1945 he said that Eichmann told him in Budapest in August 1944 that 'in the various extermination camps about four million Jews had been killed, and that two more million died in some other way, the majority shot by the commandos of the security police during the Russian campaign'. Höttl, after his release, went on to work for the American secret service in Austria. He later founded a school in the neighbourhood and in 1995, on the occasion of his eightieth birthday, received a high decoration for 'his service to Styria'.

Despite some property speculation and profiteering after the war some of the surviving refugees and outcasts – including noted writers, artists and actors – who had loved the Ausseerland did return. I have met a number of them. And strolling along the lake I also see those who were born toward the end or after the war, artists and writers of the new Austria, such as the actor Klaus Maria Brandauer. They symbolise for me that 'spacious, very self-critical, outspoken, open-minded, Europe-directed Austrian consciousness' of which Friedrich Heer, the great scientist and Austrian humanist dreamed.

Despite the shadows of the past and some real dangers of the present I am profoundly grateful to Austria and its people who in difficult days offered me not only a passport but also a new home. After all that I myself have experienced in Hungary and witnessed in other countries of Eastern and South-eastern Europe, I reject the blanket condemnation of the Austrians, the Viennese, the Ausseer or of any other national group. A critical study of history shows that human villainy knows no order of rank, that there are no 'guilty' and no 'heroic' nations, only individual villains and heroes.

The physicist Max Born has noted that there is something to be said even for catastrophes: 'For a human being there can be nothing more salutary and more refreshing than to be uprooted and to set down new roots in a completely different environment'. To be sure, I did not emigrate as a Jew nor as a hunted freedom fighter whose life was in danger. I came as a man who chose truth over lies, imperfect democracy over the experiment to create a heaven on earth. It was in the prisons and camps of Hungary not as an émigré that I learned the meaning of Popper's words: 'Those who believe they can make men happy are very dangerous men'. There was a time when I was one of these. I was and am more harsh in my moral condemnation of the Soviet-style totalitarianism than of the Third Reich because the original ideas and aims of Marxian Socialism were essentially humanistic, whereas Nazism from the outset was essentially inhumane and murderous. I therefore agree with the German political scientist Iring Fetscher that the Socialist evolution from Marx via Lenin to Stalin was a tragedy, while the evolution of the Nazi regime was the direct realisation of Hitler's racist and inhumane ideas. In view of the crimes which I myself experienced under both the Brown and Red dictatorships I feel consciously or subconsciously that I have an obligation to be a witness. In the words of Jean Améry:

> In my existence I experience and illuminate the historic realities of my epoch, and since I lived through them more profoundly than most members of my tribe I can also clarify them better. That is neither a merit nor a talent but a sheer accident of fate.

INDEX